Yoga inVision 7

Yogi Bhajan

Michael Beloved

Shiva Art: Sir Paul Castagna
Illustrations: Author
Correspondence:
Michael Beloved
19311 SW 30th Street
Miramar FL 33029
USA
Email: axisnexus@gmail.com
            michaelbelovedbooks@gmail.com

Paperback ISBN: 9781942887201
eBook ISBN: 9781942887218
LCCN: 2019903766

Table of Contents

INTRODUCTION

This is the seventh of the Yoga inVision series. It relates experiences and practices done in November, 2010 through February, 2011. These give beginners ideas of the physical, psychological and spiritual experiences one may have when doing asana postures, pranayama breath-infusion and *pratyahar* sensual energy withdrawal. Beyond that is higher yoga, which Patañjali named the *samyama* procedures. He defined *samyama* as a combination of *dharana* deliberate focus, *dhyana* spontaneous focus and *samadhi* continuous spontaneous focus. During practice these progress one into the other. If one is expert at *pratyahar* sensual energy withdrawal, one may graduate to *dharana* which is deliberate focus of the attention to a higher concentration force or person. As soon as one masters *dharana* one may slip into *dhyana* which is an effortless focus on a higher concentration force or person. Once you practice *dhyana*, *samadhi* happens as the continuous effortless focus on a higher concentration force or person.

Many persons on a spiritual path feel that they can construct a process as they advance. This idea denotes failure. After all, if the supernatural and spiritual environment, is not already there, no one can create it now. It is either there or it is not. For instance, if one intends to moves to a different country, then of course one will fail if the country intended does not exist. It has to be there prior. Similarly what you aim for as spiritual life, must be there already, or one will find that the aspiration is incorrect. This is why I speak of a concentration force or person. I could have said concentration person or divine person, or God. I did not because I do not know how anyone's spiritual path will develop.

One may leave an island in the safest boat and still the vessel may sink. One should keep one's mind open and be willing to work with fate. In spiritual development, there is providence too. What one desires to have one may not achieve. What one wishes to see may never appear.

These Yoga inVision journals show how sporadic my course of yoga was. This is after years of practice. It gives some idea of what to expect. Once you get through the lower yoga practice, you will see advancement in a more stable way but it may be incremental, accruing little by little, with bright flashes here and there.

Part 1

This birth

Basically what happens is that one takes a body. When one emerges as an infant, one is lost and does not know what one is about. This is due to having lost the reference of the previous life. We can understand this by noting what happens to people who use elderly bodies. They become afflicted with dementia. They may not know who they are and may not recognize even the next of kin.

Similarly one becomes an infant with only a reference to this life. One feels that it was the first time existing. Later as the body matures, one becomes dissatisfied with conditions. One thinks of origins.

Nature has everything under its wings. One must respect that and simultaneously get to a deeper level through reflection and meditation. One may read books about spiritual life. Gradually over time one may connect with memory from past lives. There may be a reversal in dementia where the person recognizes a relative again. The person coherently connects with the memory again.

It happens.

Process of life

This life is like getting a sentence from a judge, which says that one is to be in the prison for as long as the cell blocks hold up. The judge stipulates that you can escape if the concrete deteriorates sufficiently for you to punch your way through a cell wall. Thus for a yogi, it is a matter of waiting for a loop hole in time, and then leaving the body when the life force is weakened sufficiently for one to use it to escape.

When the body is young, the life force is very attached to it. Such an escape is not likely but as the body ages, the life force loses the attachment because of its inability to exploit the hormonal energy in the body. By training that life force to go upwards, a yogi, forcibly routes it through the spine and head. When the time comes, he or she may go to higher dimensions.

If one fails to do this, the life force will manifest in a parallel world which is adjacent to this world. As a ghost, one will experience oneself as a subtle body which is affiliated with living relatives and friends in the hope of getting one of them to sponsor one's re-entry as a baby.

I may provide valuable information but my urgency is to be sure that I can easily transfer when this body is confiscated by nature. I do not want to loop back with no resistance to the natural way of haphazardly coming back, to again come out crying from the next mother's passage.

In every life, one goes through the same struggle and effort to recap the spiritual identity. If one fails it means that again one will come back and again one will be pressed from a lady's womb. Again one will be a helpless infant, then a rude toddler, then a know-it-all teenager, then a sex-crazed young adult, then a professional or domestically involved adult, then a senior with or without social status, then an elder looking for the cure for disease, then a rickety old bag hobbling in a nursing home, and then at last a de-energized ghost in the astral world, haunting the living in the hope of being physical to participate in history.

Psychic transit

Astral Projection is mostly concerned with the now, not with the past and not with the future. But that now means the now of the particular dimension you enter in the astral world.

The psychology or subtle body is what projects which means that it becomes displaced from the physical form. This happens every time the physical body sleeps. When a person projects he/she becomes conscious of the natural projection of the subtle or astral body as it is displaced out of the physical system.

Within twenty-four hours astral projection happens when the physical body sleeps. When we become conscious of that displacement, we say that we astral project but actually we become conscious of the projection.

As for revisiting the past that is possible but to do so requires more than astral projection. It requires the power to synchronize into the record of the past which is in the universe as stored subtle energy. It is possible to do this but that will require changes in the subtle body. I use subtle body and astral body interchangeable in this correspondence.

Mostly when astral experience is gained, it is gained spontaneously and not on demand, not by desire or wish. People who practice deep meditation and some gifted psychics can induce astral projection but others experience it involuntarily.

It is possible but it is not probably. For one thing going back into another person's past is the same as going back into that person's subconscious mind. To do that one must be a great yogi or mystic.

Usually no one from a past era will see another person who returns to that time. The reason for that is that those persons will not be focused into the subconscious memory of their past life actions. Their conscious minds would have to be focused into the subconscious. One rarely has experiences of the conscious self in the subconscious. Usually when a person enters the subconscious, say as in hypnosis or in case of a psychic, he/she is not objectively aware of the situation.

If one goes back one will find that one is focused through the form one used previously but that everyone else acts as if they are robots. One will also realize that the others do not perceive one's existence as if one is an invisible person, even though one may feel that one is present and sees everything that occurs.

If one has this experience, the only way one can know when this happened is by the way the people are dressed, by the design of the houses and things like that because one cannot interact. If one tries to interact it turns out to be nothing because those persons cannot perceive one, simply because their conscious selves are not focused into their subconscious memories.

One cannot change anything. One will only find that everything is repeated as it was in the past. One does not have the power to act to the contrary.

Usually when one resumes the past, it does not have negative experiences, unless one returns to a time when there was negative historic acts, like for example going back to a scene in a war.

Malicious and criminal entities exist in the lower astral world. Unless one goes to a lower astral place, a hell world, it is hardly likely that one will meet a mischievous or domineering person.

Sometimes the astral body resumes the form one used in infancy or the form one used in a previous life and another person's body does likewise and resumes a corresponding form which was present when one was in that previous existence. One may interact with that person and carry on the relationship as before. This happens with people whom one had a disagreement with and then one makes an effort to settle the dispute.

I had a meeting in the astral world with a grandparent who helped to raise me when I was an infant. A subconscious part of her psyche wanted to continue asserting authority. Because of that her astral body assumed the elderly form used in the previous life. My astral body resumed its infant form. We argued.

I explained that she was no longer a senior since actually she took birth in a body which was much younger than mine at present. This went on for about two weeks nightly. Then the tension eased. I did not see her astral body in that old form any longer. This did not happen because I wished for it. It happened because in her subtle body there was a subconscious tension which that form released. This person has no awareness that her subtle body did this.

As I explained, the other person cannot know this unless his/her conscious mind is focused into and through the subconscious. That is hardly likely.

I was aware of it because I dedicated over 38 years to meditation and mystic practices, otherwise this may happen and I would have no awareness of it, due to not being focused into my subconscious.

To change someone's past, one would have to alter the motivational tendencies in the subconscious. This is not possible because the reach into someone's past where those motivations are located is inaccessible.

In the case of that grandparent from the past life, whose subtle body I encountered in the astral world, I had some input into that person's upbringing when that person took a child's form again. I tried to help that person with removing the dietary basis of the formation of dietary bad habits.

Even though I worked with the person's conscious self, still the person had such a need for that negative diet that the person returned to the old way of eating foods which bring on and support bad diet.

To help someone from the past, one has to reach that person in a future life and be in a position of authority to enforce corrective methods either as a medical professional or as a senior relative. Still, that will not guarantee that the person will change.

Any habit which brings with it pleasure and satisfaction, cannot be removed by superficial advice or even for enforce compliance. The person himself or herself must realize the error and then must challenge himself or herself to work against those tendencies.

When I was in the Philippines in the US Air Force around 1971, there was an epidemic of gonorrhea among some service men. This was due to sexual activity with native women. We were shown movies showing cases of incurable gonorrhea and its ghastly effects. We were told that if we contracted an incurable form, we would pass away some weeks after in pain and would be reported as missing in action in the Vietnam.

But do you think that it stopped all servicemen from propositioning the native women. It did not. Guys would get the disease once, twice, thrice, and be in pain and be treated and still go back. This is because if there is a pleasure associated with a certain habit, the pleasure offsets the effort for restraint. The individual is unable to resist because of not being able to be self-deprived.

Scenes through the third eye

During a morning practice, after some breath infusion and twisting to the right and the left, kundalini rose on the right and left side. It ascended on the right center of the body and then on the left center. It hit the collar bone and then deflected through the bones in the arm and forearm

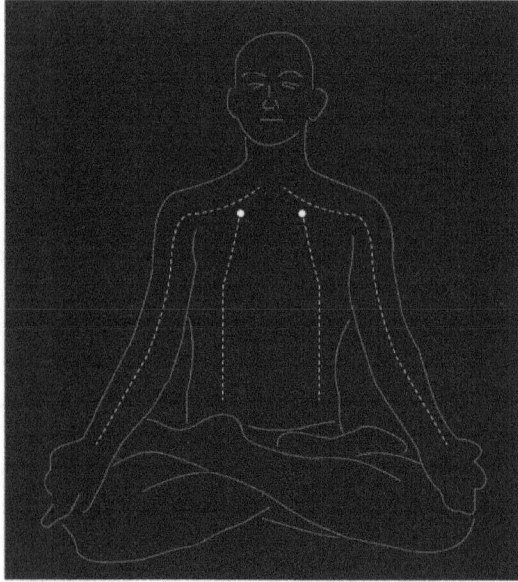

When it rose to the collar bone, it did so in the spiral energy pattern with two laser-like charges firing through the spiral energy.

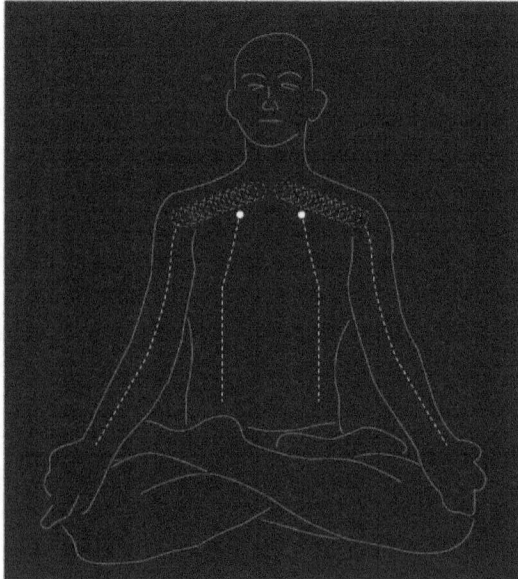

As soon as I sat to meditate, naad sound became evident. I went into it. As I entered the back right side of the head into naad, I got an energy pulse from the frontal part of the head. That came into the psyche from a person in South America. I was in South Korea which is half way around the planet, but still the person's thought reached me.

This was from a lady, who thought that I should be positioned in my next life so that I could have a relationship with her. Such thoughts serve to remind a yogi that if he is not careful, he will take a haphazard rebirth on the basis of a whimsical and perhaps costly desire energy which comes from someone and which he responded to carelessly. I did not give any attention to the energy pulse which contained this desire of the lady.

After that energy pulse was dismissed, I stayed in naad energy. Suddenly I looked forward and scenes from another dimension passed just outside the third eye at a rapid speed as if I was sitting on a rapid train and looking through a window and seeing the scenery of the landscape passing by. After about ten seconds, it turned into night in that dimension. Then I saw shadowy shapes.

Subtle attraction to breath infusion

During the meditation, a lady who is now deceased and who was a practicing yogini while she had her last body, came. She also came during kundalini exercises yesterday. She said nothing. She observed the meditation method. Because of using only a subtle body now and not having a gross body to de-energize her subtle form, her subtle perception increased considerably as compared to when she lived as a human being.

She has an interest in kundalini yoga and came to see how the kundalini moves when it is charged by breath infusion. For a yogi, it is not a good idea to have anyone on the astral side during practice, especially persons who may be sexually attracted. But if the person is a yogi or yogini it is permitted.

If someone who is sexually-attracted comes during kundalini infusion, that person will be attracted to the infused kundalini and may cause it to take a sexual route, which will in effect cancel kundalini's interest in rising upwards into the head.

Some astral persons are attracted to a yogi who infuses kundalini. They see the energy flashing through and out of the subtle body. They are irresistibly drawn to it. Some take bits of the energy, just as one may take a cream and rub on the body. They experience a bliss energy from it.

Transit to a higher dimension (November 2010)

Kundalini rose today several times during the exercise session. It penetrated the flesh and nerves in the neck. It felt like micro bubbles of bliss energy.

After that occurred, Rishi Singh Gherwal appeared in my consciousness. He explained that to have kundalini rise through the spine is insufficient for getting a yogi to a higher *loka*. The word *loka* is Sanskrit for existential zone. It is pronounced as loak or loaka, rhyming with the word cloak.

Existential zone means a place where one can exist with others who are in the same frequency range. For example on this planet there are demarcations or borders in countries, in communities and in cities. In some areas, there is high security and one can enter only with special permission. There are prisons which are designed primarily to keep people confined but which also serves the purpose to keep unconfined people from entry.

On this planet there are tight restrictions for physical existence. For instance one must have a certain type of body to live at the bottom of the Atlantic Ocean. Even if one is the greatest engineer, still one cannot live at the bottom of the ocean using just a human form. All the same the creatures who live in the deep will not survive if they were confined to a land space where humans feel comfortable.

In the hereafter, there are many existential zones, which are called *lokas*. A yogi is carefree in everything except where he or she will go after leaving the present body. He or she wants to go to the highest dimension possible, to be with divine beings, abandoning the social associations we currently promote.

The problem is that to get there, one must have a suitable subtle body which vibrates at a corresponding frequency. On this planet, sometimes even though one has friends in another country, still one cannot get a visa to visit them. It is the same in the hereafter. I may know a great yogi who reached a certain high plane of existence but that in no way gives me the right to transfer to that place. He can descend to the lower plane where I am located or he can send a telepathic message but for my entry there, my subtle body has to be suitably energized.

What happens with a yoga guru is this. After a disciple practices for some time and realizes the situation of the higher dimensions, he or she inquires of entry to those higher places. The teacher explains, "You must do this practice to get your subtle form to change to a suitable frequency."

Sometimes, a yoga guru graduates to such a high plane, that the disciple is unable to reach him to inquire about the requirements. Then a message is found in the subtle world about how to qualify. That communication may be sent by the yoga guru, or he may have left it on a subtle plane or from his existence when he was on that plane, a vibrational energy was left which gives that message.

The method of transmittance is not the issue because as soon as the student yogi made enough effort and advances, the message becomes evident. In cases where a yoga guru was unable to leave a message and where there is no energy anywhere which would inspire the yogi on the required methods, the yogi guru usually descends from the higher plane and gives instructions into the mind of the student.

Such a student has to be non-argumentative, non-critical, and very respecting of the guru, otherwise the student's attitude itself bars the student from reading the message.

After kundalini rose through the neck, through the flesh, nerves and spine, not just through the spine alone, Rishi said this,

"When one begins to do yoga, one's idea about it has to do with material existence and the exposure one had in that particular body, especially sex desire and the other ways and means of pleasure experience.

"The infant's first idea of pleasure is twofold, based on feelings and based on taste. What is the infant feeling initially besides its own body? That is the mother's body. What does the infant usually taste at first after birth? That is the mother's milk. Thus these two experiences, touching the female form and ingesting liquid from breasts are the essential experience. From this other experiences become evident.

"If you take the infant away from the mother, the infant cries. If you deprive the infant of the mother milk the infant protests.

"Later sex urge develops. The mother loses significance because the infant finds that it is attracted to other bodies of similar age for sexual expression. This is designed by nature but the infant takes it as if he or she crafted it.

"In all respects the infant is a nobody initially, a social nothing. It cannot contribute to society. It is worthless. The parents give value to it by training it in how to behave and how to function with usefulness.

"The child must attend school to increase its value to society and to achieve status for the family. Along the way, it is distracted by pleasure, especially by sexual pleasure. The two most troublesome and demanding compulsive organs are the tongue and genitals. Both organs rule the entity with an iron hand, saying, "Eat this. Eat that. Unify me with this. Unify me with that."

"Thus when the entity comes to yoga, these organs control the practice. Since there is really little use for the sexual organ in yoga, the entity is perturbed about how to get sexual pleasure through the exercises. Subsequently tantric sexual practices entered into the practice of yoga, a place in which they may be inappropriately applied.

"Kundalini is the root cause of sex desire and of the taste impulse. One must come to terms with that reality by raising kundalini and causing it to abandon its sex deployment. To do this kundalini must be trained to go upwards instead of going downward through the pleasure nerves in the genitals.

"Nature's way is to taste and then create sex hormones from what is tasted, and then use those hormones in sexual expression. First the tongue and mouth, then the intestines, then the sex hormones are manufactured, then the sex pleasure is derived.

"That is the natural way. Now let us review the yogic method. First again there is taste, then there is the intestines to extract energy from what is tasted, but then the sex hormones are manufactured and then what? Then the energy is made to go upward, abandoning the passage through the genitals.

"However if one came to yoga after having much sex fulfillment, one is tormented by the memory. One has a difficult time changing the habits of kundalini. At first when kundalini rises, a person may be surprised to find that it could give pleasure in another way by going upwards as contrasted to the natural way of going downwards through the pleasure nerves of the genitals. Later as one practices, one becomes accustomed to the upward rise and the bliss energy that is expressed when that happens.

"As one advances one must relinquish the attachment to this bliss energy and focus on distributing kundalini evenly through the psyche.

"Why should kundalini only pass through the spine, leaving the rest of the psyche without a sufficient infusement of higher energy? The entire psyche should be infused and then when one passes from the gross body, there is a chance that one will go to a higher dimension and one may be lucky to be with divine beings like Krishna and Shiva. Otherwise, yes, one may have a vision or a sudden experience at death, but it will be a flash. Then one will find oneself again entering the sexual energy of new parents on earth, and coming out again as a helpless baby. What has God to do with it? It is the natural way."

Astral world forced association (November 2010)

Just as in this physical world a person is sometimes circumstantially or otherwise forced into a certain situation, some associations in the astral world are forced. For instance here where I was in South Korea there is a law whereby, all young men must serve in the military. In the United States in the 1960's there was also a military draft order in effect. To avoid it some left the country. Others shot themselves in foot or arm. Some others pretended to be dope addicts. Some filed a conscientious objection.

It is not that a God came into the world and ordered these unwanted demands. These orders were enforced by the government. Even they, even though they are not necessarily divine personages, get a power from providence to enforce certain services.

In the astral world the same thing occurs but there it is obviously due to supernatural power. While in this world, people scoff at the term supernatural and think that it is superstition. In the astral world, supernatural power is the means of operations.

In the astral world people try to counteract supernatural power but mostly to no avail. To escape from the force of such power, one either has to take a material body or go to a higher astral world. If one is unable to do either, one must confirm to the enforced demands.

Last night I was with a man and his family in the astral world. I got there because one person whom I knew years ago, found my name on the Internet somewhere and contact me. Since that one person contacted me some others from the past used that link to find me. They endeavor to get me to do this or that service in the astral world, all based on the relationship I had over 30 years ago.

When I was with that man and his family, he tried to get his sons to do chores. They avoided having to do anything. Like usual, some children dislike serving the parents. In a child's body one may see the parent as a stooge. In which case, it is improper for one to serve, because it should be the other way around. This man's children did not like to do anything for him. I stayed with this family for about a year. I used to be willing to do things. This man appreciated that.

In the dream, he asked me to do many things. As I complied, he wanted me to encourage his sons to pitch in. The sons however were not interested. The man kept prodding me but his sons were not concerned to lift a finger.

This happens because when one takes a new body one carries from the past life, a resentment for having lost the old body and for having not got sufficient services from the family in the past life. In elderly years, one finds that one is hard up to get any services from young relatives. Of course there is no such thing as a young person, because it is just a young body with an old person in it. But still one finds that those old persons who now have young forms are reluctant to render services. One develops a resentment.

When one takes the new body, the subtle form carries that resentment in it. That becomes visible in the new body as a reluctance to do anything menial for the parents.

Unless one changes this tendency in the subtle body, it will keep acting like that in one life after another, because that is the natural mammalian way of its operation, based on the survival tendencies of the naturally designed kundalini which expresses the instinct in these bodies.

Many people whom I advised over the years, do not understand that they are controlled by the kundalini. It is hard to get these ideas across to them.

Once one gets a new body, the kundalini has sexual indulgence and status at its primary objectives. One is not interested in getting anything else. Anyone who stands in the way of one achieving that is regarded as an enemy. Even if a parent takes care of one properly, one may not appreciate the parent. These are the tendencies in the kundalini life force. Until one can comes to terms with these impulses, one will remain dead set on doing things in this hostile way.

I was stuck in that astral dimension for some time, based on the supernatural power of that man and his wife, merely because I stayed as a teenaged dependent with them for some time, some 30 year or so years ago. In the astral world, I was there like a crab in a metal cage. The crab cannot escape because the cage is designed by providence to transcend the crab's need for freedom.

After a time, I got away. The funny thing about the whole experiences is that no one else who was present there is conscious of what happened. Since they had not developed psychic consciousness, they are not objectively aware of their astral activities. The man and his wife are deceased. Their children still live physically.

Even though they are not objective to those astral experiences, still they got the fulfillment of my services to them in that astral dimension. The astral body and the subconscious psyche operate regardless of the one's awareness or lack of awareness of what happens.

I was there in that astral residence with the man, his wife and sons. The man tried to enforce his father role upon his sons, while using me as an example of the behavior he required. I knew I was trapped there. I served my time like a prisoner who has no choice. These incidences are enforced by the inscrutable power of fate.

How to get subtle energy in the thighs (November 2010)

During exercises kundalini rose with aggressive force several times into the trunk of the body. It ascended under the armpits on either side, it was like a spike energy which was condensed bliss force. It then shot through the arms.

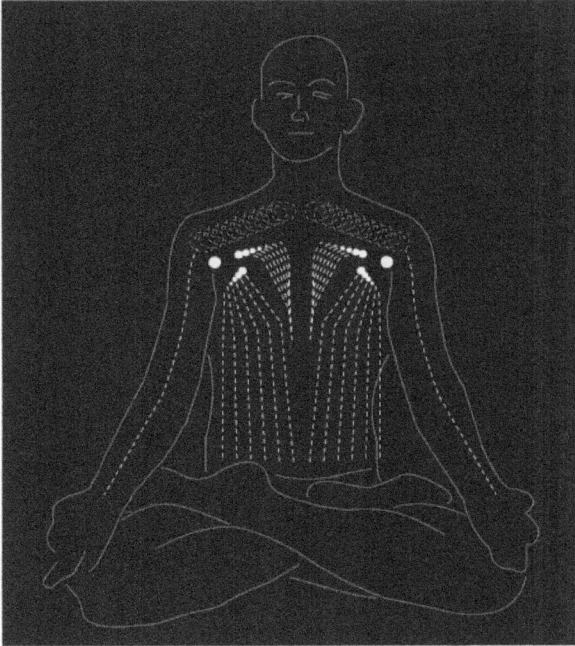

On the astral side during the practice, Rishi Singh Gherwal discussed the importance of working on what he called the lower extremities, which are the thighs, legs and feet. He opined that a yogi should keep the feet in tip top shape in as much as in yoga the head is stressed.

Rishi said this:

"The thighs are used by kundalini primarily for the creation of reproductive hormones. Hence that area is usually off limits to the yogi. The yogi should do stretches in asana postures where the thighs are targeted, so that the accumulation of blood and energy there is distributed through the body and is not collected for genital expression is sexual intercourse.

"In its natural state, the thighs are the enemy of celibacy which is a necessary for success in yoga. A yogi should spend some time reforming the energy which is created in the thigh.

"As the body gets older the legs and feet become starved of oxygen. A yogi should note that and make special effort to get the polluted blood in those extremities back to the lungs for a fresh recharge of oxygen. The psyche is one mechanism. Even though in yoga, there is focus on the head mostly, a yogi should not neglect the other parts of the subtle body.

"The physical body is a different body, but the neglect of it, causes unwanted alternations in the subtle form. In so far as the subtle form mimics physical behavior a yogi should be aware of the physical system"

In compliance with Rishi's statement, I took care to push air into the thighs especially through the bones. This is done by doing rapid breathing in a posture which stretches the thigh muscles, and keeping the attention in the thigh during the breathing. This keeping of the attention in the thigh causes subtle air to be pulled into the subtle thighs. This breaks down the subtle sexual energy which is stored there and causes it to course though the entire body instead of being channeled to the genitals.

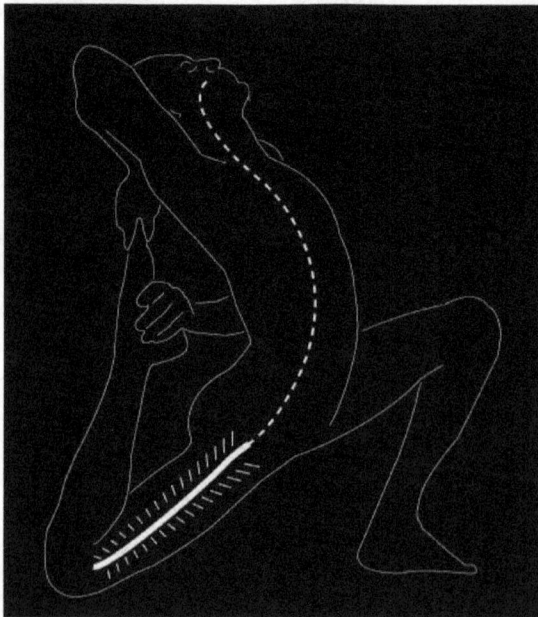

Naad: Right/Left (November 2010)

When I sat to meditate, there were two naad sounds, one at the top left and one at the top right. I tried to contact both but I found myself shifted towards the one on the top right. When I was shifted into it, I lost touch with the one on the left.

I then got an intuition to move to the one on the top left. After shifting I heard both sounds and saw colors. The one to the top right had a brown hue. The one on the left had a grey and then a red hue.

These are subjective colors which means that they may or may not be the objective colors of those zones. Subjective sight is produced by looking through concentrated subtle energy. It is pranaVision.

If one is in an aircraft above an ocean, the water will appear to be aqua marine blue. If one dives into the same water, one will see the water as being clear. The clear appearance may be compared to subjective sight since the view occurs in the medium being observed, where the viewer cannot objectify himself in reference to the medium. pranaVision enables one to make subjective observations. In the material world, people suspect subjective perception. They consider it to be illusory and imaginary but it is a valid means of perception in higher yoga.

When through intuition I shifted to the left naad sound, I became conscious of both the right and left naad sounds. They were different frequencies. They touched each other but did not mix.

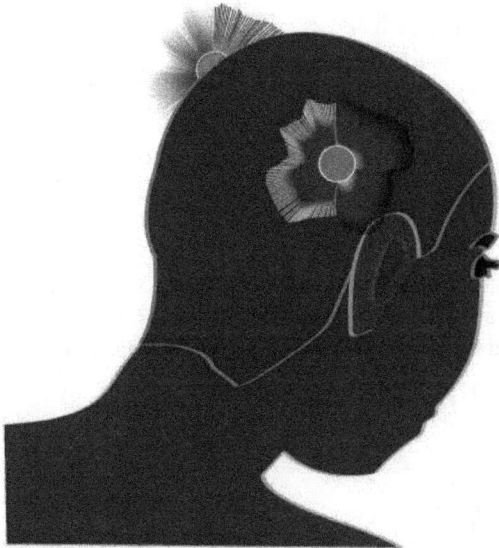

naad sound on right and left

In advanced meditation, there may be a blending of several naad sounds. This is mentioned by Krishna to Uddhava:

प्राणस्य शोधयेन् मार्गं
पूर-कुम्भक-रेचकैः ।
विपर्ययेणापि शनैर्
अभ्यसेन् निर्जितेन्द्रियः ॥९.३३॥

prāṇasya śodhayen mārgaṁ
pūra-kumbhaka-recakaiḥ
viparyayeṇāpi śanair
abhyasen nirjitendriyaḥ (9.33)

prāṇasya — of the vitalizing energy; śodhayen = śodhayet — should purify; mārgam — the passage, route; pūra – inhalation; kumbhaka – retention; recakaiḥ — with exhalation; viparyayenapi = viparyayena — by the reverse order + api — also; śanair = śanaiḥ — by graduating; abhyasen = abhyaset — should practice; nirjitendriya = nirjita — having controlled + indriyah — the sensual energy.

Translation

One should purify the passage of the vitalizing energy by inhalation, retention and exhalation, and by graduation in the reverse order, having the sensual energy controlled. (Uddhava Gita 9.33)

हृद्य् अविच्छिनम् ओकार
घण्टा-नाद बिसोर्ण-वत् ।
प्राणेनोदीर्य तत्राथ
पुनः संवेशयेत् स्वरम् ॥९.३४॥

hrdy avicchinam oṁkāraṁ
ghaṇṭā-nādaṁ bisorṇa-vat
prāṇenodīrya tatrātha
punaḥ saṁveśayet svaram (9.34)

hrdy = hrdi — in the heart chakra; avicchinnam — continuous without breakage; oṁkāram — Om sound; ghaṇṭā — bell; nādam — sound; bisorṇa-vat = bisa – fibre + ūrṇa – lotus + vat — like; prāṇenodīrya = prāṇena — by the vitalizing energy + udīrya — raising; tatrātha = tatra — there + atha — thus; punaḥ — again; saṁveśayet — one should blend with; svaram — of musical notes, tones.

Translation

In the heart chakra, the Om sound which is like the continuous peal of a bell, resonates continually, like a fibre in a lotus stalk. Raising it by using the vitalizing energy, one should blend that sound with the musical tones. (Uddhava Gita 9.34)

एवं प्रणव-संयुक्तं
प्राणम् एव समभ्यसेत् ।
दश-कृत्वस् त्रि-षवणं
मासाद् अर्वाग् जितानिलः ॥९.३५॥

evaṁ praṇava-saṁyuktaṁ
prāṇam eva samabhyaset
daśa-kṛtvas tri-ṣavaṇaṁ
māsād arvāg jitānilaḥ (9.35)

evam — thus; praṇava — Om inner sound; saṁyuktam — premixed; prāṇam — vitalizing energy; eva — indeed; samabhyaset — should direct; daśa – ten; kṛtvas = kṛtvaḥ — procedures; tri-ṣavaṇam — three times; māsād = māsāt — month; arvāg = arvāk — after; jitānilaḥ = jita — conquer + anilah — the life air.

Translation

Thus, one should carefully direct the pre-mixed Oṁ sound and the vitalizing energy, ten times, thrice per day. (Uddhava Gita 9.35)

After fifteen minutes, I found myself in the naad sound on the right side. I checked but the sound on the left ceased.

This means that the sound was still there but I was desynchronized from it. On the top of the head there was a large space which was filled with an energy which seems to be an energy of absence, a place which in that dimension was vacated of subtle objects.

Recall chambers of memory (November 2010)

During exercises, kundalini rose on one side when after an infusement of breath energy, I intuitively stretched that side. After that I repeated the infusement again by rapid breathing and then stretched to the other side, and kundalini rose with the impetus.

In some cases, when one practices kundalini may not rise on the other side, or it may rise only partially. One should practice without expecting balanced polarity. The more one practices and the more one clears various tiny tubes in the subtle body, the more kundalini will express itself efficiently in every part of the psyche.

If kundalini can blast one side of one part of the body, say the left side or right side, if one keeps doing that, kundalini will finish its infusement of that side and will of its own accord begin invading the polluted energy in the other side.

During this session after doing the breath infusions for about twenty minutes, kundalini rose evenly through the front part of the body, coming up around the navel and then into the rib cage and then into the neck. This felt like tiny frost, twinkling sparklets like energies with micro charges.

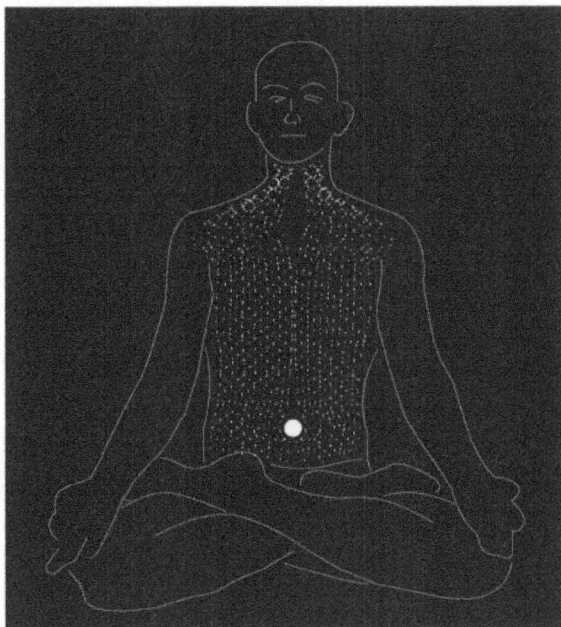

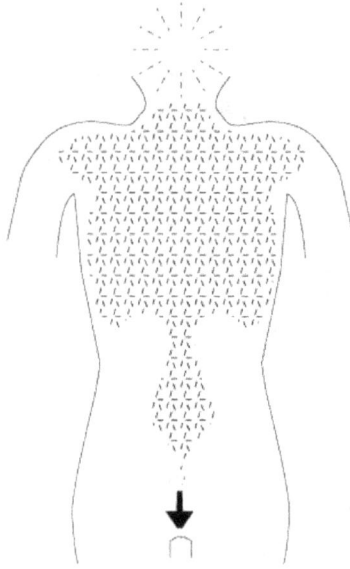

Incidentally I made an effort to file these experiences in the recall chamber of the memory. If I do not do that, I will be unable to report this since there would be no memory filed

In some cases, when the recall chamber of memory is filled, I scribble a notation quickly. Then I return to complete the exercises. Failure to make these notes or to transfer records of these experiences into the recall chamber would result in my not reporting it.

There were many great yogis who made no notes. They did not take the time and effort to transfer their experiences into the recall chambers of memory. Thus we have no record of their progress and cannot benefit from their experiences.

Science excels at keeping records. Science uses journals for filing research information. Both in the negative and positive sense this accelerated scientific development for the human race, since we have the nuclear bomb as a result as well as many things which are positive to humanity.

Rotation of Analytical Orb (November 2010)

Meditation today began with a rolling feature of the analytic orb in the frontal part of the subtle head. As it rolled in slow motion, the coreSelf followed it. There were no thoughts in the frontal part. The attempt to keep track of the activity was done in slow motion.

At about three seconds after the meditation session began, I notice the naad sound was on the right back side near the right ear. Just then I noticed that it was on the left side as well. Both sounds streamed in but the sound on the left side did not have the intensity of the sound on the right. I positioned myself on the left and the sound from that side was still distant. From there I listen to both sounds. When I did so I shifted into hearing the louder right side sound and then shifted back into hearing the quieter left side sound.

Suddenly I found myself rolling again around the analytical orb in the frontal part of the subtle head. These rolls were in slow motion. Third eye was not in operation. The orb itself was not in operation. The energy from the breath infusion caused the orb to roll over and over in slow motion as the infused energy moved around it in a clockwise manner.

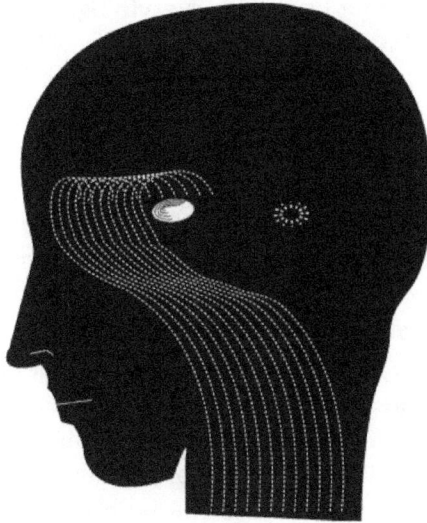

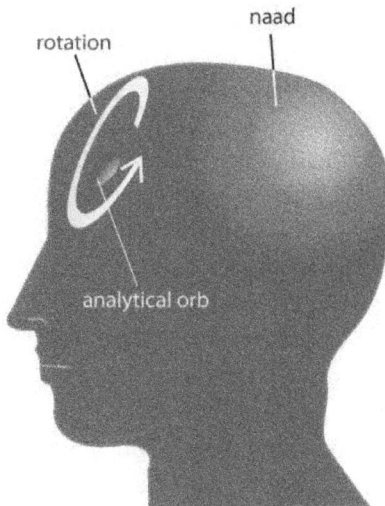

During the roll I got a flash message from Rishi Singh Gherwal. I did not see him. He was not present in my psyche. The message flashed from him. At the time I was not existentially situated to translate the message. Now when I look at it, I can read it. It said this, "When this situation is shut down it could be like this for centuries. How about existing like this for a universe's duration?"

Rishi Singh spoke about the subtle energy in which I rolled. Sometimes a universe is shut down for a time. It fizzes out. Then all entities in that situation, are left without manifested existence, without form existence. People who come to meditation sometimes make jokes about a void or a non-manifested state, and about unity with everything. Little do they know that a time will come when this universe will crash. They will have a void for billions of years with no break from it, with no diversity.

Some people wish to abandon diversity. They find ego to be troublesome. They wish to abolish it. Little do they know that a time will come when existence itself will suspend differentiation.

In Sanskrit there is a word for this which is pralaya. Laya means when something is stretch out, relaxed out of itself when something is broken down completely. The prefix pra means in total or well done, completed. When the universe is in pralaya, one may be in a non-existence, or in a no-definite-form existence and be aware of it, or not be aware of it, for billions of years.

Yogis like Rishi are aware of the epochs. They prepare themselves psychologically for such a break down in the manifested existences. If one is not prepared for it, and if one remains objectively aware when it happens, one will freak out, except that there will be no way to stop it, no way to change the situation. Just as now in the material situation we have to accept what happens politically, socially and climatically, one will have to endure that non-manifest energy state.

There is nothing like pumping your ego up about what one is about and about where one may go, when in fact, one is locked in on all sides in this existence. One is at the complete mercy of the fate.

Imagine me, that in just a short time of about sixty years, since I have this body, I plan a glorious future for myself. Where was I before that sixty year period began? What was I in control of? Who was I? Was this universe or even this planet, the ancestors of this family, concerned about me? You can see how ridiculous my importance is! My situation is one of adaptation. It certainly is not creation or production.

Our astronomers discuss storms on the large planets like Jupiter. These storms last for over a hundred years. Can you imagine a tornado for a hundred years and being as big as to cover a country like Mexico. What would you do if you were in such a storm?

In yoga, we sometimes find ourselves in dimensions which have violent climates like lightning flashes from one planet to another, with so much electricity that it is unimaginable. The sounds which emanate from those vibrations are frightening. One shivers in one's boots. This happens in other dimensions. Sometimes a yogi is fortunate to enter such places. Yoga gurus may explain that one will have to endure such spooks in the future.

Astral Body Displacement

Always try to be certain that when the physical body sleeps it has access to fresh air. Lack of fresh air increases the incidences of sleep paralysis, because the astral body will get less energy if the physical one breathes stale air, or non-circulated air or air from a dirty duct.

Rooms which have old carpeting, is bad. That would contribute to sleep paralysis, if such rooms lack continuous ventilation. Bad air from the old rugs which begin to chemically break down with age emits pollutants.

Fear of astral projection is unwarranted in most cases. The astral body separates from the physical one anytime the physical system sleeps. This means that since one took birth as this body that happened each day during sleep.

Astral awareness is the conscious observation of what the astral body did since it became fused into the sperm particle of the father. Since then, that process of fusing into and separating from the physical body, was happening. Why be fearful of it?

The astral body was separating from the physical one since the physical was in formation in the parent. It does so now and will continue to do so, regardless of whether one becomes aware of the process or not. Some persons go through their entire lives and never have one astral projection experience, but that does not mean that their astral forms never astral projected. It means they never observed it.

Predictions from the astral plane (November 2010)

There is a correlations between some physical events and what happens in the astral with the astral usually leading the physical. Just as on the physical side, we usually have to think of something before doing it, some aspects of astral existence must be worked out before it can occur on the physical side.

If one becomes aware of those aspects, one may predict the physical. In the Bhagavad Gita, Arjuna saw that warriors were wounded on the supernatural level days before those warriors were actually killed on the physical side.

That was not a prediction even though from the physical angle, one can say that Arjuna predicted the physical war on the basis of having the apparition of the defeated warriors days before their demise. It was not a prediction in reference to this world. It was a fact of what happened on a supernatural plane. Since it was a fact there, it was to be a fact here only because that level of existence presupposed this one or managed this one.

When an architect sits down and draws a national monument with all detailed plans of its layout, is that a prediction? We usually do not say so, but actually it is in the sense that after a while that drawing becomes reality as a building in the city. That is only true if the architect was commissioned by the government. If the artist was not commissioned the idea would remain as a plan only.

If one is on an astral level which feeds into this one and which controls this one, whatever one perceives there will happen here, not because of predictions but by the principle of that level being the precursor of this one.

If one is on an astral level that has little or no influence on this one, whatever occured there will never happen here. It would be factual there but never be real here, just as my blue-print of a national monument will remain in my office and never become a physical reality.

If you meet someone on the astral side and get information which proves to be true, it means that you met someone who was in a position to influence what occurs on this side. I taught kundalini yoga and meditation now for over 30 years. Most of the instructions I received from advanced teachers were given on the astral side. The truth of that comes into reality when I follow those instructions and advance further in the practice, or when sometimes I find the same instructions in books like *Bhagavad Gita*. In that way I learnt how to verify the instructions. My confidence in the memory of what happens on the astral side is reinforced.

Usually people have confidence on the physical side only. They dismiss dreams as illusion. If one opens oneself to doubtful people one will become more and more materialistic and less and less psychic. Even people whom one is related to and whom one loves may be materialistic to the core. If one shares with them the psychic experiences, they may discourage one.

There are dreams in which one works out issues and hassles in dealings between one's astral body and the astral bodies of others. There are directive dreams in which one makes contact with an astral level which is the blueprint for this physical plane, such that if one recalls what happens there, it gives one insight into what will occur here.

Dream (November 2010)

It is not a good idea to think that all dreams have significance. For one thing this presumption about dreams causes the mind to become tense.

Dreams should be seen as occurrences which are either astral happenings in a real astral world, or just imaginative mock-ups in the mind. Since the mind is involved in imagination, people have a distrust about dreams and try to relegate dreams to being imagination.

One should sort honestly between an imagination and actual dream life of astral existence.

Many things which appear in dreams have absolutely no significance, no more than the rising of the sun carries significance. In other worlds, things just happen in the astral world. Most of it has no content of impact on anything in a significant way, but it is part of the flow of real astral history.

If one takes a plane to a city, and then as soon as one gets there it rains, one never asks about the significance of the weather. When one finds oneself in an astral experience, it is similar. One enters an environment in which things occur or in which things will happen.

Yoga (November 2010)

Yoga is listed by Patañjali as having eight parts. Posture or asana is just one part. It is the third stage in the eight segments of yoga. Higher yoga or meditation is called *samyama* by Patañjali. That is the three highest parts, when done as a sequential practice.

This *samyama* is called meditation in the Western countries. People here are mostly concerned with meditation and not with the preliminary parts of the process as listed by Patañjali.

Some people are concerned with postures but only for the purpose of physical health and beauty. Yoga is for transcending ourselves as physical systems and finding everything else which is the self. In other words, besides my physical body, what I am? Yoga is the tool used to pry into that.

Yoga is an escapist thing. Those who feel locked down in the material world, like prisoners locked in a max-security prison, may do yoga. With yoga we escape from this dimension and research other places, trying to find something which is agreeable. In meditation the yogi researches other dimension in his hunt for something which suits his needs.

If he finds dimensions which involve the use of a temporary body or which is connected to a place where temporary bodies are use, he is not interested.

The highest stage of yoga, is called *samadhi* which is mostly tripping out from this place and keying in to other dimensions and other types of beings, divine beings. A yogi realizes that he needs a connection to somebody in the divine places.

Yoga is not concerned with straightening kinks in this environment, nor in becoming harmonious with it. On the micro level among the bacteria, a yogi sees that this is a *dog eat dog* situation all the way through to the top level of the human predators. The yogi has no hope of harmonizing with this or of causing this to harmonize with the self.

The idea is to abandon this and to find an already-existing place which is devoid of the *dog eat dog* profile.

Purpose of Life (November 2010)

Most persons using a human body have no memory of past lives. They have no mission in that regard. They found themselves conscious as a human body. That is all there is to it.

Patañjali said that the purpose for the conjunction between material nature and the spiritual self, is for providing self-objectivity.

$$स्वस्वामिशक्त्योः स्वरूपोपलब्धिहेतुः संयोगः ॥२३॥$$

sva svāmiśaktyoḥ svarūpa upalabdhi hetuḥ saṁyogaḥ

sva – own nature, own psyche; svāmi – the master, the individual self; saktyoḥ – of the potency of the two; svarūpa – essential form; upalabdhi – obtaining experience; hetuḥ – cause, reason; saṁyogaḥ – conjunction.

There is a reason for the conjunction of the individual self and its psychological energies. It is for obtaining the experience of its essential form. (Yoga Sutras 2.23)

Like for instance if someone is born in New York that person will be exposed to certain experiences, and if at the same time someone is born in the Sahara in a Bedouin family, that person will have a certain experience which will be quite different and which will give him certain advantages which will be useless if he relocates to New York.

What is the game plan? Some people feel that you should live in the *now* in whatever happens around you. If we take that literally, it means that if I find myself conscious as a lion cub, then the *now* for me will be to learn to kill antelope. If I find myself as an antelope foal, then the *now* for me will be to learn to eat grass.

This complies with Patañjali's statement that material nature is there to provide experience. The Sanskrit term for such experience is bhoga, which means that which is experienced. But here it applies to both desirable and undesirable circumstances.

As a foal of an antelope, if I am separated from my mother the experience for me will be that of being chased and killed by a lion. That is undesirable but it is still to be enjoyed in the sense of being experienced.

Back in the human species other experiences take place. If I took birth during Roman times, and I lived in Northern Europe and was known as a barbarian, I may be captured and made into a Roman slave. That would be an experience of White on White oppression. But if I lived in Africa during the

Colonial era, I may have been capture and transported in a ship and taken to the West Indies as a slave, which would be White on Black oppression.

Conversely, if I was a white man who was the slave owner and who got rich trading black human beings as slaves that would also be an experience. Thus even if one cannot remember past lives, one would have a mission according to the species and the era in which one assumes a body.

As soon as one is born there is a mission which will be impressed. A kitten in a New York apartment has a mission because the wealthy woman who owns it, expects it to pass waste in a specific pan in the condominium. It is expected to greet her when she comes into the apartment. It may sleep by her side when she does not have a companion.

If the kitten fails to evacuate in a pan the lady may call an animal shelter and have the animal taken away. The kitten has a mission. If it fails to format itself, its mission is changed by fate in the form of a phone call by the wealthy owner.

The creation has mission and purpose. Most is short-ranged and has no spiritual content. Most involves evolutionary drives. That means nourishment, recuperation, reproduction and protection. If one cannot discover the spiritual side to one's existence, it means that one can only serve the evolutionary drives which are compressed into the particular species one finds oneself to be at any particular time. But even in that case, there is mission.

Part 2

Kundalini in balance (November 2010)

Sometimes when doing kundalini yoga practice one may find that the kundalini comes up one side of the body and does not come up the corresponding other side. Some persons come to a yoga class with the queer idea that everything should be or will be put into balance by meditation and postures. They feel that the odd left side or hanging right side will come into position, and there will forever from then onward, be a perfect equal on either side, never ever to be displaced again.

In the human species, there is imbalance in the body since the heart is hung more on the left side. The left lung is smaller than the right one. Is this nature's fault?

If one practices kundalini yoga, and suddenly during the exercises one finds that kundalini rose on one side only, take it as it is. Do not try to put nature through a balancing act. Nature had good reason to do what it did. Observe what happened. What you can do is to cause kundalini to go further through whatever right or left channel it enters, by a side stretch for instance, by applying muscular locks on the particular side, by wiggling or whatever intuitive action or focus you feel will cause kundalini to go further up or down the particular channel which opens.

When kundalini rises on one side from a stretch on a particular side during breath infusion, I usually observe it, then I move to the other side and check to see if kundalini will course on that side. If it does not, then I observe that and continue practicing. I never stop to question it nor to put it into balance.

Some persons question me about why during some sessions breath flows easily through one nostril and is blocked through the other.

What?

I never stop to question that. It has to do with the percentage of moon or sun energy in the atmosphere. What should one do, yank the moon or tell the sun to reduce intensity?

No! We do the practice honestly and sincerely. We leave the rest to whichever supernatural agency controls it.

Perception of negativity

Even though initially one cannot see negative energy, one can feel it. It is visual in the advanced stage. We can take help from science to have confidence in that, because science can show a picture of thought forms in the brain, when certain cells in the brain fire electric charges when thoughts are conducted. In yoga one develops mystic visions which are similar to what technology shows.

The part where one identifies with the thoughts is part of the meditation practice to differentiate the various components in the head of the subtle body. If the whole head is just one thing and if one cannot differentiate the various components in the mind, then by meditation one can develop clarity in that regard.

Until one can distinguish the components of the mind, one will be subjected to identifying with whatever thoughts or images the mind constructs. There is only one way to overcome that. It is regular practice.

The word psyche means all the psychological energy that a person has. There is psychological energy in the head. It is also in the toes. The collection of psychological energies of the individual is called the psyche.

We place stress on the head but the head is not the only part of the psyche. For instance in the physical sense, the head is the most important part of the body, because if the brain malfunctions, then one is out of it, even if the rest of the body remains fit. We place stress on the head but the human body is more than a head.

Since the attention energy is in the head whatever one perceives in the body is done through that attention energy. If one perceives something in the head, then since the attention energy is there, it does not have to be focused far from its default position. If however something is near the navel or in the foot for instance, the attention must travel to that location, or a message is sent via the nerves physically or through subtle nerves (nadis) to the brain or mind. That takes a little time, micro-seconds perhaps but it is still time.

The negative force will not leave of its own accord. It enters to make an impact, to command the psyche, just as when a virus enters the body.

Negative energies, subtle forces, which enter the psyche come to it to force the psyche to do what those forces desire and to cause the psyche to develop for the benefit of such forces.

If you can make the environment hostile or non-responsive to negative forces they will leave the psyche of their own accord, or be destroyed in the psyche or remain in the psyche in a neutralized form, where they cannot alter the mission of the psyche.

Bubble body of yogi (November 2010)

This morning during breath infusion, kundalini rose from the lower torso in the form of four inch pads of beige-colored light energy. It was like a pad of ice crystals which were beige colored and which had a bliss energy content.

The first pad rose above the navel area and then it disappeared. Then a second pad appeared and did exactly the same thing. Some of the energy shot up into the neck and that felt like tiny needles of bliss force travelling upwards.

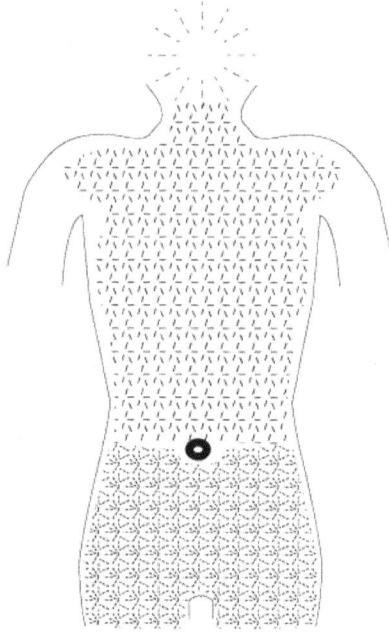

Rishi Singh Gherwal, showed how yogis achieve the bubble bliss body, which looks like an inflated psyche and which is fill with higher subtle energy. In that body the bliss force seems like tiny sand crystals, all exuding bliss happiness.

The development of this bubble bliss body, commences with the complete energization of the trunk of the subtle body below the throat. At first the neck area has a blockage which prevents the compressed bliss force from moving through the neck, but later as the practice proceeds this neck blockage is cleared. The energy reaches into the head. At that point one feels that one has a bloated bliss form which is filled with tiny bliss crystals. Just as a human being gets a feeling that the physical body is made of flesh and bones, the yogis get the feeling that there is nothing in the bliss body except tightly-compacted bliss force.

Sex organ chakra details (November 2010)

This morning I had several instances of kundalini rise during breath infusion. By doing rapid breathing in various postures, one causes the infusion to go into various parts of the psyche. This gives one firsthand knowledge about the layout of the nadi subtle tubes.

Many persons who become meditation teachers and who never did intense pranayama practice, give lectures where they describe the chakras and the nadis. Many of these teachers never experienced the layout of subtle system in the psyche.

One cannot see this system just by sitting to meditate. In the first place, most of the nadis are blocked and are in a dark condition, such that they cannot be seen. It is only when they are infused by subtle breath infusion that they become visible. Visualization does not open the nadis, neither does imagination.

At one part of this session, kundalini base energy changed into an orange color. Normally kundalini at the base chakra is a dark brown-black color, and in the darkness of the psyche it cannot be seen. In other words if one were to go down into the base chakra with a flash light, it would be so dark that even with the light one would see nothing. The darkness is so dense that it would absorb the light completely. However when there is a sexual climax, a spark of energy like a lightning flash passes from the base chakra to the sex organ chakra. Then a large explosion of energy occurs which is interpreted by the mind as the much desired sex pleasure.

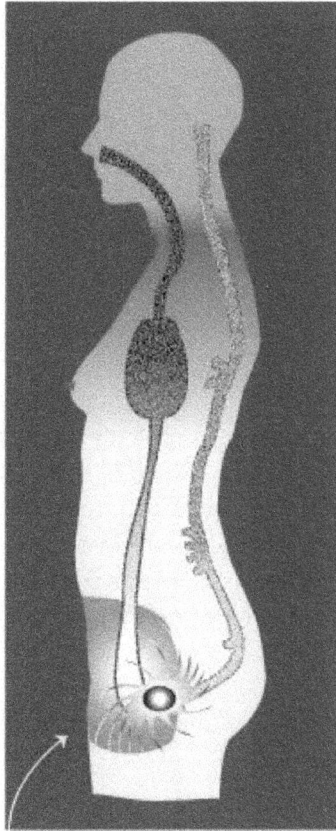

kundalini lifeforce explosion
at sex organ chakra

During an intercourse there is a beginning point when the flash spark occurs and depending on the situation the large explosion will happen some seconds or microseconds after.

Since the spark energy leaves the base chakra and travels to the sexual organ chakra, one does not see it at the base but one feels it at the sex organ

chakra. Then there is a large explosion at the sex organ chakra which is felt by the entity through the intellect, which is the means of visualizing sense phenomena. Sometimes the energy is so intense that it burns the intellect and that orb jumps back into the head of the body.

The sex organ chakra is not the same as the sex chakra on the spine. The sex organ chakra is located at the perineum nerve junction.

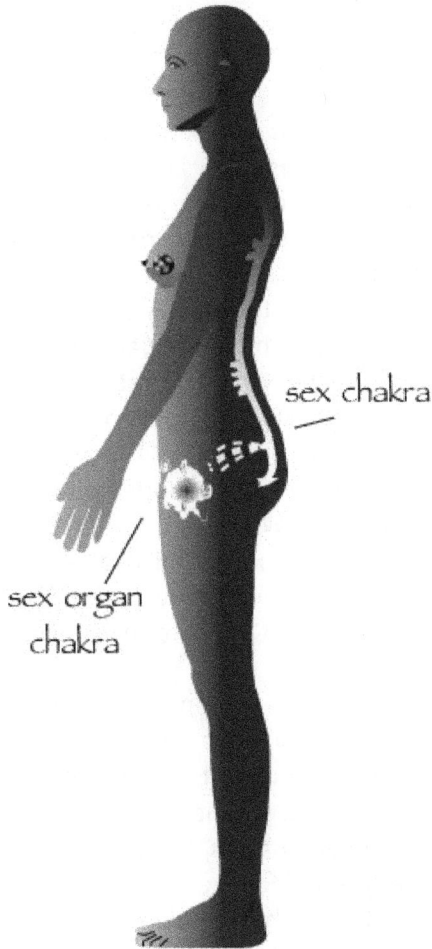

sex chakra

sex organ
chakra

After the intense explosion, the sex chakra turns black like coal and there is no visibility there, until another such explosion can be generated.

Jump kundalini (November 2010)

Rishi Singh Gherwal gave notations about jump kundalini, which is a process used by yogis, to prepare for kundalini control at the time of death.

He said that sometimes a yogi cannot get his act together at the time of death. It may come suddenly without the yogi being able to adjust kundalini just before it happens. Some incapacitating terminal diseases may cause a yogi to lose grip on kundalini during the last months or years of the body.

However, if the yogi can master jump kundalini before the body reaches a bad state in which kundalini cannot be handled effectively, then when kundalini finally leaves the physical form and is free from being responsible for it, the yogi can use the method already developed to jump kundalini to a higher chakra in the subtle body.

Jump kundalini is the method of causing kundalini's base to jump to a higher chakra. Rishi explained that jump kundalini is not the same as kundalini arousal for any purpose, like kundalini arousal for sex climax or kundalini arousal for higher awareness. In those situations the energy of kundalini moves from the base chakra but its base remains the same as muladhara chakra at the end of the spine.

Jump kundalini means that the base itself moves with the kundalini. When the yogi gets the base to move upwards from the base to the 2nd chakra or from the base to the 5th chakra, that is jump kundalini. A yogi should practice and make the base jump upwards. Preferably he should attain the power to make it jump into the brain.

The yogi should get the trunk of the subtle body and the two appendages which hang from the lower trunk (thighs, legs, feet) to be infused with a higher energy. Once that is done, kundalini's adhesive which keeps it at the base chakra is loosened. It becomes submissive to the calling power of the yogi. Kundalini becomes buoyant. Otherwise normally, it is heavy and cannot be lifted.

Kundalini settles first into the semen of the father during the formation of the semen, as the root energy there. From that it creates for itself a tail part which later becomes the blueprint for the spinal column. It is basically like a reptile, like an alligator, but with its brain at one end of its tail. When it is transferred into the mother's uterus, kundalini becomes the gravitational force which anchors the coreSelf for the formation of the fetus.

From its anchor point at the base chakra, kundalini conducts the growth and maintenance of the physical body. In the subtle body it is located in the same place basically at the base of the spine of that form.

To unhinge it one has to attack its grossness. To do so one must change its energy composition. That may be done proficiently by doing pranayama breath infusion which is the fourth stage of yoga. Some people try to use visualization and mystic exercise of willpower to command kundalini but usually kundalini ignores their attempts.

Instead of responding, it stays put at the base and directs them in getting pleasures like eating tasty foods and indulging sexually.

In the Upanishad period some yogis came to the conclusion that the most definite way to upset kundalini was through breath infusion. The idea is to sabotage the natural way of kundalini and to bring it under control so that one can be transited to a higher dimension. By itself kundalini is concerned with gross existence in a material body in any species of life. To upset that one should change its energy intake. An aggressive breath infusion practice is a sure way of achieving this.

For a beginner kundalini is deliberately raised by doing breath infusion or another effective breath ingestion practice. After repeatedly raising kundalini once or twice per day, a student manages to flush most of the subtle pollution in the psyche. Due to that kundalini gradually lose its grossness. When the student exercises, he finds that kundalini's base may sometimes relocate to a higher chakra. Then a great yogi will appear and give advice on how to pull kundalini to yet higher states.

Casual sex: where does it fit in? (November 2010)

Casual sex should be seen as a no no, because it carries consequences in one's future life. Even though it is not preferred, one may circumstantially be forced into it. The mere idea that one is circumstantially put into a position to have casual sex and one cannot refuse it, because of the emotional and sensual feelings, means that the partner involved is a part of one's fate. Everything that happens is destined, even though some circumstances do not fit into one ideals.

I cite an example when I was circumstantially forced into a sexual relationship. Once when I was in the Philippines, in Angeles City just outside of Clark Air Base, I used to go bar hopping. This was a process where on Friday and Saturday nights, many servicemen would go from bar to bar looking for women and intoxication.

There were so many bars on the main strip. It was like every building had at least one bar. At the door there were young Philippino women. Some were about fifteen or sixteen years of age. The idea was to petition a woman, take her out of the bar for the night, find a hotel, have sexual intercourse and then beat back to base in the morning.

One would have to check out the girl from the club by paying a fee to the owner. That was about US$15-40. That took care of the bar owner and the girl. One did not have to give the girl any more money but one had to pay for a room at a hotel.

After I was there for about 4 months I heard that these girls had run away from the small islands to the main island. They could not return to their villages, because they were now outcasts. In addition, they had a bill with the bar owner so that they could not permanently leave until that bill was paid.

By this time, I favored a woman. I took her out of the bar on weekends. Once I asked her what her charge was to the bar owner. I felt uneasy about her circumstance. She said that for about US$60-80 her bill would be paid.

I proposed to her that she should get out of the bar, instead of ruining her life by prostitution. She had recently got into this bar business, so I felt that she could get out of it. I spoke to the bar owner. He agreed that her bills would be paid in full for about US$65.

I scouted around with some friends (military guys) to rent a small house. I paid the rent. I paid her bills and moved her into the rented place. After about three months, I was stressed to pay the bills for food and for everything else for the upkeep of the place. Anyway I thought of making the whole thing permanent. I approached my squadron commander about getting permission to marry this girl. He used a white body and I use a black body, but he was not prejudiced in any way. He said this to me, "Yes, I can give permission but it is you who really has to make the decision to marry this woman. My view is that you should not do it."

I asked him why he did not think it was a good idea. He explained that usually when Americans marry outside of their cultural, it will work so long as the lady is in her culture but when she gets to the USA, there may be a cultural shock. The relationship may fall apart, due to cultural misalignment.

I sat in his office, not knowing what to do because this was something that I did not consider. Anyway, he told me to think it over and to return in a week with my decision. As I walked out of the door, he said this, "By the way I am married to a Philippino woman."

Later that week by chance I saw him with his wife. She was a fair-skinned Philippino woman from the higher class of Philippino society. She was extremely attractive. Because of this I decided not to marry that woman. I cited this to show that there is no such thing as a casual sexual relationship. If you meet a woman and has a sexual contact with her, it means there is something there from a past life. Providence throws that on one's path of life, to alert one to the fact that besides the present ideas, there are other consequential relationships which it intends to resolve.

None of us move through these lives without a criminal record from past lives. We have unsettled accounts and liabilities pending from past lives. Providence throws those situations in our faces at a future time.

What happened with that person in the Philippines since back in 1970-1971, is not over. It still hangs over my head. From time to time about every four years or so, I see that person in dreams. She pleads with me to care for her. This still happens. It is not over.

Casual sex with protection from disease and with some effective contraceptive means is like a clean murder. Yes, we killed the guy. He is deader than ever. We destroyed the evidence. The police are baffled. They will never figure it because we took care to be sure that there is no body to be dug up anywhere. But that does not mean that it is finished.

Each of us carries within the psyche, energies for taking care of any liabilities which will be pushed in the path of life. It so happens however that in some cases the energies cannot be matched properly because the present lay out, may not match to the layout from some past life when we had a particular relationship with the other person.

When I meet with someone in this life and there is a proposition for sex, I should consider. First of all if the woman is in need of money, that is easy if I can afford it. What I mean is this. Suppose I meet this woman at a bar and she is offers sexual intercourse in exchange for funds, then it is simply a matter of giving her the money and forgetting about the sex. That is really simple. I give her the money but I tell her that the sex is unnecessary. I wish her well. A good deed done. Instead of murdering the guy and making a clean job of it, I help the guy and get on my way. He is happy because I did not kill him. I am free from fear of arrest.

But suppose I met this other woman casually and she seems to be attracted to me but she is not at a bar. This happened in the office. She wants to have sex. She does not want any commitment from me except sex. At least that is what she says to me and that is her mood. She did this with other men before she met me. She does not want to be tied to just one man. She wants the freedom to have multiple partners. What should I do in this case?

That is like when I met the guy who had a large sum of money. He was a bank courier. He asked me to kill him and take the money. I then asked him why he wanted to die. He said that he had some domestic problems and lost the zest for life. If I killed him, he would not be a witness to my theft of the money. I would benefit in two ways. I would have the money. There would be no one to testify against me. I killed him and took the money. Someone the police traced the crime to me. Before the judge, I spoke up because I felt that it was not my fault since the currier asked me to kill him. What do you think the judge will be do? Will the judge say, "You are a law abiding citizen. I recommend that you be given the highest citizenship award."

What I am driving at is that consent for casual sex is a trap. It carries liabilities. Sex always includes emotions, even in the case of prostitutes. There is no such thing as casual sex. If you cannot see yourself having children with a woman, you should not have sex with her. It is that simple. In other words if you cannot see yourself being committed to the emotional content of a woman, then you should not make a sexual entry into her body. The reason is that a woman's breasts and birth passage are major conduits for emotions.

Did you not have a mother? Did you not have to suckle your mother as an infant? Did you not have to come out of your mother's passage to be born? If you did then maybe you forgot that those parts of her body are just as valuable as one is, because those parts were in service to cause you to be here.

Because a woman's passage is vital for us to take birth and is vital for us to get an embryo developed, we should not abuse that part of a woman's anatomy. Nor should we allow any woman to encourage us in such abuse, merely because that woman underrates her gender value.

Do not have sex with a woman if you cannot be proud of that woman as the mother of your child. Any child she produces, will begin life by being inserted through the same passage you use for sexual entries.

Kundalini sex control (November 2010)

Kundalini sex control is a complicated process consisting of getting various parts of the psyche to give up the interest in contributing to the storage of energy for sexual intercourse. The idea is to use the same energy for even distribution through the psyche and for reaching the brain. Nature arranged for this energy to be channeled to the sexual organs but if one wants to beat the system one should change the routing.

One of the areas which must be adjusted is the thighs. This area is one of the largest contributors to sexual hormone accumulation.

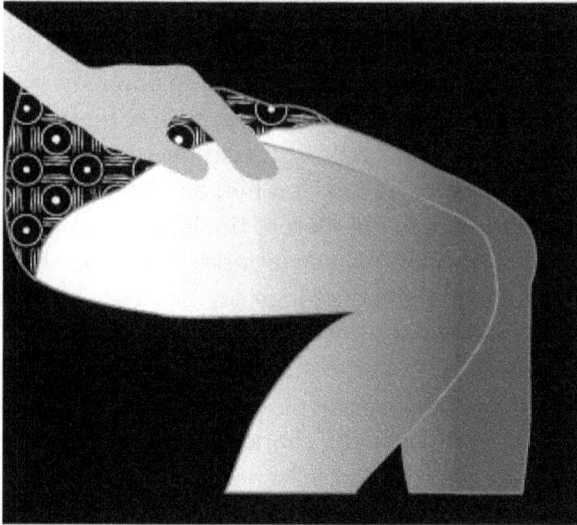

Yoga / Sociology

If a yogi fails with yoga practice, and is unable to consolidate it, he has no choice but to take recourse to the benefits which he accrued by his socially uplifting acts. As a last resort, if a yogi cannot get his act together before he loses the physical body, he falls back on his historic social account and makes use of that in his next life.

Both systems are not used. One can only use one of the systems. Social activities no matter how great and how approved and beneficial they are, will not help for yoga elevation. And yoga elevations will in turn do nothing for social upliftment.

These are two different currencies which cannot be swopped one for another. This is why we find that a person who is a great yogi may be in abject poverty. It is because destiny thinks that he has not made a sufficient social contribution to derive social benefits like others who dedicated themselves to doing socially approved acts in the material world.

The astral worlds which are reached by those who have amassed credits by favorable social activity are different to the astral worlds reached by those who perfected yoga practice. But if a yogi did not complete his practice to a certain degree, those efforts will be insufficient to cause transit to the siddhaloka astral places where great yogis live, and then he will instead be routed to astral paradises where the pious people go. Then he will return into this world through the regular route of developing a semen/ova/embryo-infancy body.

Kundalini front rise (November 2010)

Kundalini rose with intensity through the front of the chest and into the arms and forearms. This was with the intensity which is usually experienced when kundalini rises rapidly and suddenly through the spine and into the head.

When that happens if the yogi is not attentive, his or her body may fall to the ground as when the kundalini strikes the intellect, that means of perception may become disconnected from the nerves in the brain which control the body and then the coreSelf cannot give directions to keep the body standing or sitting.

Over time after many sessions of practice the yogi learns how to manage the rise of kundalini. He supervises the intellect as well as the avenues through which the energy rises through the spine and floods into the head at a rapid speed.

By repeatedly rising kundalini, the yogi gets it reoriented to the coming into the head

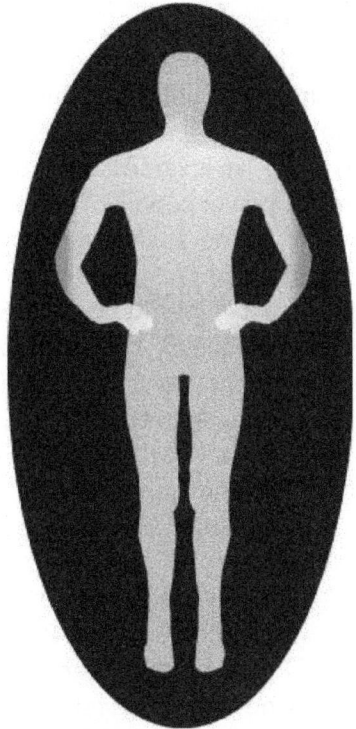

of the body. It eventually foregoes its desire to be routed only through the sexual organs.

When kundalini comes up the front of the body and into the throat and head, it feels like trillions of tiny electric shocks of bliss energy especially in the chest and throat.

Kundalini may rise through the front of the subtle body, which may be elongated and arched forward. The back of the subtle body may remained unaffected.

Kundalini hesitation (November 2010)

During breath infusion, kundalini may develop enough charge of energy to move, but then it may shiver and hesitate. Then one may lose objectivity which results in loss of control of the physical body. This could be for moments or for a few minutes.

When kundalini does not have sufficient charge from breath infusion, it will not have the power to course through the spine into the brain, but it may travel part of the way and then stop and subside.

It may happen however that kundalini moves part way, then stops, and then suddenly jumps through the spine into the brain. This may shock the yogi so that he/she loses control of the physical body for moments or minutes.

Kundalini strikes the analytical orb when it is off-guard and since that orb is the touch point between the coreSelf and objective consciousness at this time, the coreSelf also loses contact. The way the psyche is wired, the coreSelf is more like an accessory rather than being the major component, but it is the major power supply of the psyche.

It is the analytical orb which has to be protected from the striking of kundalini when it comes into the head. If kundalini hits the orb from behind, the orb will lose its contact with the body. The coreSelf will in turn seem to lose control even though what happens is that the orb lost contact. It is like a system of an electric circuit. If you cut a wire to one part of the circuit, power will no longer go to that part. All components which are wire-routed through that part will lose function in reference to the system.

The questions are:

Why does the coreSelf not maintain its objectivity even when the kundalini strikes and stuns the analytical orb?

What is the dependence of the core on the orb?

When the orb is hit from behind by it, why does kundalini stun the orb?

These questions face a yogi. Each one should research this.

One thing is certain. The delay of kundalini is usually based on a lack of sufficient energy during the breath infusion.

Sleep paralysis clarification (November 2010)

Sleep paralysis is not the same as the spooky experience one may have during the paralysis. Circumstances which occur during a paralysis are not connected to it but is coincidental. If one goes to a disreputed part of a city, and falls due to a heart attack, one may be frisked by people of that neighborhood. But that does not mean that the heart attack and the criminal elements are related. It is just that when one is disadvantaged, someone may exploit the situation. Sleep paralysis is the astral body not being in sync with the physical form, so that when one tries to move the physical one finds that one cannot operate it.

Usually when the astral body comes back into the physical system, it gets in sync so rapidly and perfectly that one does not notice the fusion of the two bodies. One awakens as the physical person. One acts with or without memory of dreams or astral contacts. But if the astral body does not synchronize properly, one immediately notices that something is amiss. One tries to move as the physical form. One finds that it does not respond as usual. One may panic. When this happens remember that it occurs due to the astral form not fusing properly into the physical body.

During sleep paralysis a ghost or a fearful apparition is present because of a fear energy in the mind. The fear energy is a psychological force in the mind. The ghost is a real being in the astral world. The fear energy causes the astral body to be on the level of existence where the ghost is present. If one eliminates the fear energy, the astral body will no longer be in sync with the ghost or fearful reality. It will be aware of a higher dimension or of one in which nothing spooky occurs.

When there are tingling sensations just before, after or during a nap or sleep, it may be part of the process of either the separation or fusion of the astral with the physical body.

Usually it is the separation. The subtle body's energy becomes super-energized when it separates from a sober physical body. If it separates from a drunk body or from a body which used alcohol, an opiate or depressant, it will become de-energized. If it separates during taking of LSD and similar hallucinogenic drugs, it may be super-energized.

Usually this takes place and the person is not aware of what happens because the person's attention is not tuned into what happens on the astral plane.

Because it happens every time the physical body sleeps yogis do special meditations to gain awareness of the separation process. How the astral body leaves the physical one is a great secret which nature is disinclined to reveal.

When sleep paralysis takes place if something is really scary, the astral body will snap into the physical one in sync. One will awaken physically. This also happens when a person has an astral encounter and feels danger. At that time the astral body is snapped back into the physical one. The person awakens as the usual physical self with fearful feelings and spooky memories.

Obligation to the deceased

Astral projection occurs anytime the physical body sleeps. It is done by nature, in order for nature to rejuvenate the physical system. Astral projection is for the most part positive. If however one enters an astral world in which departed souls take energy from the astral form that will be a drain on one's emotions.

One should determine whom one meets astrally. Is it relatives who are deceased? Is it strangers from other families? Is it souls who for one reason or the other have negative energies?

One should meditate and research that. One can meditate and contact the deceased persons without having the astral body separate from the physical one. One could see those disembodied persons and limit or bar association.

One thing is certain. Everyone owes something to someone who is deceased. We use bodies which are the result of social work of others who passed away and are on the astral planes. Many on that side of existence may claim energies from us on that basis.

How kundalini is affected (November 2010)

Kundalini practice is affected by changes in diet and schedule. Kundalini manages the material body. Any change in routine affects it. A change in diet affects the digestive apparatus and the excretion system. These affect the energy distribution of kundalini. If one changes the daily schedule, kundalini must adjust to that. This affects practice.

More or less, one should know that if one changes diet or schedule the next practice session may be different. For example, yesterday my diet routine and schedule were changed. Subsequently when doing the morning session of exercises, I did much more practice to cause kundalini to rise. In addition during the session I had to evacuate the body. Whenever that happens one should return to the session and continue the practice from where one stopped before the interruption.

One should make every effort to infuse air energy into the gap which is created by the evacuated matter. In the body waste holds energy. When it is evacuate there is a deficit space created. That should be filled with fresh air energy. In addition for evacuation the kundalini uses polluted air like carbon dioxide. This should be pulled out of the body by rapid breathing.

The basic effort in breath infusement is to extract carbon dioxide from the lungs, while infusing oxygen. Carbon dioxide increase in the body has a negative spiritual impact. It causes a decrease in psychic perception and an increase in materialistic focus.

It depends on one's objective. If one desires to increase physical focus, it would not be in one's interest to decrease the proportion of oxygen in the blood stream. In that case it would be beneficial to increase the carbon dioxide content. A corresponding feature is there in diet, where a vegetarian diet will result in sharper psychic perception while a flesh diet will increase the materialistic focus.

When doing breath infusement, the yogi should first make an effort to extract the carbon dioxide through the lungs. By doing various postures while breathing rapidly, the blood stream collects carbon dioxide from the tissues. By the pumping action of the heart blood is transported to the lungs where carbon dioxide is expelled from the body, where it is exchanged for oxygen.

During rapid breathing the heart beat increases to keep abreast to transport the infused oxygen, and similarly carbon dioxide is expelled from the system rapidly. Within about twenty minutes, most of the carbon dioxide is removed from the system.

On the subtle side, negative subtle energy is expelled from the system and a higher subtle energy is infused into it. When most of the negative force is extracted, the kundalini acquires a charge. When this charge is increased further, it sparks and jumps in one direction or the other. By the application of locks, the yogi channels this lifeForce power.

Initially the yogi cannot channel this force. It moves in an instinctive direction without his control. Over time, after much practice he/she gains control.

Why be vegetarian? (November 2010)

Vegetarian diet, is an effort to protect the self from taking birth in lower species. Any self can take a body in any other species. The selves are adaptable.

To protect the self from accidentally or impulsively being attracted to an animal species one must cultivate habits which give the required resistance to avoid animal wombs.

The only thing that protects a person from animal birth is non-animal habits. In the interim state after leaving the body, one senses birth opportunities on the basis of instinct. One does not usually have any objective say in what happens regarding where one will take birth. If one has an instinct for eating and living like an animal there is a likelihood that one may become a kitten or puppy in the next life. One cannot consciously recall what happened as an embryo and as a newborn baby, and it will be in the same ignorance in the next life.

A sure way to get an animal body is to keep pet animals. This is very good for the animal since it gives the animal something to aim for which is higher than its present status, but for the human being who keeps the animal it is a danger, because upon passing if the affection continues, the human may enter an animal parent body and develop an embryo there.

In the *Srimad Bhagavatam* there is a narration about a great yogi named Bharat. He lived in isolation doing spiritual practices with intentions to go to higher dimensions after death. Once when a tiger roared near his place, a pregnant deer got scared. It leaped across a stream. During the jump, the doe's body delivered a fawn. Since the doe ran for its life, it lost the faun. Bharat nurtured the animal.

In Bharat's next life he assumed life as a fawn. Even in that form, he had inclinations for yoga but could not practice. He lingered near the huts of yogis. He chewed the pages of their palm leaves books.

That is another method of taking animal birth after a human birth. There are many ways of doing this, according to the psychological instincts one develops and according to the route of the emotions.

Recently there was an increase in animals living in human homes. Humans always had pets but living inside the human home increased. This tells us that the animals are desperate for human birth. Perhaps this is because human beings over the past three centuries killed many animals and threaten their survival. The animals desire to be human. The problem with this is that there may also be a reversal, where humans take animal bodies because of affiliation with animal pets. If that happens then the animals will be more demanding and more influential in causing humans to treat animal-pet bodies as human bodies or as having the same value as human bodies.

Many people opted out on children. They cared for pets instead. It may be that providence will reward them by causing them to take the next body as an animal. Would that be a fair exchange?

People may get the idea that I am a vegetarian because of religious stipulation. Actually I do not give a fig about religion. I am concerned only about where I will go when this body is confiscated by nature. I will not knowingly do anything that will cause nature to guide me into an animal womb. I will do everything in my power to discourage that.

Buddha admitted to having animal bodies in the past. He saw this in meditation. His view is that it is all anguish. I do not care to be a human being what to speak of being an animal in the next life. As a last resort, if there is no alternative, I would prefer a human birth.

I could have easily raised animals instead of human babies. In fact I had dairy goats and two donkeys when I lived in Minnesota. The dairy goats were for milk. The intention with the donkeys were to use them as draught animals.

I never kept an animal as a pet, except that humans are also animals, and I kept four children. I look away even from those four children because I want to be in the divine world. There is no question of my adopting animals. If anything, I will advise students about how to effectively and efficiently take care of social obligations in caring for infants.

Diet is only a part of the method for avoiding animal birth, but it is an important step in that direction. People who have astrally projected know fully well that they will survive in a psychological form after the body dies. They should also understand that the psychology is highly adaptive. It can assume animal habits.

I have no objection to anyone eating flesh. My father told stories about snakes, turtles and many other creatures as part of his diet when he was in the Amazonian forest diving for gold as a young man. I personally think that eating flesh is great because by doing that one gets to explore the various types of taste which are available. One gets to polish one's predatory instincts by cooking the flesh instead of eating it raw as the big cats and even some aborigines do. Cooking flesh before eating it is an upgrade from the animal world. It is a hallmark of having entered the human species.

For me personally, I am not interested in exploring those avenues of experience. Because of the parental situation I ate flesh as a child, but it is not my preference.

If one gets something out of flesh one may do it. Aleister Crowley who was regarded as the Devil by Christians, left us with one important line which is:

Do what Thou Wilt Shall Be the Whole Law!

The meaning is that if you can get away with it, do it. At least until you can understand how it will hurt you.

Nature is the teacher. She shows the good way and the bad way, the way which will hurt and the way which will free one. If she gives allowance and we take it and then discover that it hurts we will eventually cease the behavior.

There is much about diet throughout my books but this verse below from the *Brahma Yoga Bhagavad Gita,* is a sample of the information:

आसुरीं योनिमापन्ना
मूढा जन्मनि जन्मनि ।
मामप्राप्यैव कौन्तेय

āsurīṁ — the wicked people; yonim — womb; āpannā — entering; mūḍhā — the blockheads; janmani janmani — in birth, in birth again;

ततो यान्त्यधमां गतिम् ॥१६.२०॥
āsurīṁ yonimāpannā
mūḍhā janmani janmani
māmaprāpyaiva kaunteya
tato yāntyadhamāṁ gatim (16.20)

*mām — me; aprāpyaivā = aprāpya —
associating + eva — indeed; kaunteya
— O son of Kuntī; tato = tataḥ —
thence; yānti — they traverse;
adhamāṁ — lowest; gatim — route
of transmigration*

Thus, O son of Kuntī, entering the wombs of the wicked people, the blockheads, after not associating with Me in birth after birth, traverse the lowest route of transmigration. (16.20)

Siddha Swami's Commentary:

Since the living entitles are hitched to a set of psychological equipment, they are to an extent limited to what such equipment allow them to perceive. Thus if one gets into a lower species of life, one will develop lowly priorities, which to one's senses, may appear as a high order of preferences. If for instance one enters the species of the big cats, like the lions and tigers, one's intellect will be inclined to analyzing methods of catching herbivores like deer and cattle. Using the intellect in that way, one will feel superior to other life forms which are not obsessed with such methods of killing other species for food. Thus even though the same intellect may be used for earning one's way to liberation and divine association, one will have no idea of such usage.

A living entity who has a leonine form in one life time, will take with him his intellect, mind space, emotional and sensual energies, along with his memory when he transmigrates to any other life form. Even if he attains the form of a human being, he will still do so with the same intellect he used in the lower species. One must know that there is no change in the psychological equipment even though there may be a change in the gross body. The subtle body adapts to any new gross form one takes but that subtle form is not changed for a new one. It is therefore important to take up the task of reforming the subtle form, since it is the same form one will use through the duration of the creation.

One remains in a lower form or goes to an even lower species, through the method of becoming addicted to the senses of the subtle body. For then, whatever is shown to one by such senses, becomes one's basis for the next transmigration. Unless one can curb the subtle body so that its quest for lower gratifications is eliminated, one will have to enter lower life forms.

Part 3

Holy Ghost or Kundalini

According to the Christian theology, the Holy Spirit is external to the person but it may saturate the person.

Kundalini is inside the body of the person. It is always there. It is the lifeForce of the body. It conducts the involuntary activities. It does not come and go. So long as the body is alive, kundalini is within the body as its life force.

Kundalini spark jump (November 2010)

The basic process of kundalini breath infusion is that the pubio-pelvis area should be fully infused with fresh breath energy. Once that is done, there is a likelihood that the energy will develop a charge which will cause it to spark over to the base chakra.

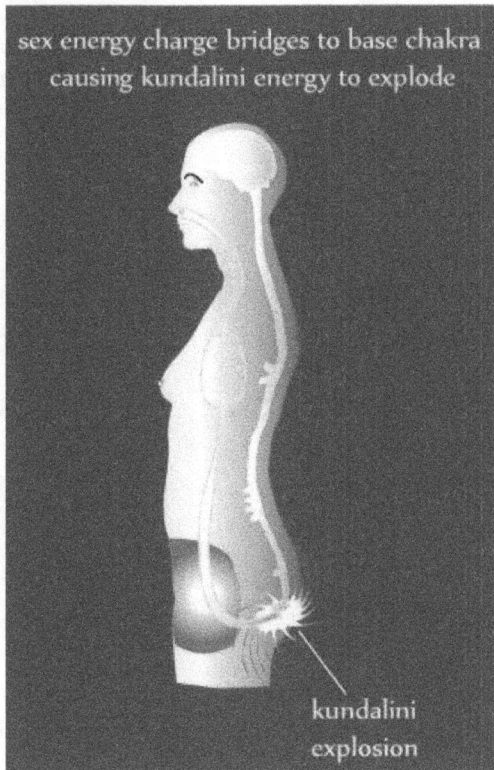

sex energy charge bridges to base chakra causing kundalini energy to explode

kundalini explosion

To get some concept of this, we can review what happens during a sexual climax experience. In a sexual experience the sexual organs generate energy until that energy reaches a certain threshold. Then suddenly there is a burst of uncontrollable energy which is called a climax

The climax takes place when the sexual organ charge accumulates to a certain level. Then there is a spark of energy where the kundalini jumps from the base chakra directly to that sex energy charge.

In the case of kundalini yoga, the charge from the sex plexus increases. Then it jumps to the base chakra. The movement is in the opposite direction. In sex the jump is from the base chakra to the sex energy. In kundalini infusion process it is from the sex energy plexus to the base chakra.

Using naad as a mantra

A Buddha Deity inspired me with a method of using naad as a mantra. This is for situations in which a yogi finds himself mentally with a requirement for dependence and use of a mantra.

Traditionally, naad is not used as a mantra, but one can intonate the Om (A-U-M) sound for a time. When that absorption gets deep, one should release oneself from the practice and listen to naad.

However I was told by a Buddha deity in South Korea, that he used a naad nam kriya which is effective. This is the first time I heard of this method.

Naad is the sound which resonates causelessly producing a high pitched frequency which is heard on the right or left side of the head near an ear.

Nam is a Sanskrit word. The complete form is namah (pronounced nuh-muh-hah). It is shortened in Hindi to nam. This word means name, nomenclature.

According to that Buddha deity, after one hears it in the head one can say the naad frequency mentally. If in hearing it, one finds that one's mind refuses to be fully absorbed in it, then one would split the mind into two parts; the part that is attracted to naad frequency and the part which is inattentive to it. The inattentive part should be made to mentally create or express a sound which resembles the naad sound which is heard by the other part. This is totally mental. No sound is made by the vocal cords.

Effects of breath infusion (November 2010)

Since there is variation in the weather energy, and in the state of the psyche of the individual yogi, one must be determined to raise kundalini daily, otherwise if one has a standard set time to practice, on some days, one will be unable to raise kundalini.

The weather changes and so does the energy content of the air we breathe, as well as the subtle air which the subtle body uses. This means that on some days, it will take a longer session of breath infusement to raise kundalini. On some days just as soon as one begins kundalini will rise but on other days, one may have to do a double or triple session to get kundalini to rise.

There is also the factor of the energy which is in the psyche of a yogi. Due to low social or astral association this energy may be depressive. The yogi must aggressively attack this energy and remove it from his or her psyche for success. This takes time, energy and attention.

An average full session of kundalini breath infusement takes about 20-30 minutes. But if there is low energy, it may take up to 40-60 minutes. Immediately after the session, the yogi should sit to meditate. In meditation one should note the effects of the infused breath. Such effects are:

- energy coursing through the trunk or head.
- spontaneous hearing of naad
- spontaneous focus on naad
- visions of lights in the frontal part of the head

- inward-outward movement of a disc of light in respect to the center of the eyebrows
- absence of thoughts and images in the frontal part of the head
- slow motion presentation of thoughts and images with ability to stop the presentation with little effort
- presence of advanced yogis or deities (divine beings) in the subtle head
- force of kundalini entering the head through the neck and going out of the head in a specific direction
- sudden descent of the yogi into the spine or trunk of the body
- appearance of scenes from the divine world in the mind space of the yogi
- appearance of scenes from the astral world, outside of the astral body of the yogi, seen through a space which opens in the center of the eyebrows.

These are some of the effects which one gets from doing the breath infusion before meditation. This is a jump start to meditation.

Uprooting kundalini

A Buddha deity in South Korea, gave an instruction about dealing with muladhara chakra. His idea is that all the work done with kundalini pans out if muladhara chakra's rooting attitude is not dealt with in a decisive way, through an aggressive attack to uproot it.

His details were:

Kundalini shakti has a tendency to get rooted somewhere. Once rooted it grows from that place and spreads itself, either as itself split into various parts or by branching out through giving access to other kundalinis which come under its subjugation because of needing to enter its establishment to get specific life forms.

Kundalini's obsession with form and pleasure has to do with this tendency to root itself. A yogi should research this to get to the root of it and to understand that this is what he must eradicate.

Jumping kundalini into the brain is preliminary. That is stressed by Indian yogis but it is really nothing because so long as kundalini's root tendency is left unhampered, the yogi will again be compelled by it, to take another material body. It may not be a human embryo. It could be any species, even the form of a sponge at the bottom of the sea.

A yogi should dive through sushumna nadi and research how kundalini is rooted in the present body. He should also delve into his time transit to see how his consciousness became rooted into the sperm particle of the father and then in the ovum of his mother, and then how through that root, the placenta developed.

This rooting system is done by kundalini but if you do not know it, how will you become liberated? Kundalini will again dictate what the subtle body will do once you depart from the present body.

When a man looks at a woman sexually, what does he see? What does he look for?

Does the kundalini use the eyes for looking to see if it can be rooted into the woman's sexuality?

The Buddha deity gave a procedure for grabbing kundalini and pulling it away from its root location which is called muladhara base chakra.

In this procedure, one should enter the spine and go downward. The coreSelf goes down through the sushumna central passage. When it gets to the base chakra, it considers the condition of the kundalini there. If kundalini is not infused with energy, the core cannot do this practice because it will not have the power to hold kundalini.

The holding action is done by grabbing kundalini mystically from the outside of the spine. Kundalini is grabbed near its base rooting place. It is pulled up. It is held firmly by mystic power, since if one does not do so, it will immediately reattach itself to the base place. I found that kundalini in that configuration felt like a lamprey eel with its head facing downwards. It has a strong gravitational pull to that base place, so that one has to exert mystic power to hold it away from that place. If one relaxes that power, it immediately reattaches itself with great compressing force as if it has a vacuum draw on that place. If one can hold it for a while say about 5 minutes, then the bottom part of it seals into a round closed shape and the gravitational force which pulled it to the base disappears. The yogi is then free to take kundalini here or there. He can turn it upwards and swim up into the head with it.

This procedure can be used when leaving a material body finally at the body's death. If the yogi can do this he would not be compelled to look for another embryo immediately upon departure from the physical body.

In the *Mahabharata* there is a description of Balram, Krishna's brother, who when he left his physical body, was seen to be like a serpent which left through the mouth of that form and went into higher dimensions. It may be that Balram used a procedure like this and made kundalini turnabout so that its downward facing direction was altered and it faced upwards went up the spine and then through the mouth of his dying physical body.

I have never seen any details of what Balram did but it must be something similar. It is stated however that Balram was using yoga kriyas of pranayama and dimension transfer.

As a divine being, Balram would have no difficulty doing this but others would have to attain practice proficiency long before leaving the body to accomplish this at the body's death.

Right now I am confronted with three objectives:

- Develop a process for extraction of kundalini which supersedes the normal process for leaving a physical body at its death.
- Write literature with details of the yoga process.
- Serve as a counterbalance in the developed countries.

The last objective is not my desire. I comply with it, as I got an instruction from a Buddha deity.

The second objective is the reason why I took this present body.

The first objective is a reality which every yogi must deal with once he or she assumes a physical form. Once a yogi gets into a woman's womb and comes out a newborn child, irrespective of why he or she took that body, the reality is that the departure from it with control of where the subtle body goes and what it will do, has to be accomplished afresh.

Taking a new body, has packaged with it, the task of carefully leaving that body in the end. Otherwise the yogi will find himself or herself recycled into another womb and into another life as a lost soul.

Even though a yogi may be sent into this world by a greater yogi, or even by a divine being like Krishna or Shiva, still the yogi has it as his task to get himself out. Those divine people are the least concerned as to how the yogi will get out or as to if he will get stuck in the material world. They assume that he or she is versatile enough to get out.

There is a story about this in the Puranas, where one of the celestial rulers named Indra, was cursed to become a pig on this earthly planet. When the time for death of that pig's body came, he used mystic power to forestall the killing of that body. His deity became alarmed at his behavior and went to him astrally. Indra then explained that he had wives and children to care for. These were others in the swine family.

Seeing the condition of Indra's mind, the deity arranged to have that pig body killed to retrieve Indra for duties in the celestial places.

This story means that a yogi or a celestial being may become so conditioned to earthly existence as to resist resuming higher dimensions. Each yogi should be aware of this and should honestly do some soul searching to see if that happened, where one became resistant to a higher plane and lost the celestial or divine point of reference.

One should not under any circumstance feel that one will be rescued by anybody. It is possible that one may be rescued but it is highly unlikely. For safety sake, one should practice, so that when the times comes, one can escape safely.

When I visited a Buddhist temple in South Korea during the month of

May of the year 2011, a Buddha deity added the third objective. He said this:

"Stay in the developed countries. Your assistance is needed. Be a counterbalance. One sadhu can offset many materialistic people. In this case your presence is needed physically."

To the right of that Buddha deity, there was another Buddha deity which is Bhaishavya Buddha or the Medicine Buddha.

When I approached this deity, He peered and said this:

"You are the one for this mission. In fact, what else should you do? I do not see an alternative. It is the only path open to you."

There was another Buddha deity to the left of the central Buddha who is Shakymuni or Gautam Buddha. This other Buddha Deity is called Amitabha. He is regarded as the Wisdom Person.

He was the only one who smiled when I approached. He said:

"Why did you approach me at the end? I am the only with the gifts for you. The others intend to employ you. Why should a friend wait to see his friend?"

He then said, "I will give you the information for the other book. Good luck to you. All information needed can be acquired easily from me."

The book he mentioned is a book published about astral projection and the dimensions into which the astral body may be enter. I completed one other book for this Buddha already, which is the *sex you!* book. Since he did not mention anything about it that is a signal that it is approved. Since Amitabha Buddha committed to giving information for the book, my lack of insight in any areas was subsidized.

Rishi Singh Gherwal also wants to see that book published. He will assist with it.

This is a resident temple building of those deities.

This is the three Buddhas at another temple in South Korea.

In the center is the Buddha who founded Buddhism, who is Shakyamuni or Gautam Buddha.

To your right, as you face the deities, is Bhaishavya Buddha, the Medicine Buddha.

To your left as you face, is Amitabha Buddha, Spiritual Wisdom Buddha.

Supernatural body

Some higher dimension experiences occur in a supernatural body which is different to the astral form. Those are difficult to identify for yogis who are physically referenced. One can sort this by developing a meditation practice in which one studies the levels of consciousness, the astral body and the higher forms which are super-subtle in reference to even the astral.

Astonishingly mystic feats are natural for the supernatural body just as walking upright is a feature of the physical form, which to an animal like a worm would be regarded as amazing.

The various bodies are facilities with special abilities. If one is transferred into any other body, one will experience that form as the self with the special powers which that body facilitates.

By a divine grace one may have a sublime experience, but more important is the fact that the experience would prove that one can be supernatural.

The mystery is how to transfer to a supernatural plane permanently. How could one abandon this drab existence as a physical form? If one has a supernatural body what is the need for a resurrected physical form. If I already have a spiritual body which is saturated with bliss feelings and which exist in a place with boundless spiritual consciousness and bliss energy, what is the point in hoping for an eternal physical form?

godBeing

Usually in the head of a human being, with eyes closed, there will be darkness or darkness with speckled pin-points of color, but there is rarely clarity or clearness in the center of the eyebrows with the eyes closed.

There is a chakra in the center of the eyebrows. When it opens one sees through it just as if one peered through a bay window. Sometimes the shape is oval, square or rectangular. Sometimes it is like a slit or is H shaped. When one looks through that opening one sees distance places in this dimension or one may view into other higher or lower dimensions.

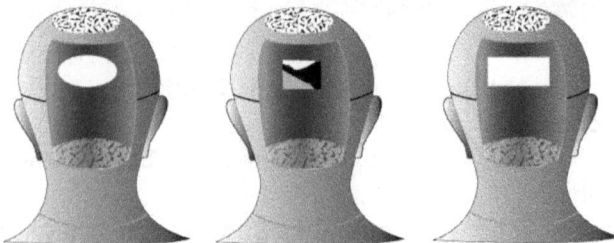

Besides that brow chakra there is another psychic organ in the head of the subtle body. When one uses that in conjunction with the third eye chakra or by itself, one may perceive supernaturally.

The location of that psychic organ, which I call the intellect or imagination orb is in a position half way between the coreSelf and the brow chakra. It is usually oval shaped but when seen it may appear to be like a cream colored jelly fish or like an oval shaped egg. This organ is the psychic tool which is used to imagine in the mind. It also functions as an eye and works in conjunction with the third eye, brow chakra.

When it does, one gets supernatural or spiritual visions which are clear and which pertain to other dimensions which are near to or distance from this world.

In some experiences, a tunnel extends from this intellect into and through the brow chakra. Sometimes one is pulled through that funnel at a rapid speed which is frightening if one has not experienced it before and especially if one holds physical reality as the reference. Over time, if one has this experience repeatedly, the fear goes away. One submits the self to these experiences willingly.

When using a supernatural body, one may transit to the level of Brahma, Vishnu or Shiva. Those are cosmic beings of gigantic proportion.

To see a superPerson is a rare experience. In the *Mahabharata* there is a story about a yogi named Markandeya. He entered into the body of one of the divine forms of a Vishnu deity. The yogi wondered as a microscopic human in the body of that person for many millions of years.

There is also a description of the Vishvarupa Universal Form in the *Bhagavad Gita* which one could read of in chapter eleven of the text.

To see any Brahma, Vishnu or Shiva divine person, one must use a body which is on par with either of those divine personalities. That is the important thing about the experience. It is not that one may perceive a cosmic divine being who wields indescribable spiritual powers, but oneself was in a divine form while perceiving the godBeing.

Infinitely large or small

In meditation or otherwise, one may have an experience where one becomes infinitely large or small. One may find that the self expands and expands beyond normal limits or that it contracts and shrinks beyond recognition. Such an experience may be frightening or enlivening.

The reason for such a contrasting experience is that the seer itself is a divine being who has somehow or the other for one reason or the other, descended into physical existence and has now identified himself or herself as a physical person.

Every so often however, the divine energy in the person's psyche expresses itself in a way which causes it to inflate or compress. When this happens that person has cosmic or microscopic experiences.

Usually these experience happen in childhood, especially before the age of nine years. After that the psychic centers de-energize. The person becomes sharply focused into physical existence and considers himself or herself to be physical being.

One may experience fear when having a cosmic or atomic experience. This occurs because one focuses into the physical world. That causes the self-consciousness to be narrowed such that a sudden release from that limitation may manifest as uncertainty. By having the experiences repeatedly one loses the apprehension. One develops confidence that the experiences will subside. One will resume the limited physical reference.

The reason for these experiences is simply that the cosmic level of consciousness wishes to inform the individual of the divine status. It reminds the individual not to maintain too sharp a focus into physical existence and not to take physical existence to be the reference, and to endeavor to return to the cosmic plane of consciousness to associate with supernatural beings.

Samadhi explained (November 2010)

What is called *samadhi* by Patañjali is rarely attained by people who meditate. This is because the social environment is hostile to deep transcendence absorption. Modern people are conditioned to concentrate for their attainments and to relax and enjoy otherwise. This has nothing to do with what Patañjali called *samyama* which culminates in *samadhi* states.

Some persons have acquired the idea that there is one type of *samadhi* but that is not factually. There are varied samadhis depending on the level of mind of the meditator.

Basically these many-featured samadhis falls into two conditional stages, which are observational and non-observational experience. In the observational stage, the meditator notes what is occurs in the particular realms for consciousness. In the superior non-observational stage, the meditator remains in the higher realm without the stress of being an observer.

An advanced yogi who does many observational *samadhi* absorptions may be of more use to us, even though his meditation is not as advanced as the non-observational stage. This is because he may inform us of what occured.

To understand this we can consider that a man plans to go to another country. His relatives become aware of his plan and commit him to sending letters describing the experience. The man consents. After arriving in that foreign place, he sends weekly letters. His relatives are relieved. They are happy to get the information about the way of the people in the foreign place.

Another man who also left that place, and promised to send letters to his relatives, became so involved in the new territory, that he has no spare time and did not remember his homeland. He sent no letters to the relatives. They were worried and perplexed and wonder if he was deceased.

Obviously the neglectful man is more absorbed in the new culture. He merged with it in a way, while the letter-sender who regularly objectifies himself to send reports, is in a sense out of touch and biased in reference to the new place.

Thus gurus who do the lower absorption samadhis, the observational ones are of much use to students. I for one, committed myself to take this body, just to do observational samadhis so that I could report of the experiences in real time. My literature may be of more value than even more advanced yogis, who do no observational absorptions.

Observational *samadhi* is called *savikalpa samadhi,* which is to say with *(sa)* intent *(vikalpa)* transcendental state.

Non-observational *samadhi* is called *nirvikalpa samadhi,* which is without *(nir)* intent *(vikalpa)* transcendental state.

In the higher *samadhi* the yogi gives himself or herself over entirely to the experience with no notational energy interacting or checking the existential situation. But in the lower samadhi, the yogi goes in with an intention to get to the higher level and to observe the passage there, the energy operation there, and the descent from there.

Due to that observation, the yogi must of necessity be limited but his report is of interest. It benefits less-advanced persons who may be inspired to practice after hearing of his experience.

Samadhi is a relocation to a higher dimension. The transit process of getting to that higher place was branded as *samyama* by Patañjali. It is the three linked stages which occur in sequence without or without jumps or digressions from one stage to another.

These three stages are:
- *dharana* (dharuh-naa)
- *dhyana* (dhee-an)
- *samadhi* (suh-mad-hee)

If one begins at *dharana* and does that efficiently, the state of mind will slide upwards into the next stage of dhyana. Or it may suddenly jump to *dhyana* instead of shifting into that gradually.

One may then remain in *dhyana* and go no higher or one may even descend back to *dharana* without reaching the *samadhi* stage. But one can also go up to the *samadhi* stage and then complete the sequence which is labeled as *samyama* by Patañjali.

These three parts of the *samyama* sequence are the three highest stages of the eight stage yoga system. This also means that sometimes when a yogi begins at *dharana* and then progresses to *dhyana* and into samadhi, he or she may find the self suddenly downshifted into pratyahar which is the stage below dharana.

Why does this happen? This occurs because the subtle body either has lower energies in it or it has somehow suddenly become infested with lower energy. When this happens, the mind will downshift without warning. The yogi will find himself or herself in the level of pratyahar sensual energy withdrawal, trying to come to terms with the mind and to rope the mind in from its nefarious activities.

If one does no pranayama breath infusion which is the stage below the pratyahar sensual energy stage, what will happen is this:

One will sit to meditate, and according to the status of energy in the mind, one will began to struggle with the mind to control its thought-image mechanism. Some may avoid that struggle by ignoring the thoughts and images. Others may observe the breath in an effort to sidestep the ideas. Some others will observe the thoughts in a detached mood stifling any emotions which arise for interaction with the images. Some others will use a vocalized or mentally sounded mantra sound in an effort to intimidate the unruly mind.

If one is successful, one will find that the mind spends more time in the thought-less image-less state, as if its thought-image producing part ceased operations. If one remains in the thoughtless state for long periods, one will find the self in the *dharana* stage which is stage one in *samyama* even though it is the sixth stage of yoga.

What is dharana? It is the linking of one's attention into a higher energy dimension or person and doing so with effort.

The flaw of *dharana* is that it is done with effort. It is not effortless. It is not natural. The natural mental state is to link and focus into this physical world and the accessory astral levels which are the basis of this place. To change that tendency one must make an effort. Nothing moves or changes without energy being expended.

Before doing *dharana* which is to link oneself into a higher plane of consciousness or a higher environment where people have divine, supernatural or super-subtle forms, one will experience the downtime of the mind.

What is this downtime? It is the stage of nothingness which occurs for a split second when the mind finished demolishing one idea and begins to construct another. Usually this occurs for a split second. It is done so fast usually, that one does not observer it. It appears that the mind instantly switches to new ideas and images without a phase of blankness. If one views a video in slow motion one cannot notice the blank interval between the frames, but there is such an interval as a technician can explain to us.

In the mind of the yogi, this interval may get longer and longer because in some meditative stages, the mind slows down and/or the perception ability accelerates.

Before one can master *dharana* which is linkage with effort, one must develop perception of the downtime of the mind. Its downtime, its blank instance, should be longer and longer, like seeing a video which is set to such a slow speed that one sees each frame as a near-still photo which slowly streams and is composed and is slowly dimmed-out from the screen, leaving a blank black screen for some seconds before another frame comes into view.

Kundalini base infusion (November 2010)

When focusing on infusing the base chakra muladhara, there is a twofold approach. The first and the simplest of the two is to infuse the base with energy so that it will move or send an energy bolt, or spark to another chakra or another part of the body.

This system is already in place. We experience it during sexual climax when the high charge of energy at the genitals, causes kundalini to jump to the sexual area. This is a spark procedure of linking, like in arc welding. Due to a power charge on one piece of metal, another piece which has a low charge is attracted.

In sex, the charge of lust attracts the kundalini, which jumps to reach it. Emotionally, that is interpreted as sexual pleasure.

In kundalini yoga the elementary way to charge the base chakra is to use the lungs, the navel regions and the groin region to force kundalini to discharge itself in one direction or another. The combined lung, navel and groin energy fires itself into the kundalini and the force explodes. To be an expert one must learn how to control that explosion so as to guide the aroused kundalini in a desired direction.

In the advanced procedure, kundalini is attacked in the same way but instead of firing the energy into kundalini, one fires around kundalini so as to unsettle and shift it from its base anchor. While in the elementary practice, kundalini expresses a moving force of energy and still remains anchored at the base, in the advanced practice it is the base of kundalini which moves.

Sometimes when the base is energized it emits laser darts of white energy downwards. If the yogi keeps the infusement and increases it further,

kundalini becomes unhinged from its anchor. Then the yogi can move kundalini here or there as desired.

Astral body is important (December 2010)

Astral projection itself without infusement of energy into the astral body, has limitations. Those who do not astral project consciously, are restricted because they have a subtle body but do not experience it objectively.

The dependence on a physical body for consciousness is a serious handicap for any person who moves through these creations. After the infant body is pushed out of the mother's passage, the spirit using that form is totally confined. He or she only breaks out through astral projection and other types of transcendental experiences.

The astral body is there regardless of whether one is objectively aware of it or not. It is essential that we strive to get an understanding of what it is and how it operates. Each infant learns to operate the physical body, how to make it walk, how to make it pronounce sounds correctly and so on. In fact the parents of the body think that this is so important, that they inconvenience the body, force it, to go to schools which are a type of confinement.

Little Johnny wants to play, but the mother takes him to a nursery where he is force to be with other infants who were also forced into that confinement. This is all done to get control of the body and to make it serve the needs of society.

Why are we not trying to get the subtle body under control and making it serve the needs of the subtle society?

Conscious astral projection is the first step. After that one should work to control the astral body, to understand what it is and how it operates. One should not wait until one is forced out of the physical form, blocked forever from entering it by inscrutable nature, and then think to observe what the subtle body is.

People made of light

When the astral body is energized to the level where it comprises of light, like sunlight or some other type of light frequency, the person lives as light in a state of light. He perceives a world which is light. He sees beings who use subtle bodies of light. In such a body one would transit to the sun and see buildings, trees, streets and people made of light.

A physical human is safe from the astral reality. One is protected by the focus on material existence but only for as long as one has a physical form. As soon as the body dies (and it will die) one will be left with the psychic self only.

Two bodies

Right now the only two bodies which are within our reach is the physical system and the astral system which is used nightly in dreams and which sometimes is experienced objectively in a subtle world during astral projection.

These are the only two systems which are somewhat under our control. As for the physical body most of us are familiar with that. The astral form is controlled by a few psychics and mystics. Most people do not recall dreams and never had a conscious astral projection.

Astral projection occurs every time the physical body sleeps and yet, many people do not experience it. Their consciousness during sleep is so dense that it makes no conscious contact with the experiences of the astral body. In other words, most people sleep-walk in the astral world night after night. They deny astral experiences simply because they have no objective take on it.

To go beyond the astral body one has to either do so by a divine grace or one has to energize the astral form to such an extent that its vibrations become alarmingly accelerated.

One should accelerate the astral body from within. This can be done by the practice of pranayama breath infusion.

Behind the physical world, there is the astral world, which is immediately adjacent to it. Beyond that immediate astral world, there is the celestial astral world where the supernatural controllers reside. Beyond their territory there is a demarcation zone. Then there is a set of dimensions in which very highly evolved and divine teachers exist. Beyond that place, there is the place of the creator-god whose mind is the support for all psychological activities below that realm.

If one gets there one is at the highest plane in subtle material existence. Beyond there is a demarcation zone where nothing exist. Beyond that there is a place which is sheer light, spiritual light. Beyond that there is a place called the spiritual world.

Patanjali gave a transit procedure for translating to higher worlds.

जात्यन्तरपरिणामः प्रकृत्यापूरात् ॥२॥

jātyantara pariṇāmaḥ prakṛtyāpūrāt

jātyantara = jāti – category + antara – other, another; pariṇāmaḥ – transformation; prakṛiti – subtle material nature; āpūrāt – due to filling up or saturation.

The transformation from one category to another is by the saturation of the subtle material nature. (Yoga Sutras 4.2)

By divine grace, one's psyche may become saturated with divine energy. As in this world, when one crosses borders or even if one jumps to a higher status in society, one inevitably must work with others. In the spiritual quest it is similar where to translate to a higher place one has to deal with a deity or with some advanced person who is resident in that higher zone.

Kundalini: What Is It? (December 2010)

Kundalini is the psychic life force in the subtle body. To understand what it is one may study sexual climax experience and the rejuvenation-sleep mechanism which is involuntary in the body.

Something regulates heart beat and breath functions. Something supervises healing in the body. That something is kundalini. The individual iSelf does not complete these actions. Even when the self is not attentive those functions proceed by an involuntary caring force in the body. That is kundalini.

When the body sleeps and the iSelf becomes unaware of it, kundalini conducts the breathing functions, the heart beat and other aspects.

In sexual climax, kundalini is aroused. It expresses itself as overpowering sexual pleasure. In times of great excitement like for instance in war time or in emotional incidences, kundalini expresses intense regret and even as very deep remorse or as intense loving feelings.

Raising kundalini up the spine into the head was done by yogis who used the pranayama breath infusion method, but there are cases of persons who aroused kundalini by visualization or focus.

Even though nature introduces one to sexual experience after the body reaches puberty, nature does not usually show one a method of making kundalini enter the brain through a sensational arousal. We can take it as a fact that generally nature has no intentions of allow kundalini to raise into the head but it does have every intention of arousing kundalini to energize the sexual organs. Therefore the place to start investigating kundalini is through sex experience.

Subtle body/divine body

Kundalini is part of the subtle body but it is not part of the divine body. In the divine body the coreSelf is the body, while in the case of the subtle body, the core is an inhabitant of that psyche.

This subtle body has kundalini and subconscious memory in the trunk of it. In its head, it has senses, memory, intellect, a sense of identity and a coreSelf.

Raising of kundalini may result in kundalini going upward through the spine, jumping from one chakra to the next. If it reaches into the neck it may go further into the head. If it reaches into the head it may go through the crown chakra *(brahmrandra)* or through the third eye brow chakra *(ajna chakra)*. Or it may pierce through any other part of the head.

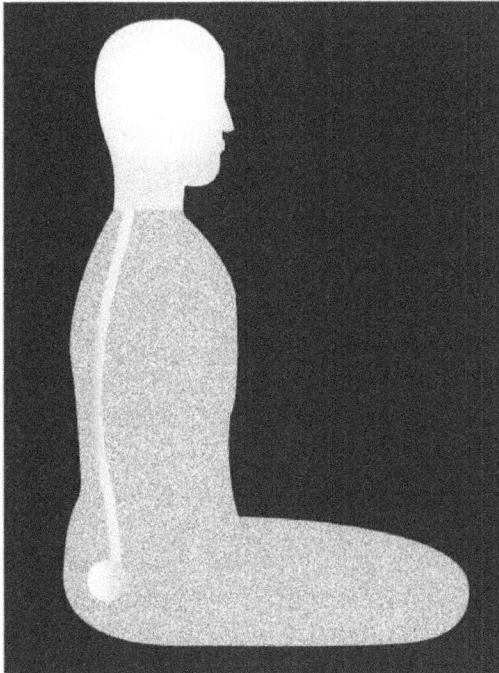

pranaVision: confidence in it (December 2010)

There is a type of vision which is vision through energy on the atomic and subatomic levels. Just as in science images are created on the basis of atomic energy, the human mind is also capable of very detailed atomic vision.

One such perception is prana vision, which is the ability to see the inside form of anything. The yogi is primarily interested in researching his or her psyche. In that case the application of pranaVision is to the various parts of the subtle body's anatomy

During breath infusement, there may be an accumulation of energy in a part of the psyche. If the yogi keeps his attention at that place, he or she may get intense sensations but there may also be vision.

If something is heated, the force which provides the heat can actually see inside the heated object. If a part of the psyche is infused with breath energy *(prana),* the self can see the inside of that part of the psyche.

pranaVision is important. The problem is to have confidence in it. If one has doubts, if one listens to the view of skeptics that may erode any confidence one may develop over time.

The best way to develop pranaVision is to practice breath infusion daily, and to pay attention within the psyche during the practice. Do not let the mind wander outside the psyche. Keep the mind internalized. To keep the mind from being distracted by external light use a blindfold during breath infusement.

Make notes about the practice. Share these with other yogis. Discuss these with more advanced yogis. Without worrying about the opinion of skeptics, explain what you saw during practice.

Intellect

The way to begin understanding that the intellect is a vision organ, is to catch yourself when you daydream or when successfully visualize something in the mind. When that happens, the psychic organ which does that is the intellect. In Sanskrit it is called *buddhi.* It is not the whole mind space which does a daydream or a visualization, it is a particular location within the mind where that occurs.

Initially one should consider the intellect as a location. It is in fact an organ, a psychic organ. Consider this: If I sat in a dark room and suddenly a firefly glows, I will consider that it happened at a location. Since it is dark and since the glow did not show the form of the insect, I will see that it happened at a location. I may not realize that it was emitted by an object. Similarly the mind space has objects within it. One is the intellect which is an organ, which can be seen when one develops psychic sensual objectivity.

Naad fusion meditation with mantra (December 2010)

A Buddha deity *(Shakyamuni Gautama)* in South Korea, gave a naad sound mantra which I was unable to test while in South Korea.

There are many spiritual systems, but I usually like to test a process before I divulge it.

This system combines *ajapa* with naad sound. *Ajapa* is mental recitation of a mantra where no sound is heard externally and the vocal chords are not involved. In *japa* the sound is said with the vocal cord. It is intoned externally with the mouth and heard physically by the ear.

For instance in some Vaishnava societies ajapa or mentally-said mantras are outlawed while *japa* or physically-said mantras are said to be the only process. In the same societies there are confidential mantras which are mula mantras and *gayatri* mantras. Some of these are called *bija* mantras. Essentially these are call-prayers for reaching certain deities and divine beings in other worlds. These *bija* mantras are considered to be confidential. They are not said physically in a loud way. In some sects these mantras are murmured. In others these mantras are said mentally only. For instance if a priest conducts a ritual ceremony for a Krishna deity, the priest cannot barge into the deity's chamber. He must first stand outside the door, ring a bell and say specific prayers. This is for alerting the deity and seeking permission to enter the sacred area for doing the ritual.

Most of the *bija* mantras concern a deity or a supernatural and spiritual being who is in another dimension, but they are a few which concerns *dhyana* meditation and *samadhi* trance states. *Bija* means seed or source-point.

For instance there is a *bija* mantra for the base chakra. There is one for the causal body. There is one for the sushumna kundalini central spinal passage. These are sounds which are supposed to cause the particular chakra or location to pulsate.

Just as in electronics, one can use a small device which projects a digital signal to open a lock or close a door, so one is supposed to use a *bija* mantra.

We find however that these mantras do not take effect. Many persons approached Indian gurus on this issue. The usual explanation is that the mantra has to be chanted with the correct pronunciation.

Really?

Om mani padme hum mantra is used primarily by Tibetan Buddhists

It is attributed to *Avalokiteshvara Buddha. Shakyamuni Buddha* said this about it:

The first known description of the mantra appears in the *Karandavyuha Sutra,* which is part of certain *Mahayana* canons. In this sutra, the Buddha says:

"This is the most beneficial mantra. Even I made this aspiration to the million Buddhas and subsequently received this teaching from *Buddha Amitabha.*"

The *Shakyamuni* deity said that when this mantra is chanted mentally, the yogi should take the *hum* intonation mentally to the naad sound.

He said that hum is harmonious with naad and is also a sound which naad absorbed with 100% efficiency. When one is told something by a deity or by someone who is in another dimension, one should check to make sure that the communication was accurate and that the source of it was valid. To do this one should test the instruction.

When the yogi sits to meditate, if he finds that the coreSelf is not interested in naad or cannot stay focus or absorbed into naad, or that it drifts in and out of naad, he should go to naad. While focusing on naad and being absorbed in it he should observe the drifting of the self away from naad. As soon as the self begins to drift, he should begin reciting the mantra. When saying the first three words he should focus on the mantra but as soon as he begins to say the last word mentally, the *hum* sound, he should loop his attention back to naad.

This procedure should continue until he finds that the self does not drift away from naad.

In terms of location the yogi would usually find naad on the right back of the head near the ear. The self usually drifts from that place to the frontal part of the brain where it is indulged in images, thought constructions, ideas and memories. Thus as soon as the self begins to drift forward in the head, the yogi should begin the mantra. When the last word, the hum sound, is mentally intoned, the yogi should loop his attention to naad.

In my experience I found that the hum sounds fuse with naad perfectly. One finds oneself again listening to naad. Since this was given directly by the deity *Shakyamuni Buddha (Gautama),* it has tremendous potency if one practice it with sincerity.

Naad/intellect kriya by Buddha deity (December 2010)

A Buddha deity showed a procedure for making the intellect become absorbed in the naad sound. Usually the intellect stays away from naad and the coreSelf alone goes to naad with the sense of identity which is more or less continuously fused to the core.

One may experience a space of about two inches or less between the coreSelf and the intellect but there is no space between the coreSelf and the sense of identity, which is fused to the core.

This Buddha deity is strict but in this discourse, he was friendly. Being one of his sons, I am careful. In some communications I am more like the son of an inferior concubine. On this occasion he was relaxed and wanted to confide some details.

He said:

"Many ascetics who are in my system and who regard themselves as Buddhists do not understand what it is to be an original buddha. They

feel that all buddhas are the same. They think that they will become a buddha on my level. "That is ludicrous but I do not interfere with that idea because it hurts only the person who feels that way. It does not affect me.

"When I taught, I divulged only what a person needed at a particular stage. Some of what I did during austerities was not described to anyone.

"The process which they divulge for a monk today is different to what I did even though some of it is exactly what I did. I do not need an assistant. I can give instruction to someone directly. If a person regards me as another buddha and not as a special unique teacher, it is not likely that such a person would have the disposition which is accommodating to personal instruction from me."

The kriya or procedure for causing the intellect to become absorbed in naad sound is based on clarifying the energy at the base chakra. Buddha deity said that once the base chakra is uprooted from its base anchor position, the analytical orb changes so that it no longer adheres to the frontal part of the head.

Then it easily moves backward in the head and no longer exhibits a stubborn tendency which is to stay focused in the frontal part of the head creating images, sounds, ideas and visualizations.

This would mean that the intellect has some subtle connection with the kundalini energy, such that if that kundalini is reformed and controlled, there is a corresponding increase in control over the intellect.

When this happens one can grab the intellect and move it back. Its power is neutralized. It seems to be a padded envelop of light frequency energy about the size of a three inch by three inch by half-inch thick object.

Part 4

Dream world focus (December 2010)

Staying longer in dreams has to do with being able to allow your physical body to rest on this side of existence. It is not so much how long you want to stay but what is your normal focus and obligations. If you have many obligations on this side of existence, those energies will draw back to the physical side. People who have good dream recall and who spend much time in dreams are usually persons who are interested in the dream side of existence, the psychic side. They are more interested in that side than in the physical level. Due to that their minds are polarized to be less involved on the physical plane.

This means that if one's dream time is short, one should check into the factors which pull one back to the physical level. Once one identifies that, one can eliminate those attractions one by one and increase the time on the dream side.

Sleep paralysis is really the astral body's inability to be synchronized perfectly with the physical one. That can happen either when the two bodies are separating or when they are about to be fused for waking the physical one.

To decrease the incidences of this paralysis, make sure that the sleeping area is ventilated such that fresh air can get to the physical body. Stale or used air causes a de-energization in the sleeping physical form which may result in sleep paralysis. Sleep paralysis may be caused by intoxication. It can be caused by the impressions left in the memory when looking at scary movies.

Mutual dreams, lucid dreams and astral projection (December 2010)

In the physical world, existence mutates at a slow place. As a result it is easy to be in sync with moving and non-moving objects. In the astral world that does not happen in the same way. There are astral heavens, astral hells and astral places which are adjacent to this physical existence and which are relatively stable but it only so for those persons who use a subtle body which has the exact frequency of the particular astral place.

It so happens that those who use physical bodies rarely experience a stable astral or dream form. As a result cases of two persons who share in one lucid dream experience in a linear way is rare.

This will change when the physical body is no longer there. After its death, the astral body, the dream form, will only be concerned with itself. It will stabilized in a particular frequency and will find itself in one astral level or another with persons whose astral forms have a similar vibrational energy.

When someone thinks of another person that thought projects through space and reaches the subtle body of the target person. It does so in an instant. If the target is asleep and is in dream consciousness, the ideas may convert into a form which resembles the sender's astral body. That body will then hold the conversation which is conducted mentally. This will happen even if it is a passing thought or a whimsical idea.

The dreaming person will think that the sender was present in the dream, even though only the thought energy was there.

On the other end of that communication, the sender will think back and forth, in response to the dreamer's thoughts. That sender may not know that it happened. Many thoughts occur without the sender's astute observation. Many are composed in a subjective way without an objective regard.

The conversion of a sender's thought into a virtual form of that sender occurs not by the power of thought projection but by the target person's dream body conversion.

Kundalini tongue loop-back (December 2010)

The following diagrams are from kundalini practice. These are instances which may occur when trying to uproot kundalini from its base. At times kundalini deviates from its normal route in the subtle body but it will keep its route in the physical system. These are instances which may occur when trying to uproot kundalini from its base. The diagram shows how kundalini was configured in the gross body, coming up into the head.

In the diagram below one will see what kundalini did in the subtle body bending the head back and looping through the tongue and back to the base chakra avoiding its spread into the head.

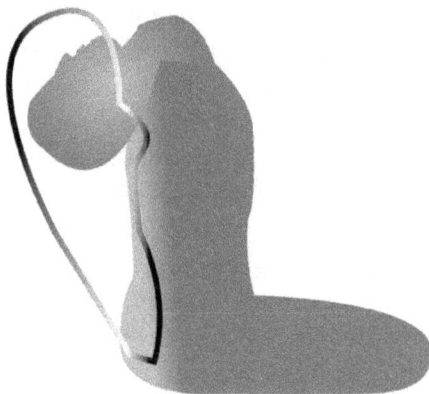

In this loop through the tongue, kundalini actually draws energy from the tongue and carries that energy to the base chakra, where it uses that tongue energy to taste the energy at the base chakra. When this first happens there is an astral electric shock.

In the next diagram the subtle body is superimposed on the physical one showing both instances occurring simultaneously. The subtle body is capable of many postures, configurations and contortions which the gross one cannot perform.

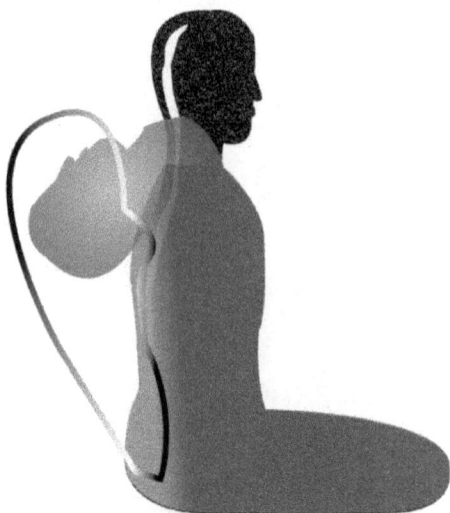

Low quality meditation (December 2010)

In the past, students of meditation questioned about days of meditation when there is no progress, when the mind remains on the normal level with thoughts and images, even though efforts are made to elevate the self.

In some sessions there is low energy in the mind. It should be considered that the mental and emotional states are a psychological weather. As in atmospheric weather, one cannot control it so in psychic energy one cannot have absolute coordination.

People continue their lives after a weather disaster with the understanding that the weather is beyond control. They become confident that it will changed for the better. But they know it may go haywire again.

This same consideration and attitude should be used in meditation, where one knows that on a certain day meditation may be of low quality. Then for sure provided one keeps the habit, it will be enriched on another day again.

A depressed or dull meditation, one that is no inspiring, one that is discouraging, should not deter practice, no more than a hurricane, or earthquake or overcast clouds will stop human beings from proceeding with their lives once the danger is past.

One should complete sessions even when a low energy saturates the mind. Be confident that it will again resume a deep experience and it will again drop to a low level. This will happen so long as one is in a world where the mental and emotional energies dip and surge.

Kundalini under military attack (December 2010)

1ˢᵗ stage kundalini attack

In the first stage the yogi has to infuse breath into the lungs and focus on that only, so that the energy of the fresh air which comes into the lungs, fully invades the lung cells and the chest cavity, including its contents like the heart and other organs.

This first stage of the attack does not affect kundalini but it is vital. As in a war one cannot attack the enemy stronghold initially. The enemy defenders must first be subdued. The iSelf must first shatter the power of the parts of the psyche which sides with kundalini against the iSelf.

The kundalini lifeForce has a protective mechanism which makes it near to impossible for the iSelf to subdue it. For instance many people feel that by subduing the ego, the iSense of the self, one can subdue everything but that is not true. The kundalini is not worried about the subjugation of the ego. Kundalini knows that the iSelf no matter what it does must directly attack for conquest. Tearing down other components of the psyche, does nothing to subdue the life force which maintains its privacy and secrecy while the iSelf makes maneuvers for self-subjugation. I said that kundalini knows. Can the kundalini know? The answer is that it can know. It has a knowing instinct. Even though that is not an objective education, it is still as effective as having one.

2nd stage kundalini attack

In the second stage of the attack, the yogi infuses breath to the navel. It will find the navel to be like a strong fortification which cannot be breached with light ammunition. Arrows, bows, ordinary riffles and the like are useless in this attack.

The efforts to crash this place, are ridiculed by kundalini. Until the yogi accumulates his breath energizing by doing rapid breathing beyond the burning point, he cannot penetrate the navel region.

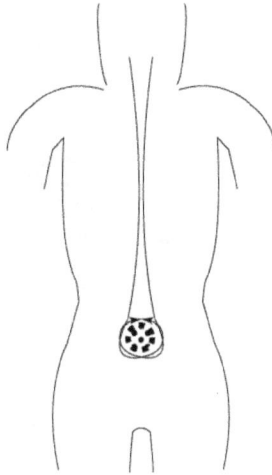

The burning point is felt when during breath of fire, there is a burning sensation just above the navel. If the yogi can tolerate that and infuse more air to increase the burn, there will come a time when one can explode the energy. At that time kundalini will hear the explosion from afar. It will be worried about the yogi's attack on its kingdoms.

Even though a yogi may cause an explosion at this place once that does not mean that kundalini is defeated. This area will be repair itself if he blows it apart, such that during the next session of exercise, he finds that it is just as it was before without the damage inflicted. He should return to this place and blow it up repeatedly until he reaches the stage when there is one final blast which completely blows this place apart. When that happens, he will find that the burning at the navel ceases. Instead, the energy traverses the navel with ease without obstruction and then targets the sex organs where it is dissipated.

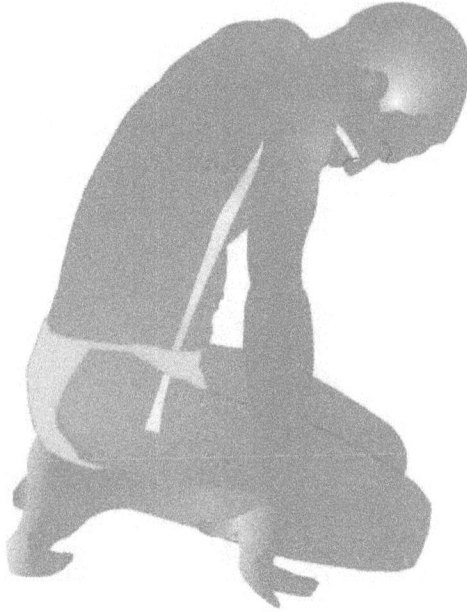

3rd stage kundalini attack

The third stage kundalini attack is complicated because the sex area which is under assault is an absorbing energy. While at the navel chakra is a repelling resistant energy, the sex area an absorbing energy which takes the energizing force from the breath energy and leaves the yogi working on and on endlessly without having an exposure to kundalini which hides behind the sex force.

The yogi must practice celibacy and must make an effort to compress the sexual energy, so as to stop the dissipation. If he can do this, a high charge will accumulate at the genitals chakra. That energy will jump to kundalini at the base chakra.

This jumping action is the first stage of a direct attack on kundalini. Some yogis get spaced out while attempting this. Others are afflicted by drifting thoughts. Some are bogged down by lack of focus. This is due to the influence of kundalini on the intellect in the head of the subtle body.

A yogi must keep the mind introspective and be determined to monitor the attention of the self. If this is done, the yogi will find that the energy of the breath which gets down to the sexual organs, mixes with and compresses the sex hormones. At the navel there is an expansion which causes an explosion. At the sexual organs there is a contraction which causes the explosion. The energy contracts to the point where it can no longer tolerate the pressure. Then it jumps to the base chakra. This is like when a charge is developed on one side of electrode of a spark plug and that jumps to the other electrode and reveals a spark.

Yoga practice demolished

Sometimes a yogi is overcome by a negative energy which cancels the desire to do practice on a particular day. This energy is a dulling force which stops a yogi dead in his spiritual tracks and causes him to neglect practice. It may last for a day, week, month or year. In some cases for a lifetime or two.

What is that dulling force? According to the Bhagavad Gita it is one of the three energy levels of material nature, the lowest one which is tagged as tama guna, dulling consciousness energy.

Last night I had an astral encounter with a lady who now lives in South America. She came astrally with her teenage daughter. Subsequently because of that association, my early morning session was discouraged. The energy for the session suddenly disappeared and left me hanging on a high ledge with no way down, not even a fire escape. Imagine if one is left on a ledge of a high building with no way into the building and no way down. It is too high to jump down. What should one do?

In cases like this when the motivation and energy for practice is dissipated by someone's or a group of persons, one should simply not be bothered but should just wait for a rescue. A yogi must be confident that negativity will pass.

The usual time for practice is supposed to be around 4 am for the latest 6 am, but at that time there was no energy for practice, no motivation. However at 8 am suddenly, I felt that the negative energy was absent. I immediately went to practice.

It appears that not only did I have a dose of bad association with that lady and her teen daughter, but I also had a dose of bad subtle energy in the atmosphere. When that energy lifted motivation for practice resumed.

Students inquired previously about why they feel dull and why they have no motivation for practice at certain times. It is not so important to know why as it is to be ready to resume as soon as the bad energy lifts.

We cannot control this universe. We cannot format reality to perfectly match what we desire. We should agree to sit it out on some occasions and wait for providence to flip in a positive direction. Association with people who have no yoga practice even if they are religious people, even if they meditate regularly, even if they are moral people of worth, will result in a downtime for practice. We must accept that and persist despite the impediments and obstructions. There is no excuse for not resuming as soon as the negative energy disappears.

Yogi Bhajan: teacher's pride (December 2010)

This morning during exercises, Yogi Bhajan appeared on the astral side. He said that I should push harder to increase the amount of infusion into the subtle body.

Before he arrived, I noticed that even though this physical body is 60 years in surviving, still I improve postures. Of course physically that has no value because ultimately, this body will be no more. Nature will take steps to erase its integrity. The value of this is for the subtle body which will exist for as long as the subtle backdrop of physical energy continues, which is for billions of years, and for as long as my coreSelf is on this side of the existential divide.

Who knows how long that will be? Taking care of the physical body just for the sake of itself makes sense only if one knows the self as a physical form. As soon as one knows the self as something else, even as a psychological unit or compartment, taking care of the physical body for its own sake, makes less and less sense.

Human beings can speak of existing forever as material forms in the future when technology and science improves, but that is a bit like in religion where there is hope that a savor will come and resurrect dead bodies, raising them from coffins in graveyards. It is a promise for the simpleminded.

My postures still improve even in a physical body which is 60 years of age. The real feature is the effects in the subtle body, which mimics what happens in the physical one. So long as the two bodies are fused, there is a give and take between them. One can use that to one's advantage by taking care of the physical one in so far as it will affect the subtle. Yogi Bhajan said this.

"Push harder. I taught these disciplines of breath infusion in the hope that somebody, perhaps one or two persons in the Western society, would take this seriously and attain the status of siddha.

"Do not play with kundalini. Get it under your thumb. Get it harnessed. Uproot it so that its instincts are abolished by infusion of energy from higher levels. Go with the siddhas. Change your status. Why stay with the human profile when something higher is available.

"It is not about religion. I was a Sikh by culture but I did not insist that anyone become a Sikh. That is not it. If you take birth in a certain country, in a certain area, the system is that you become obligated to that culture, to that ideology or religion. You may change that after leaving the parents, but still some obligation is there.

"But that is not it. That is superficial. The real thing is your bare spiritual advancement. The monkey is running. The lion is too. Which is the most proficient?

"Outstride the system! Move ahead! Do not be idle with spiritual advancement! Steal time to practice. Push harder! Push harder! Let the teachers be proud of your achievement!"

Astral association

I was stalled this morning by an astral association. Due to that I was late doing the exercise session. I did it after 6 am. Be sure that if your session is postponed or cancelled, you know why that occurred. You may not do the exercises on time each day but it is your duty to assess the influences which cause the disruption.

Do not let a day past without assessing influences which deter spiritual advancement. Knowing the sources of negative influences, will give one the power to challenge those objections head on.

At about 4 am some persons whom I used to know in Trinidad years ago, contacted me. Seeing their desire for association, I did not object even though I knew that my exercise session would be postponed. There are many unresolved issues from this life and from past lives. When one is confronted by these, one should either avoid them or deal with them.

We have issues which can be solved astrally. Some must be dealt with physically. If a yogi feels that he or she can solve all issues satisfactorily by agreeing with providence to face them in numerous situations, that yogi does not understand the flow of history.

History means that as you solve one issue, other compounding factors for which you will be implicated in the future, are created,. Providence does not solve issues once and for all. It is there to implicate the person in more faulty actions against nature, destiny and God.

Providence may be compared to a banker who services real estate loans. Homeowners get this narcissistic idea that the banker is there for their convenience but nothing could be further from the truth. The purpose of the banker is to enslave the homeowners but he has to do it in such a way, where the homeowners feel that they are free beings nevertheless.

The system of banking works well if the homeowners are set to never repay loans. As soon as the banker notes that a certain homeowner is diligent in paying on the principal and is compounding payments to eliminate the loan, the banker convinces that homeowner to refinance. This refinance causes the homeowner to feel at ease since the monthly payments are reduced and the pressure to make those larger payments is removed. But it means that the homeowner becomes more committed to the bank.

Instead of erasing the providential equations in the life of a living entity, providence increases the commitments by causing the entity to unwittingly create more obligations when he or she tries to solve problems.

Some problems can be solved on the astral planes but some must be resolved physically, which means that if there is no physical environment where they can be serviced, one will have to wait for thousands or millions of years, until suitable physical environments become available.

This a cruel system run by providence, which is rather unforgiving. When I met those deceased persons in the astral world, they lived in an astral house which was an exact reproduction of the house they used while they lived physically around the years of 1966 and 1967. They were in an adjacent parallel world. They lived there just as if they were physical beings even though it was astral. They wanted me to be with them and to do whatever I used to do at the time when I lived with them.

This scene was ridiculous as you can imagine but that is how these astral places exist. Everything was intact, their emotions, expressions, interactions, attitudes, everything, just as it was before. This is how it is in some astral places.

Buddha as a special being

In the book, *In the Buddha's Words* by Bhikkhu Bodhi, Gautama Buddha explained his unique place in human history. In one conversation he made distinction between himself and others who would take the path he laid out.

Is this for real? Is this his ego talking? I repeatedly asked persons of the Buddhist system to take Buddha, the person, into account. Without veneration for him and for the path he laid out, it not possible to use that path to its fullest extent. This is because the full method will not open itself nor be discovered in that way.

This is from pages 413-414 of the book mentioned (ISBN: 0861714911).
Excerpt:
Gautam Buddha said:

"Monks, through disenchantment with form, feeling, perception, volitional formations, and consciousness, through their fading away and cessation, the Tathagata (Tut-haa-guh-tuh), the Perfected Enlightened one, is liberated by nonclinging, he is called a Perfectly Enlightened One. Through disenchantment with form, feeling, perception, volitional formations and consciousness, through their fading away and cessation, a monk liberated by wisdom is liberated by nonclinging, he is called liberated by wisdom."

"Therein monks, what is the distinction, the disparity, the difference between the Tathagata, the Arahant, the Perfectly Enlightened One, and a monk liberated by wisdom?"

"Venerable sir, our teachings are rooted in the Blessed One, guided by the Blessed One, take recourse in the Blessed One. It would be good if the Blessed One would clear up the meaning of this statement. Having heard it from him, the monks will remember it."

"Then listen and attend closely monks, I will speak."

"Yes venerable sir," the monks replied. The Blessed one said this:

"The Tathagata, monks, the Arahant, the Perfectly Enlightened one, is the originator of the path unarisen before, the producer of the path unproduced before, the declarer of the path undeclared before. He is the knower of the path, the discoverer of the path, the one skilled in the path. And his disciples now dwell following that path and become possessed of it afterward.

"This, monks, is the distinction, the disparity, the difference between the Tathagata, the Arahant, the Perfectly Enlightened One, and a monk liberated by wisdom."

Purpose in Life

Yoga is not a religion but it did develop in the Hindu religious culture. I studied that culture extensively. I am familiar with the Christian system as well.

When one emerges as an infant, one is lost and does not know what one is about. This is due to having lost the point of reference from the previous life. We can understand this by seeing what happens to people who use elderly bodies. They become afflicted with Alzheimer or dementia. They do not know who they are and do not recognize even the next of kin.

As a baby one identifies as an infant with no other reference. One feels that it was the first time existing. Later as the body matures, one becomes dissatisfied with conditions. One figures what this is about.

Nature has everything under its wings. One has to respect that and at the same time, try to get to a deeper level through reflection and meditation. Read books which discuss spiritual life. Gradually over time one may regain some faculties from past lives, just as rarely we observe a reversal in a dementia case, where the person recognizes a relative again, regaining the memory. It does happen, even though in most cases, it does not.

Negativity predominates if one does not have a purpose in life or if one is in an environment which seems to be disharmonious with one's nature. The main thing is to gain some purpose in life.

Negativity comes about because of an innate drive to get satisfaction from the circumstances of life. If life refuses to accommodate what one desires, one becomes depressed. Life is a bigger factor than the self. Life may not respond positively to the needs of a limited self.

The self should find something that it can do in harmony with the flow of time and life. We recently arrived in a universe which astronomers estimate to be some 13 billion years in the making. It is madness if we think that this should be centered on us or that it should please us. That is insanity. Yet, most of us are afflicted with that madness.

Most people are materialistic and have no interest in researching the basis of consciousness. We must accept that and be cordial to these people. Their main concern is the material world. Even though they have no interest in spiritual life and they become hung up either in science without spiritual evaluation or in religious beliefs without scientific application, still these persons should be respected because they work day and night to build roads and buildings, to provide electricity and other products.

The trick is to appreciate them and at the same time not allow them to keep us bogged down in the materialistic lifestyle. If we do not appreciate them, our life will be a hell because we must use some conveniences which these people create.

The main thing is the spiritual practice; to keep that in order, to keep that regular, to improve on that daily. No point going to rescue anyone, if one will be stuck in the pit. A yogi must always be sure to have his getaway equipment in order so that it actually works when the time comes for escape. This life is like getting a sentence from a judge, which stipulates that one be in the prison for as long as the cell blocks hold up.

The judge stipulates that you can escape if the concrete deteriorates sufficiently for one to punch one's way through the cell wall. For a yogi, it is a matter of waiting for a loop hole in time, and then leaving the body when the lifeForce is weakened sufficiently for one to escape.

When the body is young, the lifeForce is attached to it. Such an escape is unlikely but as the body ages, the lifeForce loses the attachment because of its inability to utilize the hormonal energy. By training that lifeForce to go upwards a yogi forcibly routes it through the spine and head, so that when the time comes, he/she can go to higher dimensions.

If one fails to do this, the lifeForce will transit to a parallel astral world which is adjacent to this physical place. As a ghost one will experience oneself as a subtle body, hanging around living relatives and friends in the hope of getting one of them to sponsor one's re-entry into the human species.

I provide these insights into death and rebirth but my urgency is to be sure that I can shift when this body is confiscated by nature. I do not want to loop back without resistance to the natural way of haphazardly coming back, to again come out crying from the next mother's birth canal.

In every life, one goes through the same struggle and effort to recap an enduring identity. If one fails it means that again one will assume an embryo and again one will use the lady's passage and again be a helpless infant, and then a rude child, and then a know-it-all teenager, and then a sex-crazed young adult, and then a professional or domestically involved adult, and then a senior with or without money and social status, and then an elderly body looking for the next cure for cancer or diabetes, and then a rickety old bag hobbling along in a *home for the aged*, and then at last a de-energized ghost in the astral world, haunting the living in the hope of entering to get another embryo.

Changing the past

It is not possible to change the past so as to procure better outcomes in the present or future. One cannot do this. The conscious self is not focused into the subconscious where the motivational energies are located. One must locate the primal cause of a condition before one can create a change in circumstance. Even if one found one primal cause, there may be others which one cannot adjust. Hence there is no possibility of going into the past to produce changes currently or in the future.

I had some input into a deceased relative's upbringing when that person took a child's form again. I tried to help that person with removing the dietary basis of the formation of diabetes.

Even though the person was conscious then and I worked with the person's conscious self, still the person had such a need for that negative diet that the person resumed the previous diet which initiates and supports diabetes.

To help someone from the past, one has to reach that person in a future life and be in a position of authority to enforce the corrective methods either as a medical professional or as a senior relative, and still that will not guarantee removal of the undesirable habit.

Any habit which brings with it pleasure and satisfaction, cannot be removed by superficial advice or even by deprivation. The person himself or herself must realize the error and then must fight within himself or herself to reform the unwanted tendencies.

When I was in the Philippines around 1971, there was an epidemic of gonorrhea among some service men. This was due to sexual activity with prostitutes. We were shown movies of incurable gonorrhea and its ghastly effects. We were forewarned that if one contracted an incurable form, one would pass away so many weeks after in great pain and would be reported as missing in action in the Vietnam.

But do you think that it stopped all servicemen from seeing the prostitutes? It did not. Guys would get the disease once, twice, thrice, and be in pain and be treated and still acquire the disease again.

This is because if there is a pleasure associated with a certain habit, the pleasure offsets the pain of it which comes later. The individual is unable to resist because of not having the power to be self-deprived.

LSD and kundalini (November 2010)

Some who used LSD are afraid of raising kundalini. What is one's idea of kundalini? If one managed the switches, rises and falls and increased subtle body perception on LSD, then I do not see why one should be afraid of kundalini.

On LSD, kundalini also rises but not in a linear or relatively controlled way. Its arousal by the influence of LSD is controlled by the strength and duration of the dose. If one can raise kundalini through meditation and yoga, one would be in a better position to control it. One will not have to deal with the switches of consciousness, rises and falls which one would experience on LSD.

Let us look at kundalini in a more basic experience, which is pleasure and sexual climax. Millions of people worldwide exploit kundalini through sex experience. None are afraid of raising kundalini in that way. Why be afraid of raising kundalini up the spine. Are people going mad because of having sexual climax every day either by self stimulation or by mutual interplay? Of course some of them are. The same risk is there in raising kundalini.

First of all what method will you use to raise kundalini? Will it be meditating, sitting and waiting for it to happen by itself? Will it be breath infusion procedure? Will you go to a guru who gives touch or glance initiation? Will you join a dance session and dance until kundalini decides to move through the spine? Will you use chakra visualization? Neither of those methods is as drastic as taking LSD. Thus why be afraid of arousing kundalini

Kundalini preliminary charge (November 2010)

When doing the kundalini exercises, one must first do the preliminary charge. This is a four stage process. If this is done successfully, kundalini will rise immediately after if one continues to increase the charge. This is because kundalini will have no choice in the matter, but this does not mean that one can direct where kundalini will go. It will move in some direction, but which direction is left open because that depends on the yogi's proficiency in practice, on the blockages in his psyche and in the type of charge force which accumulated.

The four stages:

Stage 1

Charge the lung and heart fully with fresh air infusion through rapid breathing. This involves an aggressive use of the diaphragm, the main muscle involved in rapid breathing. Bhastrika is when there is rapid breathing with focus on both the in and out breaths. Kapalabhati which is easier is when that breathing is done with focus on the out breath, with the in breath occurring just as a reflex after the forced out breath.

This charging the chest region is the first stage because that is the way breathing is designed to enter the nostrils, feed through the neck and be absorbed into the lungs and be expelled from it.

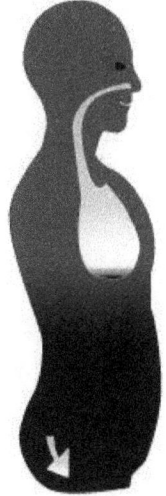

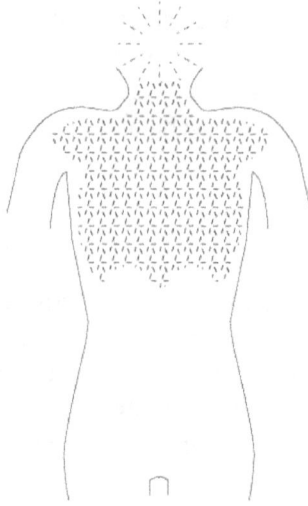

Once that is done and those cells are filled with fresh air, the rest of the body benefits from the infusion.

Stage 2

This is infusion from the chest to the navel area. This causes blockages in the navel to be shattered by the force of the infused energy. These energies are directly above the navel. They flow into the navel zone but they get locked there and do not flow out easily. When one does the infusion and the infused energy reaches this blockage, it forces its way through. It pushes the polluted energy downward.

If one is to see this psychically, one would notice that the energy reaches a dead end and cannot penetrate below the navel. There is an increase energy push from the infusion. It twirls around the navel vortex.

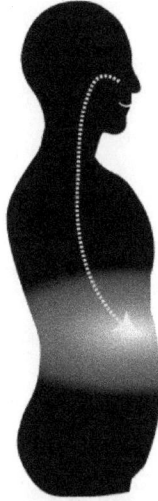

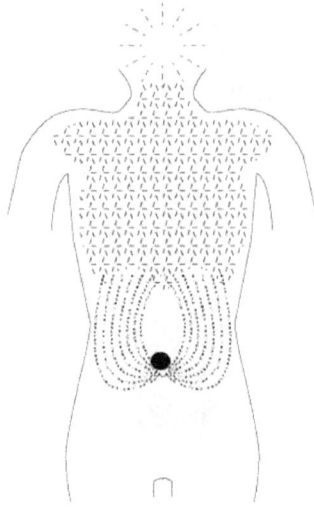

Stage 3

In this stage the energy which twirled around the navel goes downwards in a hurry, trying to meet the reproductive center. It rushes there. When it gets there instead of reaching a dead end, it enters into the reproductive area in a flush and mixes with the sexual energy. As a result of this mix the nature of the sexual energy changes. That energy loses its lusty charge. This energy then flows upwards a little and then turns downwards into the genital region.

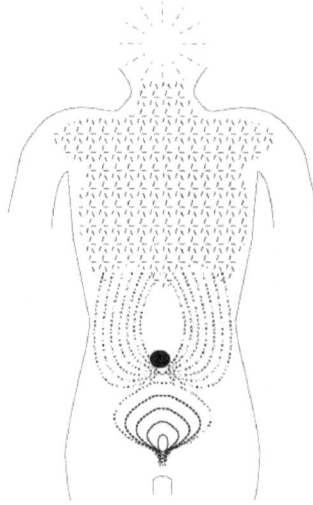

Stage 4:

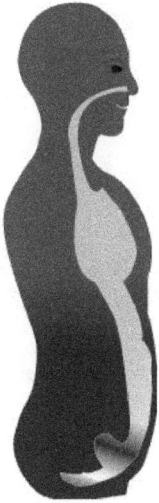

This is the last stage of the preliminary practice. This is where that energy which was mixed with the sex energy, goes in a hurry to the base chakra of kundalini. It tries to strike kundalini but at first, kundalini expresses a rejection energy in order to repel that force. The matter would end there with that rejection being effective but if the yogi continues the infusion, the charge will become more potent. It will attack kundalini and mix with it. The explosive mix causes kundalini to move from its position.

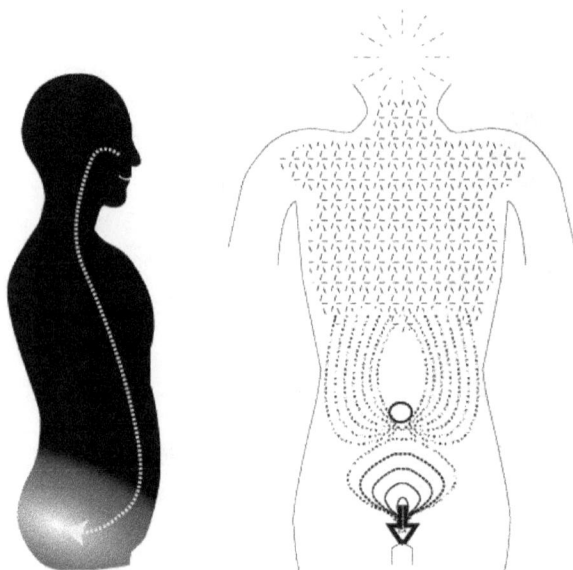

Those are the four stages of preliminary kundalini rise. During each session one must go through the stages either rapidly or gradually according to intensity of practice. A novice does this. The proficient yogi does this as well with the difference being that the master can complete this preliminary stage in the first five or ten minutes of practice. The novice may take twenty or thirty minutes.

Predictions in dreams (November 2010)

Most people consider the astral to be distinct from the physical. There is a mystique about anything psychic. For me the two existences run parallel and may be related.

I do not see the psychic side as much different to the physical. In the psychic world there is a continuity on the various levels, just as in the physical world there is a continuity.

In the astral world, history is similar to that in this physical place. There may be a correlation between some physical events and what happens in the astral with the astral usually leading the physical. Just as on the physical side, one may think of something before one does it, some aspects of astral existence are manifested before it can occur on the physical side.

If one becomes aware a psychic aspect, one may predict the physical event which is related. In the *Bhagavad Gita,* there is a story about a warrior who saw that some opposing warriors being killed on the supernatural level. Soon after they were killed on the physical side.

That was not a prediction even though from the physical angle, one could say that Arjuna predicted the death of the warriors, days before their demise. It was not a prediction in reference to this world. It was a fact of what happened on a supernatural plane of existence. Since it was a fact there, it was to be a fact here only because that level of existence presupposed or managed this one.

When an architect draws a national monument with detailed drawings, is that a prediction? We usually do not say so. However it is in the sense that after a while that sketch becomes reality as a building somewhere in a city.

But that is true if the architect was commissioned by an authority. If the architect was you or me, our idea would remain as an idea only. We are not connected into the authority system which constructs public buildings.

If one is on an astral level which governs this one whatever one sees there will happen here, not because of predictions but due to the relationship between that level and the physical plane. If one is on an astral level that has little or no influence on this one, whatever one sees there may never occur here. It would be real there but never manifest here.

If one meets someone on the astral side and gets information which proves to be true in the physical world, it means that one met someone who was in a position to influence what occurs on this side. I taught kundalini yoga and meditation, now for thirty plus years. Most of the instructions I received from advanced teachers were given on the astral side. The truth of that comes into reality, when I follow those instructions and advance further in the practice or when sometimes, I find the same instructions in books like *Bhagavad Gita*. In that way I learnt how to verify the instructions. Hence, confidence in my memory of what happens on the astral side increased.

Usually people have confidence on the physical side. They dismiss dreams as illusion. If one opens oneself to doubtful people one may become skeptical. Even people whom one is related to and whom one loves, may be materialistic to the core. Thus if one shares the spiritual and psychic experiences with them, they may discourage one from practice.

Social issues or yoga (November 2010)

For me social commitments are a sheer waste of time, and yet they are necessary. In the *Bhagavad Gita,* Krishna explained to Arjuna that the material world is a lot of hogwash, and yet Krishna advised Arjuna to complete the duties perfectly.

Arjuna was confused and asked Krishna to clarify that one should be socially attentive or take care of self-realization. Krishna explained that both things should be done; the social engagements and the self-realization achievement, Krishna insisted on the completion of duties.

In the *Uddhava Gita,* Krishna discouraged access of social duties and family concerns. He pivoted Uddhava in the direction of full time self-realization.

This means that what we do for spiritual success will vary according to our position in relation to the social world. Mostly we are involved socially because of having desires which can only be fulfilled through social interaction.

A guy went to meditate in the forest just outside a village in India. After a while he began to think that he would have to get something to eat. An old man whom he spoke to told him that if he wanted milk, he would have to get a cow.

He got a cow but the animal was miserable most of the time. There was no good pasture in the forest. This guy was advised to acquire pasture. He did this and then the cow got pregnant. After the calf was born, the guy was happy because milk came from the udders. Because of the time it took to care for the cow and calf, he later became doubtful about the whole thing. Milking the cow was time-consuming.

He was advised that he needed a wife to assist with chores. He got married. After a time, his wife showed some irritability. He asked some elders about that. They said that a wife needed sexual participation which would also produce the bonus of children.

Social involvements will multiply and utilize the time required for spiritual life. Each yogi should draw a line as to how much involved he will become. It begins by control of desires.

Patañjali told us that desire energies are eternal. If we are to believe what he wrote, the elimination of desires is out. Side-step and avoid desires. If something is a permanent reality, No one will eliminate it. One may avoid it.

A yogi should evade desires. Once a desire becomes dominant, effort should be made to fulfill it. A yogi should learn how to be resistant to and also how to hide from desire energies, otherwise he/she will have no time for self-realization.

I met many people who are at a loss about spiritual life. For me it is easy to understand what spiritual life is, because for me it is something that I reestablish.

I can remember other existences and also previous lives in physical bodies on this planet. I am desperate to get away from this. I took this body for a specific purpose which has nothing to with the social trappings that were necessary to just to have this body. I have tried to reimburse nature for using this body, to repay ancestors for using this body. Otherwise I stick to the reason why I took it.

Most people have no idea of a past life. They have no idea of a reason for taking a body. For them they are the bodies. For me I am not the body but I took the body to do something specific. Still with that came the obligation to persons who contributed to the creation of the body. These are relatives, parents, teachers, government officials and others.

The trick is to meet these obligations efficiently but not to expand them. If they are expanded that will encroach on the time which could be used for self-realization.

I raised a family with four children. I did that. I served some relatives in a fair way. For me there is not much to do other than self-realization. I do not have many desires. The main desire was the publication of books for giving information about meditation. I have done most of that as of today.

Other desires do not attract me because I can see that in the end they will fizz to nothing, or worse, fizz as unwanted obligations in this or a future life. Those who can consider only this life must fulfill desires without knowing where it will lead in this or in a future life.

If you think that self-realization is or should be your main concern, you should service social obligations head on in an efficient way. Fulfill them but do not expand them. Use every bit of spare time to push on with self-realization.

This body will die. It will be taken regardless of if one desires to abandon it or not. The father of my body was not ready to relinquish it when he laid on a hospital bed in South America and was in the last day of its life. Do not be like that. This body will be confiscated by nature.

Once you see that you should ask, "Then what? Where will I go? Who will I be?"

I needed a body to publish information about self-realization in English. I signed a pact stating that I would beget children and that I would do this and do that. I signed. I had obligations like that. I met them head on. Was it a hassle? Did it screw up my spiritual life? It does not really matter because an obligation is just what it is. It does not have to be something that one likes. Taking a body is a business contract. Once you understand that it is easy for you to know how much time is for social affairs and how much is for self-realization.

Tai Chi and Yoga, the similarities (November 2010)

Yoga is listed by Patañjali as having eight parts. Posture or asana is one part only. It is the third stage. Higher yoga is called *samyama*. That is the three highest parts, when done as a sequential practice.

This *samyama* is called meditation. Modern people are mostly concerned with meditation and not with the preliminary parts of the process as listed by Patañjali.

Some people are concerned with postures but only for the purpose of physical health and beauty. Yoga is for transcending ourselves as physical systems and finding everything else which is the self. In other words, besides my physical body, what I am?

Yoga is an escapist procedure. Those who feel locked down in the material world, like prisoners in a max-security prison, may try yoga. With yoga we escape from this dimension and research other places, trying to find something which we are agreeable with. In meditation *(samyama)* the yogi researches other dimension in his hunt for something which suits his fancy.

If the yogi finds any dimensions which involve the use of a temporary body or which is connected to a place where temporary bodies are use, he is not interested. He keeps exploring.

The highest stage of yoga, is called *samadhi* which is transiting from this place and accessing higher dimensions and divine beings.

To find what a yogi investigates in this and other dimensions see Patañjali *Yoga Sutras,* chapter three. There is a list of those achievements.

Yoga is not concerned with straightening kinks in this environment, nor in becoming harmonious with it. On the micro level among the bacteria, a yogi sees that this is a *dog eat dog* situation all the way through to the top level of the human predators. The yogi has no hope of harmonizing with this or of causing this to harmonize with the self. The idea is to abandon this and to find an already-existing place which is devoid of the *dog eat dog* profile.

Kundalini in balance (November 2010)

Sometimes when doing kundalini yoga one may find that the kundalini is aroused through one side of the body and does not traverse the other side. Some persons come to a yoga class with the queer idea that everything should be or will be balanced.

They feel that the odd left side or hanging right side will come into position and will forever from then onwards, be a perfect compliment, never ever to be disproportionate again. This is fallacy.

In the human species, there is imbalance in the body since the heart is hung more on the left side and the left lung is smaller than the right one. Is that perfect?

Kundalini / death elevator system (November 2010)

Rishi Singh Gherwal left a message in my psyche which is a basic idea of how a yogi may leave the body commanding kundalini to go up through the body and out the head. Usually death of the physical body occurs by a shutdown of kundalini from the head downwards and from the feet upwards. Kundalini uses itself as the reference and pulls all energy into itself at the base chakra. This is the mammalian way, a gift of nature.

A yogi upsets that system by causing the energy to be retracted into the head. Just as in sexual intercourse, the head consciousness goes down into the genitals to get pleasure satisfaction and pleasure bewilderment, the yogi makes an effort to pull kundalini into the head of the subtle body when death is on the verge of taking place.

Unfortunately he cannot do this if he did not mastered it prior to death. Kundalini is a creature of habit. It does not respond to compelling instructions or imaginative visualizations which it was not conditioned to perform.

Athletes become professional at a skill because of repeatedly doing that action over and over, until it becomes no more than a reflex. A yogi is a spiritual athlete. By repeatedly raising kundalini over many years while using

physical body, he or she may do the same at the time of death. The proficiency is what enables one to do this, not religion, not affiliation with a certain guru or any other factor.

Rishi Singh said that I should note that a yogi must use the jump process, which is when kundalini jumps from its base to other locations which it uses as new basis for its operation. The first jump is to the chest area or the heart chakra on the spine. The second jump is into the neck area. The third jump is into the base of the brain at the back of the head.

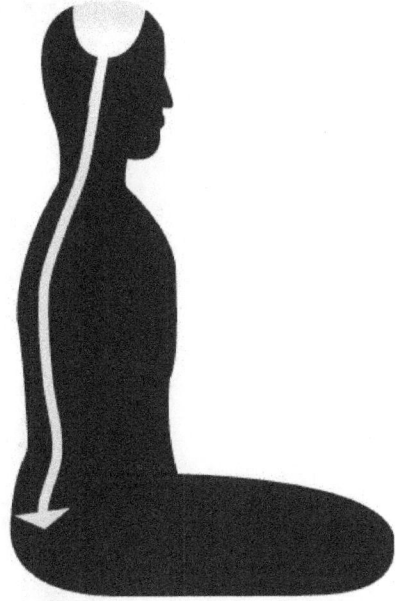

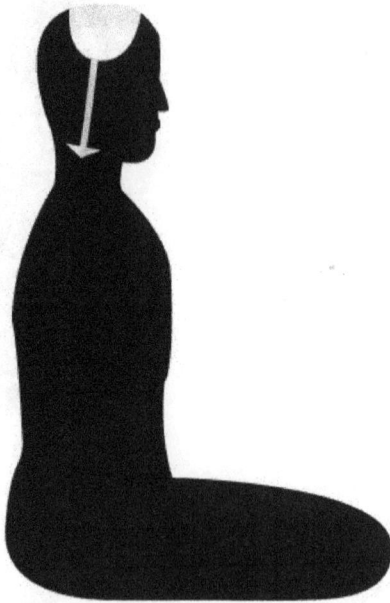

If the yogi can get kundalini to relocate that far, he is certain to reach the world where the siddha perfected yogis reside. From there he can practice further to reach the divine world. Rishi said that presently, it is near impossible for a yogi to go directly to a divine world after being deprived of a material body. The practical accomplishment to aim for is the siddhaloka places where great yogins reside, and where one can get further instruction and more association to reach the divine places.

The first jump location is the chest area or the heart chakra on the spine. The yogi has to get above the navel region. So long as he cannot move kundalini's base above the navel, he is condemned to another haphazard rebirth. Despite aspirations, his psyche will remain with the interest in sexual indulgence and nutritional accommodation. Even if by the grace of nature, in old age of a material body, a yogi gets away from sexual indulgence as a result of impotence or as a result of not have youthful sexual forms in availability, still he will be captured by nutritional accommodation, because it so happens that the primary interest of kundalini, its instinctual need, is for nutritional accommodation.

That means procurement of fat and muscle, especially fat. Kundalini looks for nutritional accommodation because if it can find that, it can live in the material world and gain sustenance. Thus it is attracted to male musculature and to female fat cells which accumulate in certain parts of the body.

The conquest of the navel is a downward push, but to reach the heart there has to be an upward push. First there is the downward push, and then there is the upward push.

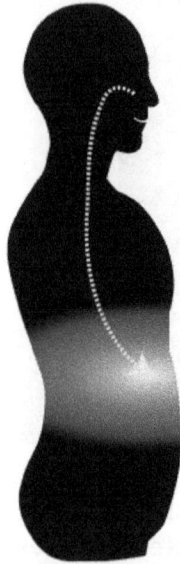

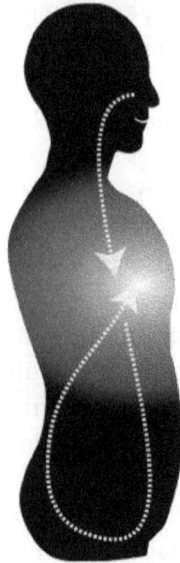

Part 5

Death Considered

First thing is to develop an interest in astral projection, which is really an interest in realizing if there is anything to you, besides the physical body. To understand this, we can consider Christianity, where they offer a deal that if one accepts Christ as the personal savior, one will get an eternal spiritual body when Christ comes back to the earth.

Their proposal is simple:

You are a material body. You will die when the material body dies. If you want to live forever in happiness, accept Christ. He will arrange so that your dead self will resurrect when he returns to the earth.

That is a fair bargain but it is terribly flawed if anyone is more than a material body. If there is a subtle body or astral body, or any remnant of energy of the personality, when the physical form dies, this proposition of Christianity has no value.

If one has a subtle body which will survive physical self-consciousness that means that one does not need an eternal physical form. Christianity loses its appeal.

How can we find out before death, if we will survive hereafter? Most people have this idea that it is not possible to do that until one dies. I declare that it can be done before death. You can astral project and test to see what you would survive as after death. The difference between astral projection and death is that at death, one is deprived of the physical body forever. One cannot reenter it no matter what. In astral projection one reenters.

It is like going to a country using a visitor's visa and going to a country on a permanent visa or going there as an exile. If you leave your homeland and go with a visitor's visa, it is not exactly the same as if one is exiled from your homeland and was force to stay in the foreign land, but it is similar because on the temporary visa, you experience the other place. Astral projection allows you to visit the subtle worlds which will become the permanent residence after the physical body dies.

Astral projection is the method of dying before you die and experiencing that. It is not true that a person cannot experience death until death actually happens. You can have that experience if you astral project regularly.

Let me be clear. When one astral projects, one becomes conscious of the displaced astral form. The astral form separates from the physical every time the physical body sleeps, but one is not always aware of the separation. Astral projection is to be aware of it.

To learn how to astral project, the first thing one should do is to develop the desire to become aware while the physical system sleeps and to be objective during dreams.

The main reason for the lack of awareness during astral projection is the tendency to be physical and to focus on the physical. If one can break this obsession with the physical, one would increase psychic perception. To begin the practice keep a dream journal by the bed side. Train yourself to recall and write of dream experiences when you first awaken.

It does not matter if there is no recall most of the time. Make the effort to remember. Jot that in a journal. This very simple act is a great way to begin dream recall.

Some dreams are concoctions of the mind, where combined old images or new images are seen in the mind. These images arise from the memory, and then the mind refashions them.

In mystic yoga one requirement is to study how the mind creates fantasies. That study is required. It gives the student an idea of how the mind operates, especially how the mind accesses memories and how it recombines subtle impressions. It alerts the student about his or her associations and their effects. The student gets insight to break the mind's hypnotic grip on the self.

I discussed how the mind imagines fantasies, but there is astral projection which is different. Sometimes there is a mix between astral projection and the imaginative fantasies of the mind.

By noting what comes to mind when one awakens one trains the mind to be aware on the psychic side and to abandon the strong focus on the physical reality.

In an astral projection one realizes that one is in a real subtle world as contrasted to being in the mind fantasies. In other words, the mind fantasies occur in the mind itself while the astral projection allow the person to see an environment outside the astral body.

In this physical world if I sit and day dream, it happens in my mind for sure, but all the same I can see outside of my physical body. There are real objects outside the body. It is the same in the astral form, in that you can see fantasies in the astral head. You can also see astral objects which are outside of the astral head.

How can one tell which is which? First explain to me how you can tell when you daydream or when you see something which is objective to the physical body, which is outside that body?

The first step is to have a dream journal.

The second step is to make efforts to astral project, after one is rested.

Rest properly. Rise and immediately recline again, preferably in a dark room which has good ventilation (fresh air access), on a firm surface if possible and on your back. Recline. Relax the mind. See if the natural system which separates the astral body from the physical one will operate.

Do not be frustrated if after 30 minutes nothing happens. When one has time try again another day.

Power not to practice yoga

Sometimes a yogi is plagued with an energy which prevents practice. The person may practice, then suddenly become dejected and hesitant, until at last practice stops completely. Then that person will avoid association with yogis.

Why does this happen?

The reason is the same reason as to why anything ceases, which is that a retardative force enters the psyche and snuffs out the desirable features. It transfers the person from a higher mental plane to a lower one, where the practice of yoga and the effort for self-realization has no significance.

Many do not realize that we shift up and down mentally into higher or lower planes, and are influenced by the energy of those levels. This is because of thinking that we control the mental faculties. This thinking causes us not to observe when we are shifted.

Once a person realizes that he or she is not a free agent and that he or she is controlled according to the mental level, it is easy to be objective and see the various forces which shift mentally, or emotionally, or physically.

Why it is that one person persists with practice, no matter what, while another diverts from practice regularly and is not consistent?

The reason is that the person who cannot persists is overcome by a negative influence. In either case, that of the one who persists and the one who does not, the negative influences are present. They are real. The negative force is a sluggish energy which causes the yogi to reduce or abandon the practice. The persistent yogi has a strong instinct for practice. Even if the negative force saturates the mind, that person practices.

Association with more advanced entities is required. No limited person can resist all negative forces without taking help from more advanced persons. Telling the self that it is powerful and that it controls, and that no influence can compel it, is very good for boosting self-confidence but it is not realistic.

Last night I was in association with some persons in the astral world. Most of these persons are related to me physically. Some were friends from years prior. In that association I related to these individuals on their level of operation, which is a lower than the one I am usually on. In any case, in this instance there was no way out, because of the pressures of fate.

By fate, we sometimes meet someone here or there. We are pressed into certain associations which may be counterproductive to self-realization. Since these situations are enforced by fate, one cannot escape them. In these situations, the best thing is to face the circumstance and perform as best as one can, with an intention to leave the association and return to the regular routine thereafter. That is what I did. There is one flaw in that approach however. One may become infected with so much retardative energy, that one cannot resume the practice.

Usually I do not absorb much retardative force. Last night was an exception. When the alarm clock rang for rising to do exercises, I turned it off and slept. This is the first sign of the success of the retardative force. It produces an attitude of carelessness which cancels the commitment for early morning practice. I did not rise for another two hours. Once I rose, I practiced. Before the practice, there was a force within the mind which instructed the psyche to forego practice for one day.

I noticed that energy. I was to consider it, when I reflected, "I will practice. Ignore the retardative influence."

It took about ten minutes of practice, then the negative force left the psyche. It was shaped like a soup dumpling. It had a light grey color. It was in the lower abdomen. It left the psyche through the front by the navel.

As soon as it left, the reluctance to practice left the psyche. I traced this energy to one person in the group of persons whom I associated with the night prior in the astral world.

One should have three obligations in yoga
- to oneself
- to the practice of yoga
- to the yoga guru(s)

Each is required. One must have such a high value for oneself, that one honors the obligation to the self to elevate the self.

One should have so much respect for yoga practice and what it can give one that one desires to always honor the practice by doing it daily.

One must have so much feeling of being accountable to the yoga guru(s), that one is terrified of having to face him or her, if one does not practice.

Three commitments are required. In Buddhism, there is commitment to the Buddha and the sanga which is the group of monks. There is also commitment to the way which Buddha established as the process of enlightenment. Essentially these three commitments are required in every spiritual discipline.

It is you. It is the discipline. It is the teacher(s) who inspires.

Negative association does not have to be deliberate to effect yoga practice negatively. It can be casual and unintentional. It is like a cold virus. If someone has it and sneezes by you, you may contract it even if that person had no intention of infecting you.

There is no sense in taking it personally. Understand that in any association with persons who are not aggressively practicing spiritual elevation, there will be a retardative energy which will put a damper on practice. With that in mind one can decide to forge the way regardless of whether a depression energy influences one not to practice.

Even though initially one may not see the negative energy, one can feel it. One should have faith that the feeling can be visual in the advanced stage. We can take help from science to have confidence in that, because science shows a picture of thought forms in the brain. In yoga one develops mystic visions which are similar to what technology shows.

The part where one identifies with the thoughts is part of yoga practice to differentiate the various components in the head of the subtle body. If the whole head is just one thing and if you cannot differentiate the various parts of the mind, then by meditation one can develop clarity about this. That comes from practice over time.

Until one can distinguish the components of the mind, one will be subjected to identifying with whatever thoughts or images the mind constructs. There is only one way to overcome that. It is the method of regular practice.

The word psyche means the person's psychological energy. There is psychological energy in the head. It is present in the toes as well. The collection of psychological energies of one individual self is called the psyche.

I stress the head but the head is not the only part of the psyche. For instance in the physical sense, the head is the most important part of the body. If the brain malfunctions, one will be out of it, even if the rest of the body is healthy. I stress the head but the human body is more than a head.

Since the primary attention is in the head, whatever one perceives in the body is done through that attention. If one perceives something in the head, the attention does not have to be focused far from its default position. If however something is in the navel area or in the foot for instance, the attention must travel to that location, or a message is sent via the nerves physically or through subtle nerves (nadis) to the brain or mind. That takes a little time, microseconds perhaps but it is still time.

A negative force will not leave of its own accord, because it enters to become a permanent feature and to command of the psyche, just as when a virus enters the body. The virus acts to take control. It engages in military conquest of the body, to kill or command cells.

Similarly negative subtle forces, which enter the psyche force it to do what those forces desire and to cause the psyche to develop for their benefit.

Hence if you can make the environment hostile or non-responsive to such negative forces they will leave the psyche, or be destroyed or remain in the psyche in a neutralized form, where they cannot hijack the mission of the self.

Sex and marriage

Marriage is designed by human beings. Nature may not endorse everything that human beings plan. Marriage as a formal agreement is the human way of trying to legitimize something which nature enforces. Nature does not care about the registration of a marriage otherwise there would be no divorce.

Take for instance medical treatment. Some humans spent millions of dollars in medical research. They send many youths to medical schools where they spend years studying the ways and means of how a material body operates. Still in modern history there is not one single case of a human being living say for 150 years.

You may have heard others speaking about a time in the future when a human body will be made to live forever. That is okay, but presently there is not a single case out of so many millions of human beings on earth, where medical science caused anyone, even the wealthiest persons who can foot the bill, to live say for 150 years. This means that to a certain extent nature does not care about our aspirations and ideas.

Look in another category: the mystic field. We have stories in the Bible for instance, about a person named Jesus, whom that book says resurrected his physical human body by sheer mystic power because he was supposed to be a divine being. But within recent history, say the last 300 years, there is not a single recorded case of this happening anywhere.

They were claims about yogis doing it in India, extending the life of their material bodies and living on in such bodies, but in India within the last 50 years, there is not a single verified case.

This means that nature is unwilling to support many of our ideas. Once one realizes that and knows that one fights a losing battle, one will relax and not tense oneself with idle boasts. If nature pressured a person for infidelity, there may be insufficient resistance. That will cause the person to yeild. This does not mean that one should fulfill every urge but it does mean that one should not hold the self aloof as being someone who is above nature.

Nature can create a circumstance in which one will either forget or neglect pledges. One cannot rely on promises. Nature has ways of nullifying committments.

For one thing one should train the self to always research who will be the child if one has an extramarital relationship. Avoidance of pregnancies is easy because of the physical and chemical contraceptives. But to be fair to oneself, one needs to always think that there will be a pregnancy. One should speculate on the past life identity of the child. The child is part of the sexual urge which one has. Even if one deprives the child of an embryo, the child's presence as part of the energy is real.

Ask a few questions:

Who will be the child?

Which ancestor is this person?

How many years of parental support will this child require?

How will I maintain this child?

How will I maintain the commitment with the other parent?

From another level ask these other questions:

How was I related in a past life to this person to whom I am now sexually attracted?

How will the relationship with this person develop in this life?

What cultural incompatible features does this person carry in this life?

Will those abrasive features cause disharmony?

Questioning oneself may not stop the sexual attraction but it may temper the attraction and reveal some liabilities.

Materialism or spirituality (November 2010)

In the infancy and youth of a body, one rides the high road of ignorance which has many places for enjoyment. One does not attend to the potential ailments which will develop in the body. The body will age anyway. Eventually one will be evicted from it and will not awaken as it. However one ignores this because of a preoccupation with acquiring enjoyment.

In the teen years one rides on a roller coaster with other youths in the hustle to be the one who enjoys the most or to be the one who participates in the action.

Subsequently that enjoyment becomes the preoccupation. When sexual maturity begins, one shifts to satisfying that without respect to the long-ranged interest of the body.

After sexual maturity develops, when one feels the interest in sexual pleasure, one considers the possibility of reproduction but since that is a drag on the current of enjoyment because it produces responsibility, one avoids reproducing. In order to attain status quo, one seeks ample money in an employment which pays to keep one in a high social class.

One ignores the call of nature to reproduce and with the help of modern science, one steps over the head of responsibility for progeny and is totally consumed by the quest for sex and money.

All the while the body is super taxed because of the wanton use of the organs. Soon after forty years one finds that the body is diseased. It threatens with ailments. One then conspires with modern science to undermine the efforts of the body to reduce sense enjoyment which it must because of old age.

Sometimes, one gets the idea that one should have a family, but with the advance of the age and with the push for status in the employment community, one again hesitates.

Life goes on with one discovering out that sooner or later one will not be the body. But there is intoxication to assist with avoiding that realization. One takes comfort by using liquor or drugs. But nature still advances. Gradually it shuts down the body. One is locked out of history.

What one puts into the mouth for whatever reason does affect the type of consciousness one experiences in the body. Eating and drinking are part of spiritual life. This is because the consciousness experienced in the body is subsidized by diet.

Consciousness as we experience it is a composite energy, part of which is based on what is ingested into the body, not only what is drunk or eaten but what is breathe into the body.

If one is careless about what goes into the body that may affect one's aspirations for spiritual development. Sometimes people wonder why a yogi restricts diet. They feel that he deprives himself of pleasure. One may consider that perhaps a yogi enjoys in some other world or in some other range of consciousness or in some other mental or emotional state, which is not available if the yogi had a normal diet.

In this world, people smoke cigarettes and drink coffee to achieve a particular type of consciousness. Some people drink liquor. Some take narcotics. These activities puts one in touch with a particular level of consciousness. The yogi also prefers a certain level of consciousness. Why bother a yogi when everyone else aggressively pursues the level of consciousness desired.

Sometimes people ask about increasing psychic perception but if the eating and drinking is counterproductive to yoga, how would that be possible. First one should determine what one will sacrifice for. If one continues eating and drinking as before, one will get the advantage of that and will not get the advantage of increased psychic perception and arousal of kundalini into the head.

One cannot have both advantages, the materialistic one and the spiritual one. Just as to advance in the materialistic society one must make certain sacrifices, one will have to adapt and change if one wants to advance in the psychic field.

Consciousness is in part a construct based on what one eats, drinks, and ingests in other ways. To up the ante one must adjust, instead of demanding higher perception while remaining with the same eating, drinking and breathing which one did and which is productive for the status quo in the material world.

Kundalini's arousal in the thighs, legs and feet. (November 2010)

After repeatedly arousing kundalini into the spine, head, chest and torso, it begins to tunnel through the thighs, legs and feet. Its arousal there is a bit different. When kundalini moves into the thighs, legs and feet (the lower extremities), it may feel like cramps with bliss feelings or as needles with bliss spark feelings.

It is not as intense as when it moves up the spine or into the head. However it is necessary to clear those lower extremities because they are part of the psyche. If one is unable to clear those areas, one will be shifted to lower astral world, after reaching a heavenly world after death.

Rishi Singh Gherwal mentioned that using kundalini yoga to transmigrate to a higher dimension either in the subtle world or in the spiritual world, is like using an elevator to rise through a building in order to get to a higher floor, while using moral values and philanthropy as a means of elevation is like using a staircase which winds around a building and climbing that staircase from the outside of the building.

Both methods are effective but the stairway path is inefficient. He said that a yogi can know how high he will be elevated just by properly rating the kundalini yoga practice. The definite way of knowing this by gauging what dimensions one experiences in dream states. It does not matter what the religion or process is, if the dreams concern mostly people using physical bodies who have little interest in advanced yoga, it means that one will be another material body on this planet or in some place which has a physical existence which is similar to this one. For such a person, the destiny after death is already revealed.

If on the other hand one reaches yogis and finds oneself practicing with them and associating with them during dreams, there is a chance that one will go to a higher dimension which is devoid of distractions and will continue the progression in the astral world without having to assume another material body as one did in this life.

Those rare yogis who associate with divine beings during dreaming, are assured of reaching divine places after death. Merely by checking the quality of the dream locations, one can tell where one will go if one must give up the body.

If it is left to the astral form, one will simply come out again as an infant from a woman's birth canal. This is because the astral body as it is, as it is unadjusted by yoga austerities, is prone to seeking out sperm and ova for manufacturing for itself another physical form. That is its tendency.

For general purposes and for purposes of traditional religion, there is material and spiritual, which means physical material like the body we currently use and the matter like the earth, rocks, water and the air we can feel or see. Those physical aspects are considered to be material in traditional religion and then things like sun light, radio waves and ultraviolet rays and so on are considered to be spiritual.

A ghost is considered to be spiritual.

In yoga, we are confronted with a third level, which is the real spiritual level. To clarify the terminology, what is material or physical in traditional religion is considered to be the same in yoga. What is subtle in traditional religions is subtle material in yoga. And there is a third level in yoga which is termed as spiritual.

A person who is evicted from a physical body, goes to the subtle world, not to the spiritual realm. This is because the subtle body which we use, which is used in dreams and astral projections is not a spiritual form. It is subtler than the physical body but it is made of subtle matter. Subtle matter is not spiritual substance.

For yoga one should learn the three categories; the physical, the subtle-physical and the spiritual.

As stated before (pages 42-43), if a yogi fails with yoga practice, and is unable to consolidate it, he has no choice but to take recourse to the benefits which he accrued by his socially uplifting acts.

As a last resort, if a yogi cannot get his act together before he loses the physical body, he falls back on his social account and makes use of that in the next life.

Both systems are not used. One can only use one of the systems. Social activities no matter how great and how approved and beneficial they are, will not help for yoga elevation. And yoga elevations will in turn do nothing for social upliftment.

These are two different currencies which cannot be swopped one for another. This is why sometimes, we find that a person who is a great yogi is in abject frightening poverty. It is because destiny thinks that he has not made a sufficient social contribution to derive social benefits like others who dedicated themselves to doing favors in the material world.

The astral worlds which are reached by those who amassed credits by favorable social activity are different to the astral worlds reached by those who have perfected yoga practice. But if a yogi did not complete his practice to a certain degree, it will not result in transit to the siddhaloka astral places where great yogis live. He will instead be routed to astral paradises where the pious people go. Then he will return to this world through the regular route of developing a semen-embryo-infancy body.

Kundalini up-spikes (November 2010)

Kundalini rose with spikes from the spinal column. Subsequently it did not reach into the brain but stayed below the neck.

Kundalini is usually advertised as rising through the central subtle spinal passage which is called sushumna nadi. On the left side of that channel there is the ida track and on the right side there is the pingala track

However besides these there are many channels or nadis, which are tiny subtle tubes. These are usually blocked so that subtle energy cannot course through them. Success in kundalini yoga means opening these tracks to allow energy to flow through them continuously.

In the beginning years of doing kundalini yoga, one should remain focused on getting kundalini to ascend the central channel into the brain. This takes some effort of daily practice. Once this is achieved, one can then divest the energy through the entire psyche.

When kundalini rose this morning, at first it hesitated to move because it considered that it would spike out instead of moving upwards. Kundalini is lifeForce. It has intelligence. It makes decisions one way or the other.

After that initial hesitation, kundalini rose promptly and spiked.

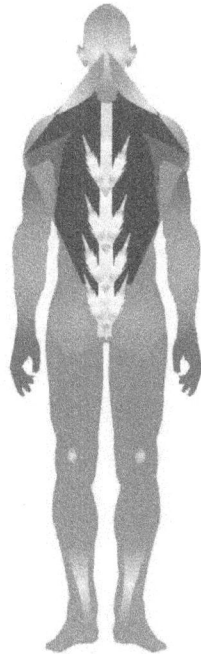

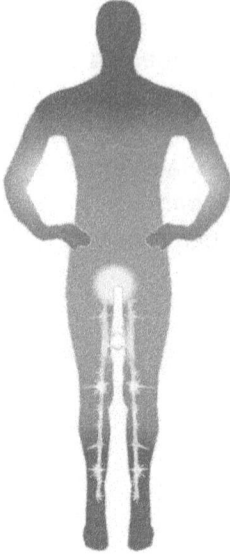

Kundalini strikes the intellect when the yogi is off-guard. The intellect is the touch point between the coreSelf and objective consciousness. The way the psyche is wired, the coreSelf is more like an accessory rather than being the major component, but it is the major power-supply of the psyche.

It is the intellect which should be protected from the striking of kundalini when it comes into the head. If it hits the orb from behind, the intellect will lose contact with the body. The self will in turn seem to lose control even though what happens is that the intellect lost contact. It is like a system of an electric circuit. If you cut a wire to one part of the circuit, power will no longer go to that part. All components which are wire-routed through that part will lose function and will not participate in the circuit.

A question arises.

Why does the coreSelf not maintain objectivity even when the kundalini strikes and stuns the intellect?

What is the dependence of the coreSelf on the intellect?

How does the kundalini disable the intellect on occasion when the intellect is hit from behind by kundalini?

These are the questions which face a yogi.

One thing is certain. The delay of kundalini is usually based on a lack of sufficient energy during the breath infusion. The yogi should gain insight about this.

In the case of the material world, we find that everyone knows his address, town or city. The residences of the family and friends are known. But hardly anyone knows anything about kundalini, the intellect, their locations and their relationships with the coreSelf.

Crazed for sex/crazed for kundalini (November 2010)

During exercises this morning there was a negative energy which wanted to stop the session just after it began. I ignored this energy and kept focused on completing the session. The energy remained in my psyche until about 10 minutes before the session concluded. After that it dissipated.

At one point I heard a voice in my head. It said, "Be sure to complete the session. Do not skip a posture." That was Rishi Singh Gherwal. About 5 minutes after I felt the presence of Yogeshwarananda. He smiled while he spoke to some persons. He gave a look of encouragement.

At one point during the session the retardative force which was in my psyche kept pressing for me to cease the practice. I ignored it but it kept asserting itself. When it applied maximum pressure, I kept practicing mainly because Rishi Singh Gherwal kept expecting me to finish the session by doing some more postures with the rapid breathing. At that point kundalini rose into the throat. It invaded the throat chakra.

In the subtle body the throat chakra bloated. The energy blocked the throat completely. The energy then spread into the head and chest. It felt like twinkles with bliss energy going in all directions in crystal white snow flakes. The top chest area of the subtle body bloated. Some of the area in the lower head which is near to the neck bloated.

This bloating happened because I effectively put on the neck lock and kept the energy in the throat chakra.

This practice session is an example of how a yogi must battle with negative forces in the psyche. It does not matter how these forces get into the psyche. The yogi must eliminate them. He can do so only by practice. It is irrelevant from whom those forces originated. The main point is to keep on with the practice and do it to the required extent making sure that kundalini rises in a full way during the session. Kundalini itself, when bogged down by the negative force which discourages practice, changes its attitude if one persists in the practice.

For students who want to know what to do with the negative energy which deters practice, the answer is simple. Do the practice. Let the practice challenge those energies.

Undoubtedly there is negative energy which discourages practice, but a yogi realizes that the negative force will never end. It is omnipresent on this level. One should not waste time thinking about it. One should be committed to completing at least one daily session for raising kundalini. During that session one should practice until one arouses kundalini.

In this respect modern people in the developed world set an important example in the way they persist for sexual indulgence, where they do everything possible to increase sexual indulgence and where they would even destroy their careers and marriages, to get as many sexual indulgences as possible. We can learn something from their persistence.

As they are sex crazed, we should be eager to raise kundalini daily. They raise kundalini through the genitals using partners of the same or opposite sex, or they masturbate, or they use external sex aids, or pornographic films or aphrodisiacs. They do everything possible to worship at the shrine of the genitals. They indulge in oral sex, genital sex, anal sex and whatever else can be done to expand kundalini's arousal in a sexual way. From them we can get some idea of how determined one can be to raise kundalini up the spine and into the head of the subtle body.

Floating astral forms

After meditation this morning, I found myself in an astral dimension in which the human bodies floated on water, the way ducks float without effort on their part. There are many of these astral dimensions. Each has its own facilities which are contrary to what we experience in this material world.

One other queer feature of that astral place, was that if a material did not want someone in proximity, that person could not approach it. Even the inanimate objects there have will power and desire. They express themselves by an attracting or repelling force.

I noticed this when my astral form floated near a shore line where there was a pier. I tried to step on the pier but it refused to accept me. When I expressed that desire I was repelled from it by a will power force within it.

While I was in that astral place, my body was in a lotus posture. After a time I was near a stream of water. A lady I knew while I was in South America some years ago, came there. She was in a small boat-like contraption, moving on the water. When I greeted her, I realized that she did not recognize me. She was in that parallel world but without memory of her earthly existence. She was in total ignorance of a past life, just as we discovered ourselves in these bodies as the son or daughter of parents but with no memory of a past existence.

Transiting to the astral world is tricky. Usually one does so without prior memory. Some meditators feel that since it frees a person from negative biases the loss of memory is good. However, it also frees a person from positive and useful biases as well. It leaves a person with innocence as a thin coating over massive ignorance.

One does not automatically continue with only good biases. The subconscious chamber in which the biases are stored has both the good and bad prejudices in a compacted form. If one loses that, one loses both aspects, the desirable and undesirable ones. Such a condition would be like that of a child who has no understanding of good or bad, right or wrong and who would eat garbage if it was placed before him or eat ice-cream as well, who would desire what is harmful and also desire what is harmless, without knowing what is what due to a lack of discrimination. Innocence includes massive ignorance.

In kriya yoga, the subconscious chamber of memories and instincts is checked and rated by the yogi for the elimination of undesirable traits and the support and reinforcement of desirable ones. This is taught as the first and second stages of yama and niyama but both stages continue through all the advanced aspects of yoga. The yogi maintains proper social behavior within the psyche itself. He disciplines various parts of the psyche in their interactions with other sectors.

Buddha past lives technique (November 2010)

During meditation I got a mental procedure from Buddha. This is a purely feelings maneuver. For instance to move the right thumb, one has to execute a mental order or a willpower movement but if the nerves to that thumb are damaged, the order will not manifest as a physical act. In that case, there is a mental principle but no corresponding physical action.

In yet another example, you may imagine moving thumb and not execute a mental order. In that case, there is only an image in the mind with no corresponding mental physical act. These are three distinct actions. One should work in meditation to honestly distinguish each maneuver.

Skeptics feel that there can be no clear distinction in these acts but there can be. It does not have to be proven to anyone. The proof manifests in the yogi's development by progress in meditation.

Buddha gave an instruction for a mystic action through which one can delve into history to research past lives. This is a simple procedure as I will describe. Even though it is simple, one will have no success doing it if one did master the art of stopping the mental imaging and sounding in the mind. Stated precisely, unless one practiced to stop the involuntary thinking functions as instructed by Patañjali, one will have no success doing this, because one will not be in the dimension or vibration where this procedure operates.

Here is the instruction:
- Get the mind space into a condition where there are no thoughts or images and no effort is required to keep the mind in that blank state.
- Listen for naad sound in this back or side of the head.
- Check to see that the self is attracted to naad and that its attention naturally holds to the naad sound with interest.
- Move to the back of the head, while remaining focused on naad.
- When one is sure that one is in the back and that one still hears naad and is still aware of the entry point of naad, and is still moving backwards, look forward.

- There should be some shimmering light and a flash of an image or of many images. These will be sights from past lives.

If nothing is there, this procedure is too advanced for the yogi. Still one should practice until something appears.

Re-ordering the components of the mind (November 2010)

When doing asana postures with or without breath infusement, a yogi should practice the relocation of the attention energy, the intellect and the coreSelf.

These three components are in the head of the subtle body, but they can be moved from the default positions. A yogi, must by all means learn how to relocate these. If these are not relocated, their power or lack of power will continue unabated to the regret of a yogi.

For one thing the lack of power is something which plagues the coreSelf. The authority over the coreSelf is something which usually resides in the intellect. The sense of attention has a bad habit of doing whatever the intellect commands even at the expense of the coreSelf.

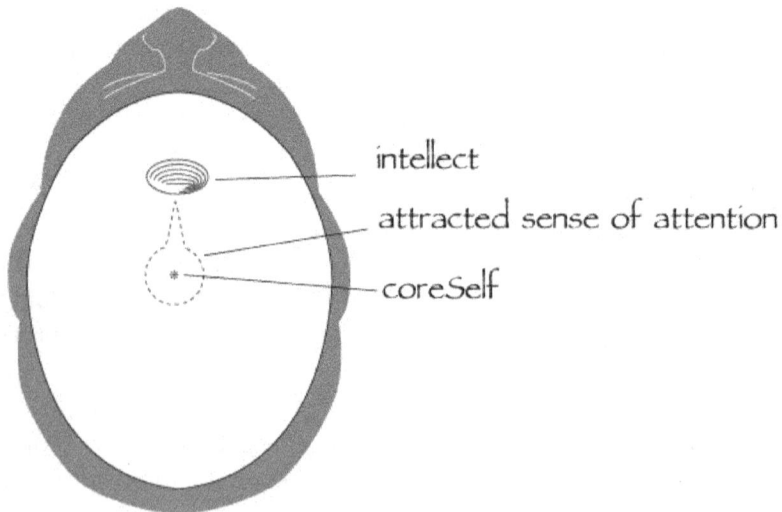

intellect

attracted sense of attention

coreSelf

This can be re-ordered by the yogi if he or she simply practices to relocate these components. Asana postures help considerably in this even though the asanas are only physical postures.

If someone takes a large needle and suddenly plunges it into my arm, my attention will immediately go to that place in the physical body. However it will not remain there, the attention will impulsively relocate to the subtle head. This jump to the puncture spot and then relocation into the head, will happen so rapidly and reflexively, that it may be unnoticed. In yoga, the inability to trace the movements of the attention must come to an end. One can achieve that by a daily meditation practice in which one uses special techniques.

When doing postures with or without breath infusion, always be attentive to the part of the body which is stretched, tensioned, relaxed, or energized. When one does so the attention and intellect will make attempts to relocate to those parts of the body. In some cases, the attention and/or the intellect may refuse to relocate. In other words, these subtle organs will produce a resistance and will remain in their default locations. In fact the intellect may not simply refuse to relocate, but it may insists that the attention be involved in something which the intellect imagines.

In that case, say that I am doing the bow pose that would mean that my stomach area is arched. My back is under-arched. Still the intellect thinks of something else and engages my attention in that thinking, such that my attention has no idea that my trunk is arched.

I do the posture. People see it. They think that I do the posture properly. Still within the psyche, very little attention is given to the pose. This is an example of what not to do when doing postures.

The intellect and the attention should be engaged in the posture and should be relocated into the stretch and into relaxing the stretch.

Since nature has many hidden systems, and since most of her methods are unknown to the selves using bodies, even those using human forms, it takes much research to figure nature's operations. Nature conducts this universe, the life that we individually have, with us being massively ignorant. One should recognize this power of nature.

Kundalini rises in various ways, up the spine, up the front of the body, up the middle, and sometimes it rises up the left or right side.

One should observe this. One will not know every ascension of kundalini because unless one is in an observational position while kundalini is rising, one will not know how kundalini rose. Many students experience a rise of kundalini. If one asks a student to explain honestly what happen, he may not have a clue, except to say he felt this or felt that or he lost awareness, and then became conscious of himself as the body after blacking out.

The student should demand of himself or herself that there be a detailed observation. This does not mean that there will be one, but it means that the mind's observational capacity may develop the perception.

In the end, one must pilot oneself out of this body or be evicted from it, forced out of it by nature in whatever way nature sees fit. If one learns how to manage and influence kundalini, how to know its methods and its potential for improvement, later when one must leave the body, one may pilot the self to a higher plane.

There is one big problem everyone faces once the body hits about 50 years of age. That is how to get out of this body finally? How will that take place? Will I help myself out of this? Or will it be out of my hands and in the hands of nature to do whatever it may?

The particulars of how kundalini rose, up the front, back or wherever and how it subsided and retreated, should be observed in detail, no so much to explain to others but to know for oneself its formats.

In most persons, the kundalini is stranger to them than their next door neighbor. Even though it is in the body, they have no idea of it. Nature will push every living body to its death. That is certain. The individual psychology of energies will survive, but in what condition? How will it be bundled?

Motivation for mindfulness (November 2010)

Meditation is a bit like everything else, in that one does it because one has to, or because one chooses to. Many things we do are done merely because we must perform these actions. When someone instructs one may not like that because one feels that one should be in control. Many actions are done on impulse as one is forced by emotions and moods.

When we consider the situation, we find that there is no purpose for living. We discover that we go from day to day aimlessly or are driven by trends which were introduced by others.

Traditionally, people learnt meditation is ashrams, either in India, China or Japan. What is an ashram? It was a boarding school. Just as today, in the modern societies, every child is forced to attend school, to learn grammar, how to add and subtract and so on, so some children used to go to an ashram to learn meditation.

But if a child is in an undeveloped country, or say in a tribe in the Amazon, that child is not compelled to attend school. There is no government enforcing school attendance. Thus the child has no interest in language and calculation.

Then suddenly a missionary comes or an American from the Peace Corps. That person causes the child to study English and Math. But the child finds that he does not like it.

When he is given homework, he does not do it. He does not feel motivated.

When Buddha set out to meditate, it was because he lost motivation for social life. He decided,

"I will no longer participate in social dealings. That leads to a dead end. I saw the end of this, as death of the *me*, death of the body. Until I can see some sense in this, I will not participate."

With that he left his infant son, attractive wife, concubines, status as a Prince, everything. He went into the night with determination to find if there was something besides being born as a human infant, growing up, having sex, begetting children, being overtaken by ill health and then dying helplessly.

Think about it. Am I having sex because I desire it? Did I invent copulation? Did I give my body the urge?

Mindfulness came to us in a tradition from Buddha. Maybe by reading about his life, one may get inspiration for doing the practice.

Nature: The Superpower (November 2010)

Before becoming a physical body, one must have an astral form which will be used by nature as a blueprint for the physical system one is to become.

The natural process is that nature does most of this. It uses the self as a psychic power supply. Due to primeval arrogance, we are obsessed with what we can do, but if one checks closely one will see that everything desired was already enacted by nature.

Kundalini base infusion (November 2010)

When focusing on infusing the base chakra muladhara, there is a twofold approach. The first and the simplest of the two is to infuse the base with energy so that it will move to send out an energy bolt, or to spark to another chakra or another part of the body.

This system is already in place by nature. We experience it in a very obvious way during sexual climax when the high charge of energy at the genitals, causes kundalini to jump to the sexual area. This is a spark procedure of linking, like in arc welding. Due to a power charge on one piece of metal, another piece which has a low charge is attracted.

In sex, the charge of lust attracts the kundalini, which jumps to become unified with it. That is interpreted emotionally as sexual pleasure.

In kundalini yoga the elementary way to charge the base chakra is to use the lungs, the navel region and the groin area to force kundalini to discharge itself in one direction or another. The combined lung, navel and groin energy fires itself into the kundalini and the force explodes.

To be an expert one has to learn how to control that explosion so as to guide the aroused kundalini in a specific direction.

In the advanced procedure, kundalini is attacked in the same way but instead of firing the energy into kundalini, one fires around kundalini so as to unsettle it and to shift it from its base anchor position. While in the elementary practice, kundalini expresses a moving force of energy and still remains anchored at the base, in the advanced practice, it is the base of kundalini which moves.

Some times when the base is energized in that way, it emits laser shoots of white energy downwards. If the yogi keeps the infusement and increases it further, kundalini becomes unhinged from its anchor position. Then the yogi can move kundalini here or there as desired.

Struggling to breathe during OBE

Struggling to breath or inability to move the physical body and sometimes the astral one, is normal in out-of-body-experiences (OBE). Generally it is called sleep paralysis. It is really paralysis of the physical body but only in reference to being able to operate that body with the willpower as usual.

This paralysis may occur upon leaving the physical body or upon trying to repossess it. It is a paralysis in the sense that the willpower of the individual is unable to operate the body as it usually does when the body awakens. This is interpreted by the mind as a movement resistance.

During astral projection the willpower is transferred from the physical brain to the head of the astral body. Thus one cannot operate the physical system. When the astral body returns and tries to fuse into the physical one, if it is unable to synchronize perfectly, the individual experiences a non-responsiveness of the physical form.

To cause the astral body to synchronize properly, the person may manipulate the breath or make a sudden movement with the astral form or just wait for that body to synchronize properly.

This feels weird, restrictive and unnatural. The person becomes fearful, panics or enters a state of anxiety.

In the effort to operate the breathing, if the person holds the breath long enough, both bodies will snap into synchronization but sometimes when one does this, the two bodies quickly separate again. One finds the self back in the position of being unable to operate either body. It feels as if both forms are stiff and unmoving. This may cause further panic. Eventually however the astral body comes in sync. The person rises as a physical body.

If one can hold the breath in or out long enough the astral body may snap into place.

There are three important things to know about sleep paralysis:
- If the body is in a room which has little or no ventilation, that condition of breathing stale air may cause increased incidence of sleep paralysis. This is because the astral body and the lifeForce in

the physical system do not get sufficient energization from the stale air.

- Taking of alcohol, narcotics or sleep-aid drugs or any drugs which affect the nervous system, can cause increased incidence of sleep paralysis.
- Looking at scary movies can be a cause of sleep paralysis.

The main thing is to understand what it is and not to panic when one finds the self in that position but to be confident that if one cannot cause the astral form to snap in properly into the physical one, still the condition will pass within seconds or minutes, unless of course one has a serious accident and the body goes into a coma or unless one has a medical stroke or some other nerve system degeneration.

In some experiences which relate to astral projection, lucid dreaming and transiting to other dimensions, there may be a thin line between imagination and subtle reality. This is why some people are skeptical about psychic experiences. Some dismiss it as being unreal hallucinations.

In yoga and meditation, we accept the truth that the psychic perception has flaws. We should research and figure the degree of error and then regard it.

Nobody will pluck out his eyes, because he does not have 20/20 vision. We have to agree to use the imperfect eyes because it is better to have a malfunctioning eye that no vision. In the same way one should use the subtle body but should be alert to its misconceptions.

If one meditates with care and patience, one will gradually come to understand what the malfunctions are. Taking that into account one could adjust for the errors in psychic perception. That is better than being a skeptic who aggressively dismisses psychic perception because it is not 100% accurate.

By persistence in meditation, one comes to know the thin line between imagination and actual mystic perception. One may understand the relationship between visualization and reality. Sometimes visualization serves to promote actual psychic experience which is reality.

There are many who have such a sensitive mind, that their visualizations cause them to transit to real subtle states. This happens even though the initial visualization is creative imagination in their minds.

A buzzing sound may be heard when the astral body is super-energized. Sometimes in these experiences there are also loud thunder claps in the subtle body and even subtle lightning. These may cause fear because if one is still referenced to material existence, that reference will produce a fear response.

When the astral body is energized to the level where it is made of light, like sunlight or some other type of light energy frequency, the person lives as light and will perceive the world which is there and beings who use subtle bodies of light.

Such beings are people like Jesus Christ. In such a body one would also rapidly transit to the sun and see buildings there, and trees, and streets and people made of light energy only.

In relation to meeting God or the Supreme Being directly, that idea is there because in the Judeo-Christian system, there is focus on one Supreme Being in exception to everyone else. However in reality, there are multiple expansions of Godhead.

Bhaktivedanta Swami explained it aptly by explaining that Godhead was plural in the sense that there is one Supreme Personality of Godhead but they are innumerable Personalities of Godhead Who exist in parallel and in coordination to that Supreme Person. This means that to be realistic we should release ourselves from the Judeo-Christian idea and face the fact that our relationship is with divine beings not just with the Supreme Divine Person. If one's mind is open one may have experiences of meetings divine beings who reside in the spiritual universe.

Presently we have a phase of history where we see that the developed nations which are Judeo-Christian, have the predominant global influence.

The Muslim society realized that this is the situation. In an effort to reverse the situation radical Islam opposes it. Since Jesus Christ is the predominant deity at this time, they cannot reverse that. This does not mean that everything the Christians and their Jewish friends do is right. Some of it is criminal from any angle but still Christ has the main authority over the planet. The other deities of the other faiths are subordinately functioning, at least in terms of global political control and enforced cultural dominance.

One can meet Jesus Christ. He uses a sunlight body in the subtle world. If one's astral form is energized to that level, one can see him. There is no need to doubt the experience. Do not try to prove the psychic experiences to those who are skeptics. Does not harbor doubts. People do not harbor doubts about technological gadgets even though these fail and are imperfect.

The main thing is to realize that even though one is safe from astral reality and one is protected from it by the focus on material existence, still that protection is only valid so long as the physical body lives. As soon as that body dies, and it must die, despite our science, one will be left with the psychic self only.

Why not take time out and develop an understanding of the psychic side even the flaws in it.

In the system of yoga there is cosmic kundalini (lifeForce), cosmic intellect, and cosmic sense of identity Apart from these there is the supreme divine person.

Each of the selves, you or me, have a sense of identity which is permanent. It cannot be eradicated. It causes a tremendous suffering as one transmigrates in various species of life, but still one cannot be rid of it. There is a pure flawless state of that sense of identity, but presently we have no idea what that pure condition is.

It is explained in the Puranas that when the Supreme Being initiates the creations, trillions of limited selves become aware of themselves here. These spirits are given some psychological equipment, of which the sense of identity is part.

It is similar to what happens when a baby emerges. Soon after a name is officially assigned. In some countries even a number is given. The child is tagged. When these creations are initiated by God, there is created a vast cosmic pool of intellects, and another pool of senses of identities and one for lifeForces.

Sometimes it happens that a person through meditation or just by sheer divine grace without effort on his part, gets to reconnect to the vast cosmic energy.

When this happens one sees a light overhead or in the distance. It appears as a vast blinding cosmic apparition. One or two rays from that place strikes on either in the head or chest. When this happens one feels as if one's existence was translated to a celestial or divine level.

There is also a bliss energy which enters one because those cosmic pools are saturated bliss energy.

An experience like this may last for just seconds, or minutes and for longer, as the case maybe. Usually when the person resumes physical existence there is a residual effect which may last for minutes or even hours or days but eventually it diminishes. One finds oneself back with the usual human social consciousness. This may happen even to persons who have no history of meditation.

The only two bodies which are within our reach is the physical system and the astral system which is used nightly in dreams and which sometimes is experienced objectively in a subtle world as astral projection.

These are the only two systems which are somewhat under our control. As for the physical body most of us are familiar with that. The astral one is only within control of a few psychics, mystics and the like. Most people do not recall dreams and never have conscious astral projection.

In respect to that, I say that astral projection occurs every time the physical body sleeps and yet, people say that they do not experience it. Either

I do not know about it or their consciousness during sleep is so dense that it makes no conscious contact with the experiences of the astral form. In other words, most people sleep-walk in the astral world night after night and deny astral experiences simply because they have no objective take on it.

To go beyond the astral body one may either do so by divine grace, or by energizing the astral body to such an extent that its vibrations become alarmingly accelerated.

For instance in the space industry, by expensing large amounts of energy, by burning super-fuels they send rockets beyond the earth's gravitational field. This causes an acceleration, even though it is an external one with the burnt fuel leaving the spacecraft. In the case of the astral body one accelerates it from within.

Beyond the physical world, there are the astral dimensions, which are adjacent to it. Beyond that immediate astral world, there is the celestial astral realm where the supernatural controllers like Jesus, Indra and others reside. Beyond their territories there is a demarcation zone. Then there are a set of dimensions in which very highly evolved and divine teachers exist. Beyond that place, there is the place of the creator-god whose mind is the support for all psychological activities below that realm.

Beyond that there is another demarcation zone where nothing exist. Beyond that there is a place which is sheer light, spiritual light. Beyond that there is a place called the spiritual world.

Patañjali gave this information.

जात्यन्तरपरिणामः प्रकृत्यापूरात्॥२॥
jātyantara pariṇāmaḥ prakṛtyāpūrāt

jātyantara = jāti – category + antara – other, another; pariṇāmaḥ – transformation; prakṛiti – subtle material nature; āpūrāt – due to filling up or saturation.

The transformation from one category to another is by the saturation of the subtle material nature. (Yoga Sutras 4.2)

However by divine grace, one's psyche may become saturated with divine energy, which may cause translation to higher places.

There is a spiritual practice whereby a person can infuse the psychology with energy from a higher place? It can be done through yoga austerities.

Patañjali explained what yoga is. He gave instructions on how to do it. As in this world, when one crosses borders or even if you move to a higher social status, one inevitably must work with individuals. In the spiritual quest one will be confronted with the same thing, where to translate to a higher place one must deal with a deity or with some advanced person who is resident in that higher zone.

Samadhi practice (December 2010)

The idea of doing yoga practice which includes meditation, is to develop familiarity with higher bodies and to learn how to use these, so that after leaving the physical form, one can go to the divine world.

A living entity requires an environment. By the grace of nature, we are familiar with this physical place. If we fail to develop an interest in another higher location, we will definitely return into this world as an infant in some species.

This will happen because we are only familiar with the physical body.

Many people meditate but how many become aware of even the astral body, what to speak of the super-energized astral form or a spiritual form which is full of bliss energy. Just as they meditate and become aware of subtle states, and then they return to bodily consciousness, they will do the same thing in the afterlife, except that it will be subtle body consciousness since the physical form would be lacking.

There were cases of yogis who jumped into a super-subtle or divine form and left the physical body to die. Usually this does not happen because usually a yogi has to use the time destiny allotted him in a particular body.

One has to be very advanced at meditation practice, to jump to a higher form. Usually a yogi waits until there is a loophole in time or a downskip in the kundalini's hold on the physical form. When he catches that slot in existence, he influences kundalini to leave the body and so the body dies.

It is hardly likely that someone can do this in the modern setting because there are many distractions that ruin or at least slow down meditation progress, such that a yogi will be unable to develop the required proficiency to make a sudden transit and escape from the routine of death of the physical body.

Mahasamadhi usually means that a proficient yogi enters into a trance state and attain a higher dimension at the time of death of his or her physical form.

Maha means great. It also means final. *Mahasamadhi* is the final trance state of a yogi. There is this opinion that *samadhi* is a practice of merging into the Supreme, but if you really want to know what *samadhi* is read a reliable translation of the *Yoga Sutras of Patañjali*. He listed several types of *samadhi* and tells how to accomplish these.

Usually in India, disciples give their spiritual master the benefit of doubt about attaining a high level trance state at death. In some cases this is just the faith and expectations of the disciples and nothing else. Every spiritual master does not enter into *samadhi* at death, but instead merely go over completely into their subtle bodies on some level which is adjacent to this physical place.

Food in South Korea

In Decenber, 2010, I returned to the USA from being in South Korea for about 3 months. It took about two weeks for my system to be purged of the chemicals in the water and food in South Korea.

When I first got there, a cyst I used to have when taking inorganic produce acted up along with a fistula track which lay dormant and which used to be irritated once in a while.

The cyst went out of whack to such an extent that the entire right thigh was inflamed. It was painful. I asked my son to take me to a clinic offbase. His wife (a native of South Korea) directed us to a clinic. The physician directed us to another place which specialized in fistulas.

By the grace of providence, I had a superficial surgery and had to stay about one week in the clinic under observation. The expenses for all this were borne more or less by my son with me chipping in a small amount which I could afford.

I tried to get some information from the surgeon on the cause of these anal fistulas but to no avail. In any case, I am certain that it was caused by inorganic produce.

Usually the antibodies in a human body, react to bacterial invasion mostly but in my body the antibodies also react to chemical invasion. In an infant and child body, my body used to break out in sores or have cysts from simple actions like eating too many sweet fruits.

However it took two weeks after getting back to the USA to get my body under control regarding the taste of the saliva in the body. There are some weird chemicals in South Korean produce. That is for sure. In two weeks my taste resumed. There was however another definite indication about this which is the nerves in the teeth. In my body the nerves in the teeth are very sensitive such that if I eat sugary foods, I immediately feel it as a super sensitivity in the teeth. But the same thing occurs with chemicals.

My teeth acted up in Korea but since I am not a person to be running to physicians, I bore on with it. Actually I am glad that I did, because now I see that the teeth have lost the sensitivity at the same time that the saliva taste has lost its chemical composition. This verifies my conclusions.

South Korean farms are using strong chemicals in the fertilizers used in their fields. They did this for many years, such that the water under the ground is now saturated with these chemicals. In addition the spices and salts used in cooking are being manufactured from strong chemicals perhaps things like ajinomotoo (MSG).

On the labels of food products in South Korea there is a long list of items. I cannot read Korean script, I had no idea what those chemicals were. Chemical ingestion will be one of the major problems for human beings in the future as the chemicals in food slowly but surely alter the genetic codes.

As human beings we are so smart and intelligent that we may victimize ourselves out of being able to reproduce. Then the material world which is no near and dear to us will become off-limits by the actions of our intelligence. Funny is it not, how intelligence which is supposed to remove ignorance can itself be a cause for stupidity?

The holy grail of chemicals is such a thing, that it is impossible to explain to people what is really going on, and without reason, people even physicians, disbelieve that chemicals in fertilizers cause problems in human health and fertility.

I am not saying that the low birth rate in South Korea is due to chemical fertilizers alone. As elsewhere South Koreans aggressively use contraceptives to prevent pregnancy, but even that is a chemical attack on the reproductive system. That may cause genetic alterations in the Korean bodies, alterations which may have undesirable effects which we cannot see.

As we try to get the upper hand over nature, we may in the process push ourselves further under nature's restrictions. Sadly we are in this together, sink or swim. One or two correctly-perceiving individuals on a sinking ship have absolutely no impact on the overall situation which is that the boat will sink and even the best swimmers on board cannot swim an ocean.

Ultimately our pride in human accomplishment and human battering of nature may cause failure. When nature ends the opportunity for human species to exist on this planet, it will be a long period of millions of years, before we can again get human bodies somewhere somehow on some rare planet somewhere.

Part 6

Physical body mimics astral form (December 2010)

Last night in New York, there was a huge influx of astral bodies, floating up from South America and the West Indies. This was due to the weather pattern in New York which was influence by winds from the Caribbean.

I was visited by several people from Guyana. Some of those persons have little astral awareness. Their astral bodies are heavy and do not transport long distances usually.

There are verses in the Bhagavad Gita, where Krishna mentions that by the weather of the sun and moon, a person's astral body will reach a destination at the time of death, because of the solar and lunar influences.

Closer to home however is the earthly weather pattern which affects the astral bodies, giving them more power to move about or curtailing their movement and restricting them to certain areas.

Do not wait to figure it out. As you pay attention to weather reports which predict physical circumstances, you may observe the astral environmental conditions.

Lucid dreaming is when the astral body is desynchronized from the physical one but it is still located in the same space as the physical system.

Astral projection is when the astral body is desynchronized from the physical body but it is also dislocated from the physical body and is not in the same space.

In both cases, the same astral body is used but in lucid dreaming, there is residual awareness of the physical form, while in astral projection usually the person is totally unreferenced from physical reality.

As there is an astral hand and astral fingers, there is also astral genitals. In a case where a person lucid dreams and has sex experiences, more than likely there will be a wet dream. Because of the closeness of the subtle and physical bodies, the physical one may mimic the subtle actions.

However in astral projection, the physical body does not usually mimic the astral one, and therefore there is sex experience with no evidence of it on the physical side, no wet dream.

Kundalini: What is it? (December 2010)

Kundalini is the psychic lifeForce in the subtle body. To understand what it is one may study sexual climax experience and the rejuvenation-sleep mechanism which runs involuntarily in the body.

Something regulates heart beat and breath functions. Something supervises healing in the body. That something is kundalini. The individual iSelf does not do these functions. Even when the self is not attentive these functions proceed by an involuntary caring force in the body. That is kundalini.

When the body sleeps and the iSelf becomes unaware of it, kundalini conducts the breathing functions, heart beat and other aspects.

My next life in ignorance (December 2010)

Last night there was a wave of astral bodies which came to New York from Trinidad. Some persons whom I knew there came to see me, particularly a lady who was a headmistress of a school and who is now deceased.

After her astral body arrived, it was transferred back to Trinidad. My subtle form did not follow it but I perceived everything she did. I communicated with her just as if I was in Trinidad.

She was busy giving directions to other teachers. This was in the astral world. I decided to check to see if they were teaching at a school in the astral world and if the teachers she directed were departed souls. Some were departed but most were still using physical bodies. This means that even though she was long deceased this person still supervises certain educational activities in Trinidad.

This is similar to gurus or pastors, even some politicians and other social figures who wield power and control from the astral world after the physical body dies. Sometimes they do this for five or ten or fifteen years. Then the influence wanes. As soon as it does that they crave embryos. They acquire a body and repeat history as leaders in human society.

In the case of the powerful religious heads, like Jesus Christ for instance, these persons rule for centuries from the astral world. Their religious influence and ideas prevail as they inspire human beings to enforce their doctrines and spread faith in their glories. For a yogi, this is confusion. A yogi sees this everywhere. He sidesteps this.

After that lady's astral body went back to Trinidad, it stayed there for about ten minutes giving directions to others. Then it returned to New York. We discussed some issues which I was involved in when I lived in Trinidad around 1967. Then another lady who was a neighbor to this headmistress appeared. She was happy to see me.

I check on the way she found me. It was through the movements of the astral body of the head mistress. Their astral forms are linked in such a way, that if one goes to a place, the other one can without foreknowledge instantly find that location.

I spoke to them. I tried to pare down some consequential energy which I acquired while I was in Trinidad. Neither woman was interested in reducing down the involvement. Seeing that this was their mood, I cooperated because that was the only way out of the situation.

The astral bodies are the bane of yogis. These forms retain impressions from all interactions. These impressions must be resolved in future lives in desirable and undesirable ways.

Providence keeps a log of one's activities and uses the energy which is expressed in the performance of desirable or undesirable social situations to construct new circumstances in which it places the actor in a future life. The ignorance of the actor about reincarnation does absolutely nothing to stop providence from doing this. Hence it makes sense to escape from nature's way of action and reaction.

Patañjali instructed yogis to shut down this astral system of expressive seed ideas which will cause a yogi to take haphazard transmigrations on impulse without control. For sure, the astral body is a danger to a yogi.

Base chakra wash-out (December 2010)

This morning during exercises kundalini spiraled up both sides of the trunk of the body. That was with a bliss energy which was like four inch spikes of glass moving upward under the shoulders. I got an instruction. It was an order from a Buddha deity in South Korea a few weeks ago. I should press on to wash out the base chakra. Rishi Singh Gherwal gave an estimate of a two year practice to get that chakra fixed in the desired way.

Many students who come for yoga instructions expect instant results, like when they go to department stores and can get an item at a cheap price any time of the day or night. It is too bad that yoga is not like that since human beings are mostly motivated for instant gratification.

There are numerous diagrams about kundalini; some from ancient yogis who left sketches in manuscripts and some from modern people who feel they know something about kundalini. I published strange diagrams, based on my experiences with kundalini.

Despite diagrams, a yogi should have an open mind and not try to superimpose on kundalini some other configuration from a diagram published by me or anyone else. Have an open mind, so that when kundalini moves, you can know of its whereabouts and influences.

When working on the base chakra, I perceive it by subjective pranaVision to be a brown energy which has the shape of a 3/8 inch thick disc which is about 3 inches across and which is like a brown cloud of energy. This is a dark or light brown energy. As I infuse it more and more, the brown energy is dissipated. It becomes clear and translucent.

Our psychic criminal acts and the resultant effects will find us either in this life or the next. If one becomes liberated the energy of it will stay in this dimension and will latch on to some other soul who will be victimized by it.

Nature is reactive to whatever one may do. There is always a return-effect or boomerang energy which will loop through future time and strike the performer.

I may forget what I did in the past life, and I may be absorbed in this moment, but Time never forgets what was done. It victimizes even those who have no memory of what they did in the hoary past.

The subtle body has a subconscious compartment but in advanced yoga, this is regarded as a memory storage compartment. While it is subconscious to the average human being it is conscious and compressed to the yogi.

Subconscious means what is below the threshold of objective observational awareness. A yogi can use special tools of insight to read the information in the subconscious. Every unfavorable act of the past, even incidental criminal acts in past lives, can be dealt with effectively in the subconscious, rather to wait until such acts burst out by the sprouting action of inscrutable time.

To deal with such acts, one must learn how to enter into the subconscious stockpile of energies and apply neutralizing force to the residual potencies which are just about to burst into consciousness.

A criminal, if he or she can reach the law enforcement officials before they write a warrant for arrest, may absolve himself of previous crimes committed. Once a warrant for arrest is release, he or she has to go through a court procedure. Thus if he or she could compensate society beforehand, a full-blown imprisonment may be avoided.

There are so much energies from the past lives which are about to fructify, that a yogi should actively develop subtle consciousness so as to meet obligations from the past head on to counterbalance providence's upper hand.

Pituitary / pineal glands

Pituitary and pineal glands and other such organs do play a part in psychic perception but still these physical organs are not the focus in yoga practice. For instance sometimes when a person is having an astral sex experience, the physical body mimics the experience and emits sexual fluids even. Still the yogi is not concerned with what happens on the physical side because his focus is astral.

Interim state before birth (December 2010)

What would it be like to remain for years as an embryo? There are many views about when the soul takes residence in an embryo. Some say that it happened the moment of conception which is when the sperm of the father embedded itself into the egg of the mother. Some say it happened after 3 months or some odd number of months of pregnancy. And yet there are others who say that it happens when the embryo is pushed out of the mother's body.

Regardless I feel that in such a discussion, one should take into account that the self may be deprived of its objectivity. In a subjective state, it cannot gage its position as to whether it was stalled for days or years in the period of formatting an embryo and getting it ejected from the womb.

Subtle bodies meet (December 2010)

Subtle bodies sometimes meet to hash over incidences of the past which formed complications in the lives of individuals. Last night, suddenly I found myself in the presence of a couple who are now divorced and whose child was abused when I lived at a Hare Krishna farm in West Virginia.

Even though they were separated for some years now, both the man and the woman acted as if they were still together. In other words, their subtle bodies moved back in time to hash over the problems they had when the son was abused by a teacher in the religious boarding school.

My physical body was located in Brooklyn NY while I met with these persons who came astrally to the location of my physical body. Suddenly the three of us were relocated astrally near to the boarding school.

The man looked at me for an explanation of what took place. I described the sexual orientation of the teachers who were at the school at the time. I was there. I had a responsibility. I explained however that I was not an authority in the school. I was a junior teacher. They were seniors above me. Those persons were of homosexual orientation.

This was a religious society from India, but it stressed renunciation. The teachers were under that pressure. Some who had a homosexual orientation before coming into the society, shifted completely into that to take care of their sexual needs, except that since they were in a male boarding school situation, they satisfied those needs by sexually abusing boys who were in their care.

These two parents carry with them the negative content of their neglect of their son. They were told by their guru, who founded the Sect, that the movement was pure and that the senior people were surrendered and pure or near to pure but what they got in return was some very ugly consequences.

As we poured over the facts, there was the realization that much of what happened was beyond their control. Their surrender to that guru was terribly flawed. His promises about the school and teachers were worthless statements. His guarantees were baseless claims.

This was painful for these two individuals since they really endeared the founder and thought he was blameless.

These two persons used white bodies. The woman carried some prejudice towards other races. She did not express this to me years ago when her son was in the boarding school, but tonight she apologized for her indifference to me some years ago.

In an argument I had with her when she lived in the community, I explained that when the Biblical prophet Moses came down with the commandment of "You should not kill," it was in reference to human beings and not to all species. She immediately went to the leader of the community who was the most senior disciple of the founder of the Sect. The founder cited that biblical stipulation as support of the Indian idea of not killing cows. He extended the commandment to domestic animals and claimed that God inspired Moses in that way. But his interpretation contradicts Moses' acts as a carnivore.

I was then summoned to the leader of the community. He riled me about the issues saying that what the founder said was infallible.

This lady apologized for the incidence and also for mistreating me in any case because I used a black body. I told her not to be concerned because I do not carry resentments over social injustice.

Moses could not have received a commandment not to kill cows because the sacrifice of animals was part of the Jewish system of worship to their deity. The stipulation about not killing in the Old Testament was for not killing human beings, and only in reference to human beings who were not offensive to the Jewish tribes. But the founder of the society used the commandment to say that Christians should heed the commandment and not kill cows, as if the Jewish deity was concerned about cows the way Krishna, the deity of the Sect, was concerned about bovine animals.

Low quality meditation (December 2010)

In the past, students of meditation questioned about days of meditation when they seem to make no progress, when the mind remains on the normal level with thoughts and images, even though efforts are made to elevate the self.

I considered this over the last two days, when there was a low energy during my meditation. The answer to this is to consider that mental and emotional states are a kind of weather. As in atmospheric weather, one cannot control it and one knows that for sure, so in psychic energy one cannot have absolute control.

People continue their lives after a weather disaster for the very reason that they assume that the weather is beyond control and they are at its mercy. But they are confident that it will change for the better and then will again go haywire.

This same consideration and attitude should be used in meditation, where you know that on a certain day your meditation was of low quality and then you know for sure, that provided you keep the habit, your meditation will be enriched on another day when the mental and emotional atmosphere is favorable.

A depressed or dull meditation, one that is not inspiring, one that is discouraging, should not deter practice, no more than a hurricane, or earthquake or overcast day will stop human beings from proceeding with their lives, once the danger is past.

Continue the meditation even when it is of a low quality. Be confident that it will again resume a deep experience. But it will again drop to a low level. This will happen so long as one is in a world where the mental and emotional energies dip and surge.

Failure to raise kundalini (December 2010)

Yesterday someone requested that I address the issue of failure to raise kundalini even after doing kundalini yoga exercises for up to one hour. This is bhastrika pranayama practice with asana postures.

There are various reasons why kundalini will or will not rise. There is no set reason. It is not that simple. At this time of year, since it just past the June 21 solstice date, the sun gives most of its energy to the northern hemisphere. This means that there is an overload of sun energy in reference to moon energy, which decreased. During the winter the moon energy is maximized. Then it flips in the summer months.

The full moon was on the 15th and now the moon phases out, which means that its influence decreases. There is more than 50% solar energy. This is good in a way and it is bad in a way.

For those who do kundalini yoga, but who are not proficient in compressing the hormonal energy, this is not so good since the solar energy may cause that energy to be in dispersal. For raising kundalini that energy needs to be in concentration and compression.

Besides the sun and moon, we have to deal with the association of the persons whom we are involved with from day to day. This association may positively or negatively impact us so that it requires more focus during the practice.

The main instruction however is to keep the daily practice, no matter what, no matter if kundalini rises or not. Do not train yourself to expect kundalini to rise as a reward for doing the exercises. Do not train yourself to be a pleasure-needing result-oriented yogi. If kundalini rises, that is okay. If kundalini does not, you should do at least one daily session aggressively.

Let me explain something else. When I travelled to the USA from the Philippines sometime in 1972, I was at an air base in a place called Baldwin which is just outside Kansas City Missouri. I learned the formal way to do asana while I was in the Philippines. I was tutored by Arthur Beverford. I discovered that this procedure was not aggressive enough. It so happened that while I waited for discharge papers, I took a trip into the Kansas City. Near the university I saw a poster with Yogi Bhajan's picture with a notice about kundalini yoga practice. When I saw that I felt that this was the practice I needed.

This image is the picture of Yogi Bhajan which was on the poster:

I attended a class. When I asked if there was an ashram in Denver, the teacher said that there was but he told me that the yogi was in California or New Mexico. When I got to Denver some weeks after, I went to the ashram.

Later I resided there. Yogi was not there but his seniors students were present, a man name Brian and another name Prem Kaur.

Needless to say, we were required to rise at 3.30 am, then clean up and report to the meditation hall. The exercises were gruesome. You had to do postures under supervision while doing breath-of-fire. In some poses you had to keep breathing for about 10 minutes. It was aggressive but effective. Later on Yogi Bhajan came to the ashram. At the airport, when we greeted him, he carried a small bag. One disciple asked Yogi to go to baggage claim for luggage. He replied, "Baggage? This is my baggage. I travel light."

Yogi Bhajan was very simple but with exercises, he was strict. Students did the exercises twice per day. There was no promise of happiness or even of kundalini raising. There was the commitment to do the exercise twice daily. That was it. After a session one did meditation then and there, either reclining on the back or sitting up with spine balanced.

That is how I got this practice from him. That is how I give it others. In other words, if one has happiness as the main objective, this is not the process. But if one reached a stage where one wants to influence the impact of kundalini on the psyche, this process is suitable. One should be strict. A person cannot bring kundalini under his thumb if he is not strict.

Kundalini is a dictatorial force in the psyche. To regulate that one should be strict. Kundalini is a cruel dictator. With an energy like that routine assault and conquest is necessary.

Kundalini will force one for sex, masturbation, dishonesty or disagreeability. When it cannot get satisfaction it will be impulsive. It will betray the coreSelf for pleasure, to kick whatever or whoever to fulfill its desires. With such energy if one is not strong and if one cannot muster the strength to practice daily, one will never control it.

Penthouse yogi (December 2010)

The main disturbance while doing asana posture and breath infusion is random thoughts which come in from the psyche of others, who just happen to be thinking of the yogi at the time of the exercises or whose thoughts arrived at the psyche of the yogi while focusing on exercises.

Even though a thought is a tiny psychic energy it comes with potency. It can distract the yogi. This is because the initial receptor of thoughts is the psychic touch sensation. This sensation in turn, transmits received thoughts with rapid speed to the intellect function of the mind. This function has direct access to the coreSelf, just as the private secretary of an executive has access to the office of that important person.

The psychic touch sensation is not under the control and command of the coreSelf. Its director is the intellect. It does not care about the particulars of the coreSelf. The core does not have direct access to the touch sensation functions.

At any moment a private secretary may barge into the office of an important person and make an announcement, without considering if it is an interference. This is exactly what happens to the yogi, when the errand boy of the touch sensation runs into the office of the intellect which is like a private secretary to the self because then the intellect forces its way to the core and makes the announcement about a sensual intrusion.

Imagine a scene in which an important man is tucked away with his lover in a penthouse bedroom, high over a city in the most prestigious building in that place. He indulges with his darling and is at the moment just before reaching the climax of the experience.

Suddenly the door of his bed room opens and in comes his secretary with what she considered to be an important message. "My dear sir", she says, "I am here to alert that there is an ant on my desk?"

This is the kind of disturbance a yogi may get when he does a session of exercises or meditation. It is for this reason that the ancient yogis discovered and introduced the process of pranayama, which is breath infusement for suspending the interference of the intellect. With breath infusion the yogi can suspend the functions of the intellect for a time.

Patañjali alerted that this intellect is the nuisance for yogis. He suggested that it should be disabled. Of course Patañjali's proposal is absurd for a beginner because a student yogi may not distinguish the intellect. He may not know how to discover it as a component in the psyche. He may feel that his analytical ability is an indistinguishable part of his mind or his very self. The attack of thoughts upon a yogi who is doing kundalini practice must be dealt with effectively if there is to be progress in the practice.

Repeated defeats suffered by a yogi, gives the yogi firsthand experience about his lack of control of the psyche. It lets him plan to increase his knowledge of the outlay of the components of consciousness. By being repeatedly defeated in the effort to directly manhandle the analytical functions, the yogis comes to the honest conclusion that the coreSelf is a loser in the psyche, a mere slave to sensations and mental analytics. He awakens to the reality that he fights an internal war for control of the psyche.

Yoga practice demolished (December 2010)

Sometimes a yogi is overcome by a negative energy which cancels the desire to do practice on a particular day. This energy is a dulling force which stops a yogi dead in his spiritual tracks and causes him to neglect and forget practice for a time. It may last for a day, week, month or year. In some cases it endures for a lifetime or two.

What exactly is that dulling force? According to the *Bhagavad Gita* it is one of the three zonal influences of nature. It is the lowest one which is tagged as tama guna.

Last night I had an astral encounter with a lady who lives in South America. She came astrally with her teenage daughter. Due of that association, my early morning session was cancelled. The energy for the session disappeared. In cases like this when the motivation and energy for practice is dissipated by someone's or a group of persons, one should simply not be bothered but should wait for a rescue. A yogi must be confident that discouragement will pass. It may take some time. One may be battered as if in a hurricane but still it will pass.

The usual time for practice is supposed to be around 4 am, for the latest 6 am, but at that time there was no energy for practice, no motivation, nothing. Suddenly at about 8 am, I felt that the negative energy was lifted. I immediately went to practice.

It appears that not only did I have a dose of bad association, but I also got a dose of bad subtle energy. When that energy lifted, the motivation was reestablished.

Students inquired previously about why they feel dull and why at certain times they have little motivation. Actually it is not so important to know why as it is to be ready to resume as soon as the bad energy lifts.

One cannot control the universe. One cannot adjust reality to perfectly match what one desires. One should agree to sit it out on some occasions and wait for providence to flip in the direction desired, to give the energy boost desired.

Association with people who do not have the yoga habit even if they are religious, even if they meditate, even if they are moral people of worth, will result in down time for practice.

Uddhava Gita Explained (December 2010)

Uddhava Gita Explained is the largest book I published. It includes a full index. The page count is 740 pages. The size is 7 X 10 inches.

Of the spiritual information from India, the Uddhava Gita is the most complete instructions for people pursuing a serious spiritual life.

While in the *Bhagavad Gita,* Krishna successfully pressured Arjuna to live in the material world with a yogically-attained sense of detachment while fulfilling social duties, in the *Uddhava Gita,* Krishna discouraged that and insisted that Uddhava distant himself from social concerns while focusing out of this dimension into whatever is the spiritual world.

Intellect submission (January 2011)

This is a meditation procedure shown by Rishi Singh Gherwal this morning. This has to do with using naad sound to control and condition the intellect. Rishi said that this is done best immediately after doing breath infusion practice but it can be done without that, even though it will not be as beneficial.

There are three psychic components and three locations to use in this meditation.

components:
- naad sound at the back of the subtle head
- coreSelf surrounded by sense of identity
- intellect

locations:
- location of naad sound
- default location of coreSelf as it is surrounded by sense of identity
- location of intellect, front part of head between brow chakra and coreSelf

Naad sound is sometimes located at the right, left or center back of the head. Sometimes it is all-surrounding. It does not matter where it is located. Go to the location.

The coreSelf is surrounded by a sense of identity. Even though these are two distinct supernatural objects, they are regarded as one reality in this meditation, just the way the filament and a glass bulb is regarded as one object, as a bulb.

No effort should be made to separate the coreSelf from the sense of identity in this meditation. The sense of identity is not the problem. For this meditation the target is the intellect.

It is usually unseen but it becomes manifest indirectly by its thought, idea and image constructions. The yogi should focus on the location from which thoughts, ideas and images arise and should accept that the invisible orb is located there even though it is imperceptible.

Just as when there are thoughts, ideas and images, the yogi knows for sure that the intellect functions, he/she knows that it is silenced when it does not generate conceptions. This organ has a higher function which will be manifested to the yogi if he or she adheres to Patanjali's instructions. It is used as a visual orifice to see into higher dimensions.

With or without doing breath infusion prior, the yogi should sit to meditate and should at first endeavor to reach naad sound. If the yogi finds that naad sound is not recalled during the meditation and the yogi is diverted to something else, he should note that after realizing that the meditation was dominated by distractions.

In some sessions, a yogi even though he/she began with an intention to meditate in a certain way found that five, ten, fifteen or more minutes passed without any idea of naad sound and with absorption in other ideas which were produced by the intellect. When this happens the yogi should make a mental note and should use that experience to realize the power of the intellect over the self.

The natural arrangement of the psyche is that the orb should dominate the self. The yogi should realize this and then endeavor to change this. Constant effort at this in meditation will result in success over the long term but there will be disappointment and frustration time and again. Still the yogi should persist.

The procedure is this:
- Sit to meditate
- Reach naad sound
- Double check to be sure that the core adheres to naad and is not pulled forcibly to the frontal part of the subtle head to be under the dominance of the intellect

Remaining in the naad sound, the coreSelf should reach forward and touch the invisible intellect and make an attempt to pull it back. If it does not move back the coreSelf should without it, simply move back into naad.

One of two things will occur.
- The coreSelf will retrieve its touching energy and the intellect will move to the middle of the head abandoning its intentions in the front area.
- The intellect will retain the self's touching energy and self will feel itself being pulled to the orb forcibly.

If the orb is resistant when self moves back into the naad sound, the self should simply insist of itself that it remain there and for that meditation session it should abandon all attempts to influence the orb. The orb will be silent as if it does not exist, such that no thoughts, ideas or images will arise.

If on the other hand, the self finds that when it pulls back its touch energy, the orb willingly moves back, then the self should return to focus in naad and should retain only a slight observation of the orb which accepted the naad influence.

Origin of desire

Desire comes from the causal body. We have a subtle body which we experience in different vibrational stages in the astral existences, but there is another body which is a zone of condensed ideation energy. That is where the desires originate. On that level the desires cannot be fulfilled, just as dry seeds in a sealed jar cannot sprout.

If the seeds are put in a moist environment they will sprout and if after they are placed in soil, they will evolve into full blown plants. When released from the causal body, the desires first become known to us in the subtle body. Later they motivate us to manifest them physically.

Personal history is involved. Who can deny that? In a way personal history is insignificant because the desires are like viruses in that they can penetrate the mind unknowingly. Then one assumes that it is one's individual desire.One endeavors to manifest it. From that angle we are pawns of desire.

The zone of unfulfilled but known desires is different to the zone of unfulfilled unknown desires. Those which are known are like desires for more sex after one reaches puberty and has the experience. As soon as one has the first experience, other desires for it surfaces in the mind. Then one procures sexual opportunities to fulfill the emerging desire pressures.

However if we regard a three year old for example. At that stage there are dormant unknown desires which remain unmanifest to the infant. Another example of this is the eggs in the ovary of hen. The hen lays eggs every 36 hours or so but she is not aware of the eggs until they reach a certain stage of development. Once she becomes aware of them the sitting and clucking begins. She is not at ease with a particular egg, until she expels it. That is like unfulfilled desires.

However other eggs are in her body. Some are the size of a pin-prick. Some are so small that we need an electron microscope to see them. Those are like the unknown unfulfilled desires.

The origin of the condensed unknown desires is the pre-existence. As such it is causal, meaning that even though it is not evident, it caused this existence. Hence transcending that, to find out about that, is near impossible.

If something existed before I did and is now unmanifest and if it was instrumental in my being here, to discover it would be a daunting task.

Spiritual natural forces placed the factors of our pre-existence here. There is absolutely no place for logic in such matters. It is only about observing what took place if we can and accepting that as the reality, just as we are dependent on the sun, regardless of who or what placed it there. We can do nothing to either show that it makes sense or that it makes no sense. We are helpless in that regard.

Cause and effect do not always make sense. Our minds and the need for order and logic cannot bully everything into a logical sequence of events. Much of this, we must accept as super-reality.

Intellect discovery

This is a three phrase procedure shown by Rishi Singh Gherwal.

- **Phase 1**

The yogi sits to meditate after doing pranayama breath infusion or even sitting without that practice. He/she finds that there is a high pitched frequency (naad sound) in the head. Sometimes this sound is heard on the right side or in some other area or zone.

The yogi becomes aware of his or her central presence in the head of the subtle body. This is the coreSelf but it is surrounded by an invisible energy which is the sense of identity.

Along with this there is the intellect which is the place where the thoughts, images and ideas arise and are shown graphically or otherwise in the mind. The objective of the yogi is to curb this psychic organ but initially the yogi has to put aside that idea and listen to naad sound.

How long should a yogi remain in first phase varies from student to student. However one should remain listening to naad and being aware of the limits of the coreSelf's intense radiation and its contact with the intellect. Practice this for as long as is necessary to feel that it is natural to be in contact with the naad listening zone

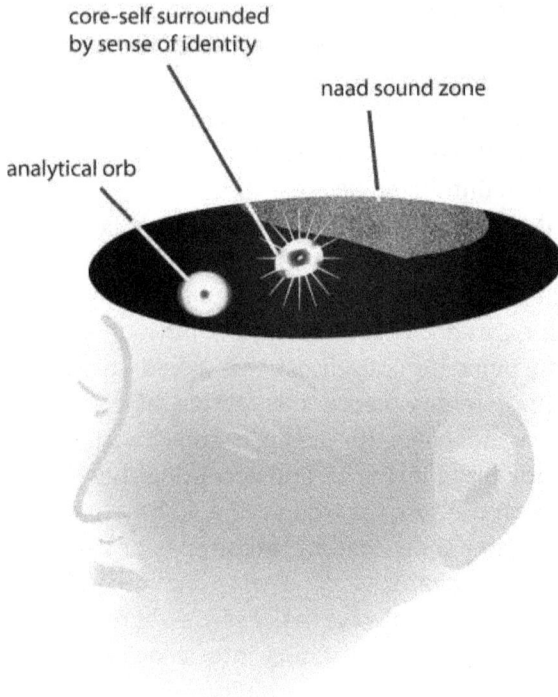

core-self surrounded by sense of identity

naad sound zone

analytical orb

- **Phase 2**

In the second phase, the coreSelf moved into the naad sound zone. It has to do this for its own protection so that it does not fall under the influence of the intellect. Since it is natural for the coreSelf to be under that unwanted influence, it must take help from naad to transcend the hypnotic effects of the intellect. Gradually as it listens to naad, it is nudged into the naad zone. The intellect becomes almost non-existence. The coreSelf is free from the intellect's influence for the time being.

Rishi said that even though Patanjali instructed the yogi to attack the intellect outright that cannot be done successfully in the beginning. The core must acquire sufficient strength to do this.

Rishi said,

"In the Bhagavad Gita *there is a statement suggesting that the coreSelf is higher than the other mental components and that it should dictate to those components but in reality, this is not the case. The reality is that one has a psyche which is out of control.*

"To bring it in line with Krishna's ideas will require adaptations and changes in the basic structure of human psychology.

"The coreSelf has the potential which Krishna suggests but initially it cannot realize its power. For instance, we know that an alligator is superior to a dog in strength but this statement is flawed.

"A small alligator which is about one week old cannot successfully bring down an adult dog but an adult alligator can.

"Similarly so long as a human being has not evolved sufficiently he or she cannot control the components of the psyche. A certain degree of maturity is required. In the case of the infant alligator, it stays under the protection of its parent. Dogs cannot attack it. In a similar way the coreSelf should take shelter under the naad sound until it can execute Patanjali's instructions.

"The yogi should remain in naad and should do whatever is necessary to keep the coreSelf there. If it leaves that influence and then finds itself under the influence of the intellect, it should immediately return to naad, just like the infant alligator which runs back to its parents when it strays away and finds itself confronted by a vicious dog."

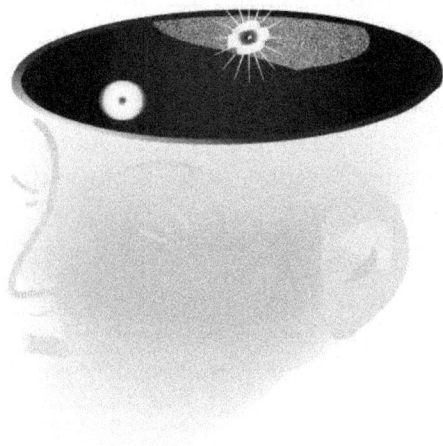

• Phase 3

In the third phase, the intellect moved backwards from its usual position in the frontal part of the subtle head.

This action occurred because the intellect became lonely for the association of the coreSelf. There is magnetic draw between the sense of identity and the intellect. When the coreSelf which is surrounded by the sense of identity, moves into the naad sound and becomes absorb there, losing interest in the intellect, that intellect finds itself being pulled to the core.

Since these are not the natural locations of the intellect or the coreSelf, both factors will return to their respective positions as soon as the yogi ceases to endeavor to keep the coreSelf in the naad zone.

So long as the intellect is nudged backwards away from its natural location, it will remain submissive to the core and will make no effort to create compelling ideas, images or sounds.

Rishi said that while remaining in this position in location with the naad sound, the coreSelf should directly peer into the intellect and should observe that the intellect's creative activities do not occur. It is harmless here. It does not display its diabolical attractions but it will resume the schemes as soon as the yogi is no longer taking shelter in naad.

This is a very important stage of meditation since it gives the yogi an idea of how to handle the orb without empowering it to create images, ideas and sounds which distract one from transcendence meditation.

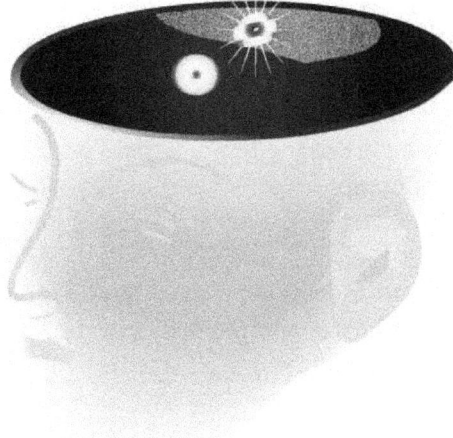

Sleep in partnership with memory (January 2011)

Patanjali listed memory and sleep as two of the five operational modes of the mind. He considered these to be troublesome and advised for their suspension. Why does the psyche operate in such a way as to suspend certain memories and keep them out of reach of the coreSelf?

Why does the psyche invoke stored memories even at times when it is inconvenient and when the self has no desire to hash over certain undesirable details from a past experience. How does memory convert into instinct as stubborn tendencies in the psyche?

Kundalini spike through naad (January 2011)

I did breath infusion for twenty minutes, then kundalini was induced to leave base chakra. It coursed through various parts of the body. Gradually it was felt as it passed through the neck into the head of the subtle form. Once it courses into the neck, one should try to guide it somewhere. The usual two locations are the brow and the crown chakras.

These are called *ajna* and *brahmrandra* chakras respectively. *Ajna* is Sanskrit for knowing or realizing. With the brow chakra one can pry into reality and get perception of other dimensions and situations. Brahmarandra may be translated as hole of brahma or aperture through which one would gain a glimpse of spiritual existence.

Rishi instructed that at some point in development, a yogi should heed Patanjali and make the effort to cease the independence of the intellect. The Sanskrit for the intellect is *buddhi*. In chapter two of the *Bhagavad Gita*, Krishna gave the discipline for curbing this psychic adjunct.

This orb is known as *jnana chakshus* and *jnana dipa*. *Jnana chakshus* is the organ which gives direct visual *(chakshus)* perception in an objective way *(jnana)*. *Jnana-dipah* is the organ, which by, its own light *(dipah)* gives perception in an objective way *(jnana)*.

The big mistake made by people who have no psychic perception is that they regard this orb as a part of the brain. Others who are yogis but who did not developed psychic perception consider the organ to be non-existence but when questioned they assert that even though it is invisible it is an integral part of the mind.

Rishi instructed that the intellect should be the main focus of attention but that such focus must be done while taking into account its independent operations, the relation the kundalini life force has with it, and the self's lack of control of it.

When kundalini rises into the head, if the yogi finds that he can direct this energy, he should for this practice, direct it to the intellect. If kundalini is in the head and the yogi finds that he or she cannot direct it, the yogi should try to reach the naad sound and then from that perspective, determine the next action.

There will be some times during meditation, that the yogi finds that kundalini entered the naad sound zone of its own accord and that it caused a spiked energy to rise out of the naad zone.

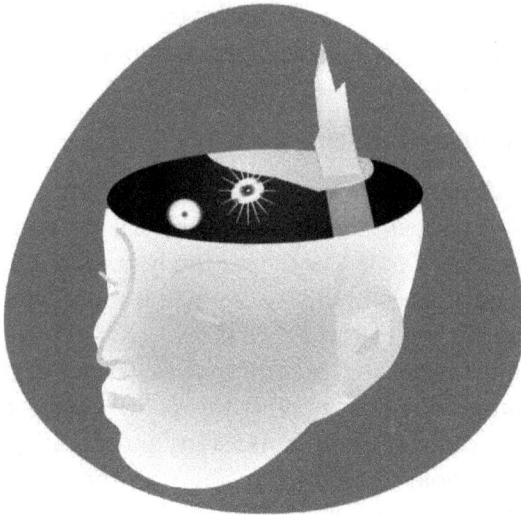

After observing that the kundalini entered the naad zone and that it spiked upwards in the back of head, one should enter the spike at the point where it shoots upward above the naad zone. The yogi should remain there and observe the type of consciousness which results.

See this diagram and notice that the coreSelf moved into the naad sound just where kundalini spiked up through the sound.

Intellect entry (January 2011)

This is an advanced practice which one may do if one gets the intellect into an attitude of submission. Rishi Sing Gherwal gave this procedure. A similar but more advanced procedure was given by Yogeshwarananda in which the intellect moves under the crown chakra, is fused into that chakra and takes a bell shape under the crown.

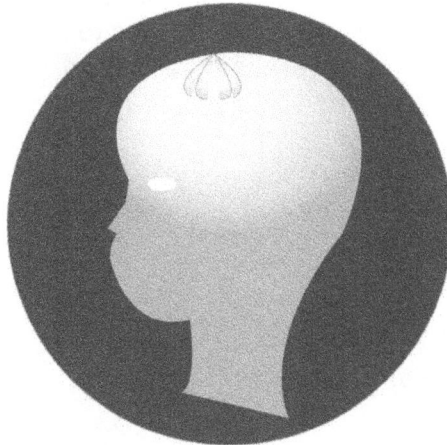

Yogesh's procedure is too advanced. One would have to be in isolation for some years in order to practice that method.

Rishi's method is as follows:

Always get kundalini raised into the head. Then use kundalini to attack the intellect repeatedly. This means that kundalini is focused into the place where the orb usually creates thoughts, ideas and images.

When during breath infusion practice one finds that the intellect created a thought or that it has sensed one which was created by someone else, one should direct the breathing energy to the location where the local or foreign thought appeared. One should do this aggressively and do battle with the intellect to subdue it.

As soon as one ceases the infusion and sits to meditate, one should focus on the naad sound and move the coreSelf back into the naad. When this is completed and the core remains in the naad and the intellect has no compulsions or demands but remains quiet like a frightened mouse which is afraid of a cat, then one should as the coreSelf step into the intellect.

If one does this and one finds the observing self in the center of the space of the intellect, it will feel as if one stepped into a transparent bubble. One will know if one achieved this because one will be able to move back into the naad sound and then step into the bubble again.

One will not be able to do this if the orb is resistant to the coreSelf, in which case, one should remain with naad and continue the practice of being in naad in isolation from the intellect's influence.

Because of the location difference between naad and the intellect, this practice is definite and is not imaginative. These aspects have their particular location just as the eyes are located in one place on the face and the nostrils are located in another. This is not a mergence experience where everything is one. In this experience these aspects are distinctly sorted.

If one is unable to move into the orb as described, one should not worry about it or feel undone. Simply keep practicing to move the coreSelf in the influence of naad. Keep confronting the intellect until you are no longer afraid of it, and until the coreSelf has stamped out the intellect's independent notions.

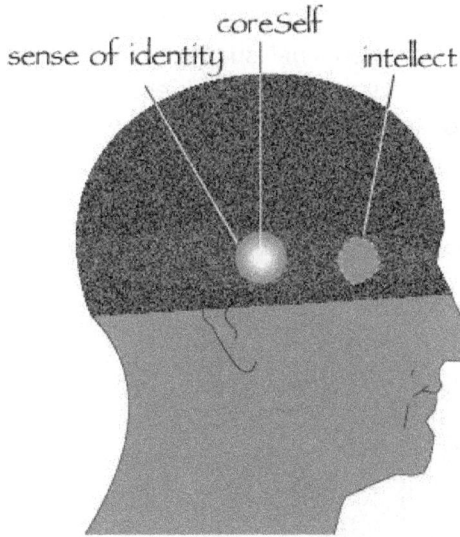

sense of identity   coreSelf   intellect

In the above diagram, the default locations of the intellect and the coreSelf are given. Even if a yogi can relocate these, they will resume these locations as soon as he relaxes the control.

Examine this other diagram.

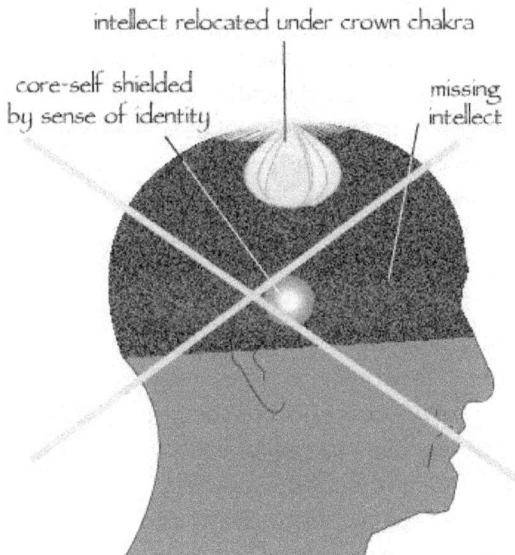

intellect relocated under crown chakra

core-self shielded
by sense of identity

missing
intellect

In that diagram, I gave a procedure shown by Yogeshwarananda some years ago. Unfortunately this diagram is useless unless one was isolated with the right techniques for some years. In that diagram the crown chakra (brahmarandra) is activated. The intellect moved to a location under the chakra. In doing so it assumed a bell shape.

Yogeshwaranda discussed this in his *Science of the Soul* book. Within my subtle head he demonstrated this.

Examine this diagram.

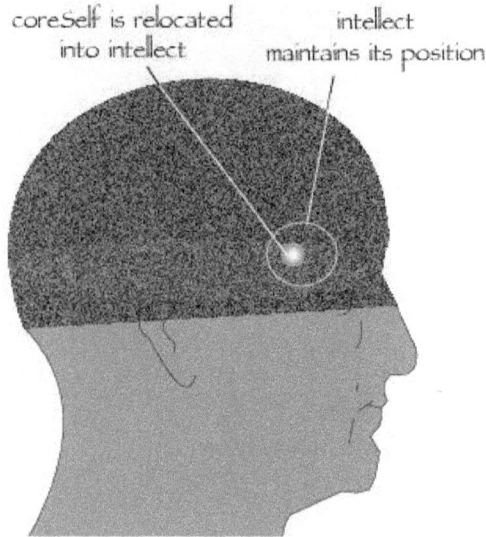

coreSelf is relocated into intellect

intellect maintains its position

In that diagram, the coreSelf moved from its default location. It entered the intellect which is in its standard location.

To achieve this, the core should first locate, listen to and then move into the naad sound. When the core detects that the intellect is submissive, it should make the attempt to move into the orb.

Clarification: astral projection/lucid dream (January 2011)

Think of two kinds of astral projection; conscious and unconscious. In conscious astral projection the person becomes aware of the subtle body when it is separated from the physical system. In unconscious astral projection, the astral body separates but the person is unaware of it.

Astral projection as we normally use the terms means only being conscious during an astral projection. Each time the physical body sleeps, the astral one separates but we are not always conscious of the separation. In some cases a person becomes aware of the separation minutes or hours after it occurs. This means that one may become aware of the astral body in the astral world long after that body was displaced from the physical system.

Lucid dreaming means that you become aware of the astral world even when the astral body was not displaced from the physical system. In that case the mind is totally attuned to the astral body and is not specifically aware of the physical one, only slightly aware of it.

Regarding if dreams are different to astral projections that depends on how dream is defined. A dream which is merely ideas in the mind which appear to be real to the dreamer is not astral projection. However, one can be in an astral projection and interpret the experience as imagination while in fact it is an experience in an objective astral dimension.

How to tell the difference?

How does one tell the difference between thinking of going to the airport and actually driving to the airport physically?

Whatever method one would use to differentiate those two experiences could be applied to imaginative mental experiences and actual astral actions in an astral world.

Some herbs or drugs can cause the subtle body to be displaced from the physical system. The difference is that when using a drug, it is like when one rides on a roller coaster. Once one is strapped in and the machine starts one cannot get off even if one does not like it. One must exit only when the machine stops.

Part 7

Dreaming while fully awake (February 2011)

One may find the self to be dreaming while it is awake. This happens when the subtle body needs to separate from the physical system. It may occur when one remaines awake for too many hours or when one works strenuously.

When the physical body is awake it is a composite of the physical and subtle bodies. After these bodies remained fused for some hours, they must separate. No human being or animal no matter how powerful that person is, can keep those two bodies together in the awaken state forever. At some point the physical system must sleep. Eventually the physical body will fall asleep. When it does, the physical system goes into repair mode, which we interpret as sleep or as dream and sleep or as astral projection, dream and sleep.

After being awake for some time if one does not rest, one will fall asleep. But if one does not doze and sleep as nature requires, one may enter into a hallucination. This hallucination is usually interpreted to be mental nonsense but in fact it is vision of other realities.

As the life force in the body takes actions to put the physical system to sleep, and as the person resists that sleeping tendency the subtle body begins to separate anyway. As it does, the person's attention is shifted to the subtle side, the psychic side. That person begins to perceive the subtle or psychic existence and sees into a dimension which is subtle.

Note that the same process takes place if the person were to recline and sleep, but the difference would be that there would be no perception of the subtle world. The person's mind would skip that experience, because of not resisting the drowsy feelings.

A fear of these experiences is not really a solid conclusion because if one were to enter into that hallucination, one would not remain there and one would return to the physical system as soon as the life force which keeps it alive during sleep, requires one's attention. In other words, one experiences that every time one sleeps and one resumes the body and awakens as the social self. The same thing would happen if one resisted sleep except for one small detail that if one drove a car, one would fall asleep. The car would crash immediately.

The death of the body would not be because one could not get back into the body. It would be because one shifted into another existence by the life force in the body. It would be because one dozed, and the physical body was no longer controlled by the objective mind.

There is no need to fear coming back from an astral experience because one has such experiences every time one sleeps except that one does not recall the experience. Astral projection and lucid dreaming means conscious astral projection and conscious lucid dreaming with stress on the word conscious. We have the experiences but we do not recall because the objective mind is disconnected when the experience take place.

I would suggest that one practice meditation and study the movements in consciousness when going to sleep and when rising from slumber.

Just as when a person needs rest, and if he keeps driving or whatever, he will doze and have hallucination (which are real experiences of other dimensions), so a person can have astral experiences when taking a rest or nap immediately after a full rest.

Get a full rest. Lay on your back with your eyes closed or covered with a dark cloth or in subdued lighting, and in a quiet place.

If you are lucky your astral body will separate. You will experience astral projection consciously. Or you may have a lucid dream experience.

But by all means get rid of the idea that you will not come back, because it is natural that the lifeForce resume objective consciousness to the physical system, just as it conducts breathing without one's help, and just as it causes one to awaken as the physical self after resting on a daily basis for so many years. The lifeForce is reliable for this. We live only because of that reliance that we awaken after sleeping. Everyone is confident of that.

Intellect bruised (February 2011)

Here are some ideas of Rishi Singh Gherwal.

His principle is that a yogi should first raise kundalini by using pranayama breath infusion. Once kundalini is awakened and moves from the base of the spine into the head and into other parts of the body, the yogi should attack the intellect which is experienced as thinking and ideation.

After kundalini is raised, the yogi should direct the infused breath energy to the intellect. Question is this: If one cannot see the intellect or if one has never seen it, how should one direct the infused energy to it?

This is done by directing the infused breath to the thinking/imaging area in the head. As soon as a memory or image appears, note where it is. Direct the infused energy there. Eventually you will know the general whereabouts of the intellect. The intellect is egg-shaped. It is in the head in the front part of the brain.

This is its appearance when it is silent and unseen.

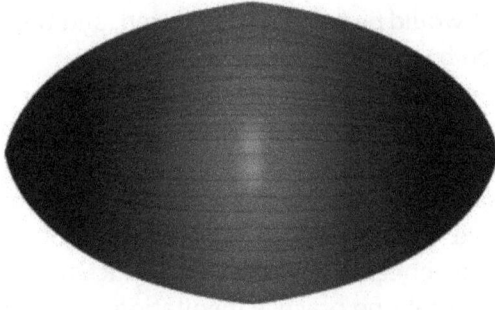

This is the intellect when it is hit by a thought from someone else. The light on the right is the impact of the thought.

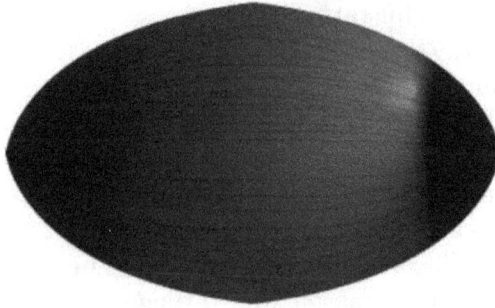

This is the intellect when it is bruised by a thoughts from someone else. The light on the right is the bruised area.

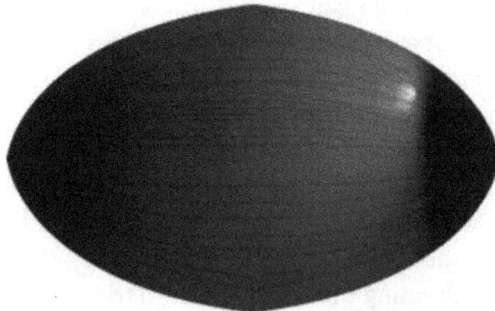

If the idea or thought came from someone else it will hit the membrane layer of the orb and then it will either bounce off or it will create a bruise mark like when a person is hit with a hard object, and a bruise appears on the skin.

This bruise mark on the intellect will then produce an inner spike energy which will spread through the organ and will become a thought, image or idea. If the idea, thought or memory was from the meditator, it will appear inside the intellect like magic without a bruise on the membrane of the orb.

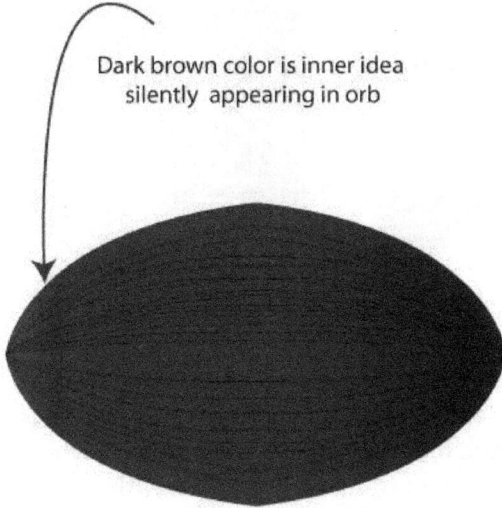

Dark brown color is inner idea
silently appearing in orb

inner idea developing of its own accord
It begins to attract the core self to view it
core-self experiences the attraction
as a lack of total darkness in the mind,
and as a picture or idea or image emerging

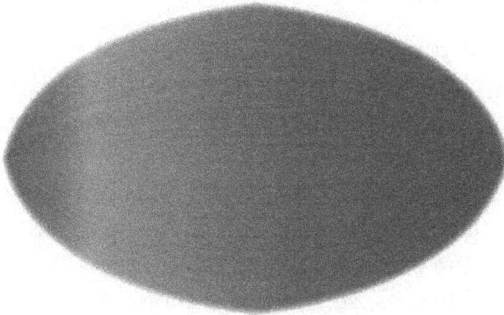

inner idea comes alive in the mind
due to receiving energy input
from the attention of the core-self.
Core self for its part is fascinated with the image
which it sees as if it was positioned in the orb

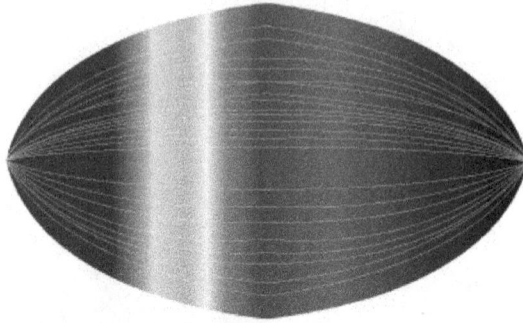

The thoughts/images from the inner edge are from the meditator (internal source) and thoughts/images from the outer edge are from someone besides the meditator (external source). A yoga guru may however enter the mind space and transmit a thought within the mind. That idea will not hit the outer surface of the intellect from the outside. It would only expand within the intellect just as a self generated thought would. Memories act likewise where they penetrate the intellect before being seen by the coreSelf

There are two sets of thought images which come from outside the intellect. Those which are foreign to the psyche of the meditator and those which are from his memory.

Geography of the psyche

The psyche is a compartment, a container for psychic selves, psychic equipment and psyche energy. This psyche may be called a self. However for the details of yoga, it is a container which has within it one or more selves with psychic equipment and energy. The convention is to regard the psyche as a self but for keen observation the psyche must be regarded as a container.

This container is the subtle body, which is also called an astral form. Just as in there is skin of the physical body which contains organs, muscles, bones and various types of tissues, so there is a subtle membrance for the subtle body which contains psychic stuffs, psychic organs and coreSelves.

When one enters the psyche one discoveres more than one component. The coreSelf is only one factor. In fact it is not always the dominant feature. It may act in a sobordination to some other part. It may be compelled by psychic energy or by the intellect which is a perception aparatus.

There is an outside which is inside. We know very well what is outside the physical body. That is an environment in which there are other bodies and other animate and inanimate objects. But there is a similar situation on the inside of the psyche where the self will find itself in a mental or emotional environment which is outside of the coreSelf.

Just as in this world someone's body is outside of my body, so in the subtle environment within the mind, the kundalini energy is outside of the coreSelf and so is the memory and other psychic objects. Most meditators are oblivious to the psychic objects. For them the psyche is all one without differentiation.

Thoughts and images which come from other psyches and which penetrate the aura, immediately latch on to the intellect, just as when viruses enter the body, they latch on to cells and do damage for their own survival. Thoughts which are foreign to the psyche slam into the subtle membrane of the intellect and bruise it. In that bruise, the said thoughts spread their energy and take control of the intellect. One is then forced to view the ideas.

The only thoughts which bruise the orb are those which come from an external psyche. But there are thoughts which come from outside the intellect but inside the psyche which also penetrates the orb but they do so without bruising the psyche. Those are thoughts from memory and sensual energy which assume thought forms once it inhabits the intellect.

Because these thoughts are native to the psyche they do not break in. they enter silently without bruising the membrane of the intellect. These other thoughts come from the kundalini, and from the memory compartments and also from compressed energies in the causal body.

Think of a situation where I have two sons. My wallet is in my house. One son goes to the wallet and removes $100. Later the same night a burglar smashes a window enters my house and removes $500. The burglar is like the thoughts from outside the psyche. The son is similar to the thoughts from kundalini, memory or causal body. Everything outside the house is outside my room and everything that is in the house and which is not in my room is also outside the room.

My son did no damage to the structure of the house. The burglar did. Yet in another consideration my son stole more money than the burglar.

Compelling thoughts

By convention of nature, the self is compelled to view the thoughts. The compulsion comes from the thoughts and not from the coreSelf. Mostly the self is helpless in this matter.

The thoughts and images do burst in the intellect but not necessarily in the center of it. According to the nature of the thought it will burst here or there, appearing to be random even though in fact it is ordered. Because our psychic senses are undeveloped we fail to differentiate the location of particular thoughts.

The thoughts and images burst for display in the intellect. The self is compelled to see the illustrations. It is forced to position itself to view them.

Clash of thoughts

If two thoughts hit the intellect simultaneously or if an external thought hits the intellect at the same time when it shows an internal thought, there is a struggle between the two energies and one supersedes the other, such that the coreSelf must accept the priority of the stronger idea. Sometimes after giving that thought its demanded attention; one tries to locate the other thought energy but sometimes that other through energy is destroyed in the clash with the other stronger thought which took precedence over the mind space.

Sometimes when this happens the coreSelf regrets that it lost contact with that other thought. It tries to retrieve it but if it was destroyed it regrets the lost, just like when a woman has two children and when she is away, one kills the other. She regrets the dead infant but all the same she is compelled by motherly instinct to care for the vicious child anyway.

Third eye beam-light (February 2011)

In meditation this morning the following occurred. This was meditation after breath infusion which raised kundalini into the head and then breath infusion which caused the intellect to be direct struck by the breath energy.

At first in meditation, I instinctively identified and moved into the naad sound. I noticed small thoughts hitting the intellect but the orb was not responding to the thoughts because it was struck by the infused breath energy which I did just prior to sitting for meditation. The orb was still under the spell of that energy. Thus it did not resume its usual acceptance of thoughts which strike its membrane.

I remained in naad. Suddenly there was a light ahead of me. It shone in a vast darkness. This changed into a third eye light which shined like a search beam in a dark sea which had fishes everywhere. The fishes were startled by the light. A few moved to come to the light but the light moved away from them. It moved at about 5 miles per hour. I could not tell how deep in the water it penetrated. As this happened my central consciousness was still in the material body but its full focus was on the light and its spread through the dark sea.

This continued for five minutes. Immediately after this, without any span of time intervening, the subtle body suddenly and without any notice separated from the physical form. Both bodies were in lotus posture. The subtle body maintained that posture.

Suddenly the subtle form was in the air near a place where people walked by a beach. There was a seawall made of rock and concrete. The subtle body accelerated to twenty miles per hour. It rushed towards the rock. I knew that it would not crash into the rock but still when it got near the rock, the rock seem to emit a fear energy as if it did not want the body to crash into it.

The body then rose up just before hitting the sea-wall. After this it coursed through the sky and went to a place where people moved near some tall buildings.

While this happened the subtle body used third eye vision and not dual subtle eye vision. This is unusual. Usually when one is in the subtle body during astral projections; it uses dual subtle-eye vision.

I modified but could not fully control the speed of the subtle form. It moved on its own. I could not control where it went. It acted as if it was programmed to make the movements. After about ten minutes, the subtle body suddenly resynchronized into the physical one.

This experience shows that the subtle body may sometimes act on its own. Rishi Singh Gherwal's opinion is that if one energizes the subtle body by raising kundalini and then energizes the intellect which is in the subtle head, one will get such experiences. He said that the influence of hesitation and inertia discourages yoga practice.

Instead of thinking that one can order the subtle body to have these experiences, one would get success in a rapid way if one made certain that one infused sufficient energy into the subtle system.

One must struggle and eliminate the laziness energy in the psyche. It operates on the individual. This is why one person practices and another does not. The negative energies must be confronted and defeated individually.

Some conversation between Krishna and Arjuna

Read this discourse.

अर्जुन उवाच
अयतिः श्रद्धयोपेतो
योगाच्चलितमानसः ।
अप्राप्य योगसंसिद्धिं
कां गतिं कृष्ण गच्छति ॥६.३७॥

arjuna uvāca
ayatiḥ śraddhayopeto
yogāccalitamānasaḥ
aprāpya yogasaṃsiddhiṃ
kāṃ gatiṃ kṛṣṇa gacchati (6.37)

arjuna — Arjuna; uvāca — said; ayatiḥ — indisciplined person; śraddhayopeto = śraddhayopetaḥ = śraddhayā — by faith + upetaḥ — has got; yogāccalitamānasaḥ = yogāc (yogāt) — from yoga practice + calita — deviated + mānasaḥ — mind;

aprāpya — not attain; yogasaṁsiddhiṁ — yoga proficiency; kāṁ — what; gatiṁ — course; kṛṣṇa — Krishna; gacchati — he goes

Arjuna said: What about the undisciplined person who has faith? Having deviated from yoga practice, having not attained yoga proficiency, what course does he take, O Krishna? (Bhagavad Gita 6.37)

कचिन्नोभयविभ्रष्टश्	kaccinnobhayavibhraṣṭaś
छिन्नाभ्रमिव नश्यति ।	chinnābhramiva naśyati
अप्रतिष्ठो महाबाहो	apratiṣṭho mahābāho
विमूढो ब्रह्मणः पथि ॥ ६.३८ ॥	vimūḍho brahmaṇaḥ pathi (6.38)

kaccin = kaccid — is he; nobhayavibhraṣṭaś = na — not + ubhaya — both + vibhraṣṭaḥ — lost out; chinnābhram = chinna — faded + abhram — cloud; iva — like; naśyati — lost; apratiṣṭho = apratiṣṭhaḥ — without foundation; mahābāho — O Almayy Kṛṣṇa; vimūḍho = vimūḍhaḥ — baffled; brahmaṇaḥ — of the spirituality; pathi — on the path

Is he not like a faded cloud, lost from both situations, like being without a foundation? O Almighty Krishna: He is baffled on the path of spirituality. (Bhagavad Gita 6.38)

एतन्मे संशयं कृष्ण	etanme saṁśayaṁ kṛṣṇa
छेत्तुमर्हस्यशेषतः।	chettumarhasyaśeṣataḥ
त्वदन्यः संशयस्यास्य	tvadanyaḥ saṁśayasyāsya
छेत्ता न ह्युपपद्यते ॥ ६.३९ ॥	chettā na hyupapadyate (6.39)

etan = etad — this; me — of mine; saṁśayam — doubt; kṛṣṇa — Krishna; chettum — remove; arhasy = arhasi — you can; aśeṣataḥ — without reminder, fully; tvadanyaḥ = besides you; saṁśayasyāsya = saṁśayasya — of doubt + asya — of this; chettā — remover of doubt; na — not; hy (hi) — indeed; upapadyate — he exists

You can, O Krishna, remove this doubt of mine fully. Besides You, no other remover of doubt, exists here. (Bhagavad Gita 6.39)

श्रीभगवानुवाच	śrībhagavānuvāca
पार्थ नैवेह नामुत्र	pārtha naiveha nāmutra
विनाशस्तस्य विद्यते ।	vināśastasya vidyate
न हि कल्याणकृत्कश्चिद्	na hi kalyāṇakṛtkaścid
दुर्गतिं तात गच्छति ॥ ६.४० ॥	durgatiṁ tāta gacchati (6.40)

śrībhagavān — the Blessed Lord; uvāca — said; pārtha — O son of Pṛthā; naiveha = na — either + eva — indeed + iha — here on earth; namutra = na — nor + amutra — above in the celestial regions; vināśaḥ — loss; tasya — his; vidyate —

it is realized; na — not; hy (hi) — indeed; kalyāṇakṛt — performer of pious acts; kaścid — anyone; durgatim — into misfortune; tāta — O ideal one; gacchati — goes down permanently

The Blessed Lord said: O son of Pṛthā, it is realized that neither here on earth nor above in the celestial regions, does the unaccomplished yogi lose his skill. Indeed, O dear Arjuna, no performer of virtuous acts, goes down permanently into misfortune. (Bhagavad Gita 6.40)

प्राप्य पुण्यकृताँल्लोकान्
उषित्वा शाश्वती: समा: ।
शुचीनां श्रीमतां गेहे
योगभ्रष्टोऽभिजायते॥६.४१॥

prāpya puṇyakṛtāṁllokān
uṣitvā śāśvatīḥ samāḥ
śucīnāṁ śrīmatāṁ gehe
yogabhraṣṭo'bhijāyate(6.41)

prāpya — obtaining; puṇyakṛtām — of the performer of virtuous acts; lokān — celestial places; uṣitvā — having lived; śāśvatīḥ — many, many; samāḥ — years; śucīnām — of the purified person; śrīmatām — of the prosperous person; gehe — in the social circumstance; yogabhraṣṭo = yogabhraṣṭaḥ — fallen from yoga; 'bhijāyate = abhijāyate — is born

After obtaining the celestial places where the virtuous souls go, having lived there for many, many years, the fallen yogi is born into the social circumstances of the purified and prosperous people. (Bhagavad Gita 6.41)

अथ वा योगिनामेव
कुले भवति धीमताम् ।
एतद्धि दुर्लभतरं
लोके जन्म यदीदृशम् ॥६.४२॥

atha vā yogināmeva
kule bhavati dhīmatām
etaddhi durlabhataraṁ
loke janma yadīdṛśam (6.42)

atha vā — alternately; yoginām — of the yogi; eva — indeed; kule — in the family situation; bhavati — is born; dhīmatām — of the enlightened people; etad — this; dhi = hi — indeed; durlabhataram — difficult to attain; loke — in this world; janma — birth; yad — which; īdṛśam — such

Alternately, he is born into a family of enlightened people. But such a birth is very difficult to attain in this world. (Bhagavad Gita 6.42)

तत्र तं बुद्धिसंयोगं
लभते पौर्वदेहिकम् ।
यतते च ततो भूय:
संसिद्धौ कुरुनन्दन ॥६.४३॥

tatra taṁ buddhisaṁyogaṁ
labhate paurvadehikam
yatate ca tato bhūyaḥ
saṁsiddhau kurunandana (6.43)

tatra — there; tam — it; buddhisaṁyogam — cumulative intellectual interest; labhate — inspired with; paurvadehikam — from a previous birth; yatate — he strives; ca — and; tato = tataḥ — from that time; bhūyaḥ — again; saṁsiddhau — to perfection; kuru-nandana — O dear son of the Kurus

In that environment, he is inspired with the cumulative intellectual interest from a previous birth. And from that time, he strives again for yoga perfection, O dear son of the Kurus. (Bhagavad Gita 6.43)

पूर्वाभ्यासेन तेनैव
हियते ह्यवशोऽपि सः ।
जिज्ञासुरपि योगस्य
शब्दब्रह्मातिवर्तते ॥ ६.४४ ॥

पूर्वाभ्यासेन tenaiva
hriyate hyavaśo'pi saḥ
jijñāsurapi yogasya
śabdabrahmātivartate (6.44)

pūrvābhyāsena = pūrva — previous + abhyāsena — by practice; tenaiva = tena — by it + eva — indeed; hriyate — he is motivated; hy (hi) — indeed; avaśo = avaśaḥ — without conscious desire; 'pi = api — even; saḥ — he; jijñāsuḥ — persistently inquiring; api — even; yogasya — of yoga; śabdabrahmātivartate = śabda — spoken description + brahma — spiritual reality + ativartate — instinctively sees beyond (śabdabrahma — Vedas)

Indeed, by previous practice, he is motivated, even without conscious desire. He who persistently inquires of yoga, instinctively sees beyond the Veda, the spoken description of the spiritual reality. (Bhagavad Gita 6.44)

A person who did not perfect yoga practice in a past life, must take another human body sooner or later, and will more than likely do the practice again even if that person has no training in yoga in the new life and even if that person is born in a family or society where yoga is not used.

Krishna said that the yogi is inspired with the cumulative intellectual interest from a previous birth. By that he strives again for yoga perfection. By the grace of previous practice, that person gets experiences and feels inclinations to yoga.

Social contact, family life and the like does have value. It is just that it has mostly nil spiritual worth. If one takes another body, one will have to take recourse to whatever social contributions one made in previous lives. On that basis one may get another body.

Stated differently:

The social life has value in terms of the allowing choice opportunities for rebirth in selected families and under select conditions. As yogis we do not care about that value, because when all is said and done one cannot get out of material existence by patronizing sociology. It only increases one's involvements and causes one to be more intertwined in the various providential (karmic) complications.

All the same we should take care socially not to hurt anyone and to not be criminal in intent because that causes unwanted backlashes from nature and other persons. Nature may appear to be haphazard and random but it is methodical and mathematical. It is exacting in dishing out reactions for the beneficial or criminal acts.

One does not know who will be one's future mother and father, or who will assist one to influence a couple to be the next parents. It is worth it to handle everyone on the social plane with care.

Naad meditation

Naad sound is usually heard either on the left or right side by the ear. It may be heard in the back part of the head. It is a high pitched frequency which resonates always even when it is not heard. The frequency may change if one meditates on it. To some persons it is a boring sound but it is a source of shelter to yogis. It allows a yogi to escape from the harassments in the frontal part of the head.

Naad is the ultimate free mantra. One only needs to listen and become absorbed. It shelters from the harassments of the intellect which creates images and sounds which distract the yogi.

The key issue about naad is location. Where does it originate, from which direction? Can the yogi enter it? Is the yogi repelled from it?

Third eye vision

The third eye may open as a square shape, as a rectangular shape, as an oval shape, as a circular shape and also as a haphazard shape. It is simply an opening like a bay window. It is not like an eyeball. One sees through it just as if one peered through a window.

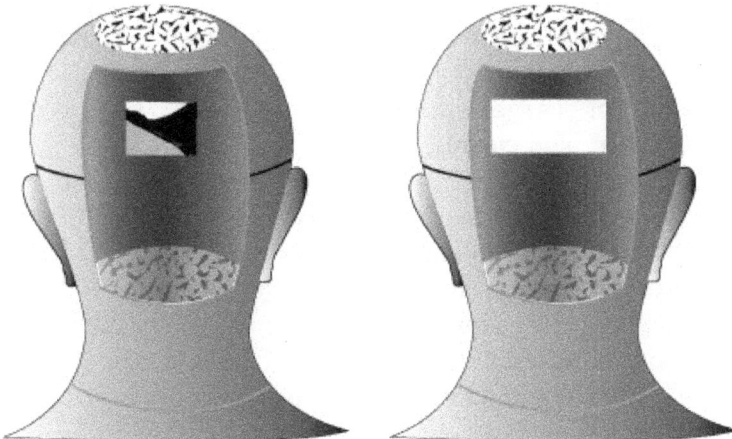

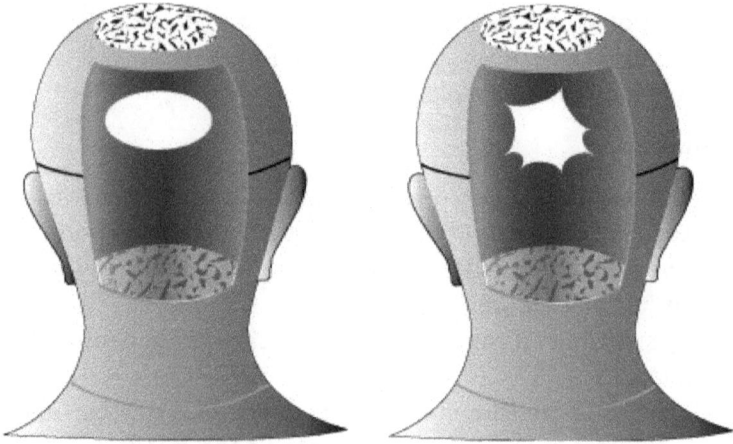

The actual eye which sees through the third eye is the intellect. The intellect is itself an eye. Many people who have third eye experience feel that the brow chakra is an eye. That is incorrect. It is simply an opening. The eye is the intellect which is the singular eye of the supernatural body.

Using that orb we see also through two subtle eyes which are on the face of the subtle body. We also use the orb to see through the two physical eyes.

In all cases, except when using pranaVision (atomic sight, sub-atomic particle vision) or using the spiritual body, one must use the intellect to perceive either though itself only or through it in conjunction with other perception adjuncts.

When one meditates one should abandon preconceived notions. Check the mind carefully to be sure that it is free from preconceptions. This means that one should not engage with the ideas of the mind. Instead one should go to a part of the mind chamber where the shananigans are nonexistent. The preferred place is the naad sound. Once a yogi is absorbed in naad, he may come forward to see if there are any notions elsewhere in the mind. If there are none he can peer forward to the brow chakra.

If they are some notions and idea, the yogi should retreat into naad. He should wait there for the unwanted mental activities to disappear.

A yogi should be blindfolded for this type of meditation. It is best to use a dark fabric. If he is in a completely dark place, that is best. The mind is very sensitive to light. If it detects light even light which passes through the bone of skull, it may become anxious and anticipatory which may result in the creation of unwanted images and sounds.

If the third eye opens when one is in sunlight the opening may not be distinct. In fact it may not be seen. One may not realize that it operative. It is best distinquished when one is in darkness or when the head is blindfolded. Even great yogis went into dark caves and meditated to facilitate this vision.

Caves were used because sunlight does not penetrate and one's psychic sensitivities may increase exponentially in such environments.

Why practice yoga?

The question as to why one should practice yoga may arise from time to time. Especially since one will not get transcendental experiences during each session, why should one practice? How should one go about pushing oneself to practice if one feels that one should practice but one is discouraged by the yoga itself?

Yoga may be a cause for discouragement because it does not always bring with it transcendental experiences or meaning full realizations.

Again why practice?

If one practices to please oneself or to live up to an ideal or aspiration, how will one continue with the practice if the ideal or aspiration is difficult to attain? If one does not achieve the desired accomplishment, why should one continue doing it, especially since other activities like social involvement for instance, brings immediate physical benefits?

If one practices to please a teacher, why should one continue practicing if the method does not yield results or if the results are hard to come by and are rarely experienced. If out of a year of practice, one will get about 7 or 8 meaningful realizations and transcendental experiences, is it worth it?

The motivation for practice has much to do with why a yogi continues or discontinues the method. For me, there may be three motivations. Any of these is sufficient for me to continue with or without immediate results which would give satisfaction and sense of accomplishment. Those reasons are:

- Obligation to yoga gurus to comply with their request for practice
- Sense of purpose to myself, feeling that the practice reinforces myself.
- Sense of duty to inform and encourage others who need the information which I offer and which is derived from practice.

The individual psyche

During meditation this morning Yogeshwarananda entered my subtle head. He make the following statements.

Success in yoga comes about through an all—out effort to study the individual psyche. General statements and ideas about the composition of the psyche does not help. The scheme, the process, was given by Patanjali. Krishna also discussed the details.

These procedures serve as a map so that a beginner can realize what he attained and what he must accomplish.

Only in the human species can one get the upper hand to challenge the layout one is given by nature. This species is the location for the greatest social demands.

Unless one finds a way to efficient service the social obligations or to side step them without negative reactions, one cannot be a successful yogi. A human body is only a means for social participation in the history of the world. You participate either as a rich or poor man, a famous person or a nobody. That is normal. But to side step that and study the individual psyche, that is an attainment which one must struggle to achieve because nature will not give that easily.

In general terms the struggle for that may be termed as yoga, even though Patanjali ironed out a specific definition and process.

Some say that yoga is unity or advaita, but the flaw in that is this: Who or what controls that unity? If the individual is not ultimately the controller over his unification into or distinction from the Whole, then a discussion about unity is mere talk and nothing else.

You emerged and found yourself as a unit of energies. Did you cause your appearance? If you did not, the discussion over your permanent unification with the Whole is baseless. Until we can communicate with the original cause of this diversity, the idea of advaita or ultimate unity is meaningless. The diversity is here to stay. No one can get rid of it. Even great yogis who merge into cosmic consciousness as they define and experience that, find themselves again as individual units after such experiences.

There is a place where one can go into cosmic energy and remain there but for how long? Since one is not the ultimate controller, one cannot be absolutely sure that one will not again emerge as an individual composite in the creation. One does not have that power. Why not admit it and work in a practical way to improve the individual psyche which one has?

This is why I stress that one should accept oneself as a composite unit and work from there to understand the ins and outs of one's individual psyche. Why keep on hawking over something one did not control, cannot fully control now, and will not control in the distant future.

You have an individual psyche. That is what you are. Work with that. Bring that to order. Know the details of that. Get the best service from that. Reform that. Refine that. Keep that on the highest plane.

Location in meditation

Location is important in inSelf Yoga™ even though it has little or no importance in many other meditation methods. inSelf Yoga™ is concerned with clarity because in samadhi one can get lost and one may believe many vague and indistinct conceptions and realizations.

If for instance I am located in London and I state that I am in Brazil or that I am the center of the universe, you can understand that something is amiss with my sensual perception. In inSelf Yoga™ one gets bearings or sense of direction from locations.

If I run off with the idea that I am God and that I am everywhere and am everything, it will be difficult for me to have clarity. I may be happy with the *absolute me* idea and my sense of omnipresence but it will be an abrupt departure from reality. Thus, location is important.

Naad sound comes from a certain place where the subtle material nature borders the spiritual nature. That place has a supernatural content. Its resonance is naad sound. According to how near you are to it or how far, that is how you hear it. Still it will come from a certain direction because the material nature is situated or it manifested from a certain place on the edge of the spiritual nature.

The biggest problem for people who want to meditate is to realize what the coreSelf is and also what the intellect is. People usually think that the intellect is their understanding or reasoning ability. They do not see it as a psychic object. One should strive to get that clarification.

It is your psyche but it has components. What are the components? How do they interact? What is the function of each component? What is the observing self's relationship to each component? What is the self with or without the components? Do the self lose power to act if it is separated from another component?

If my right arm is severed, I cannot do certain task as quickly as before. If both arms are severed I would be more handicapped. I am a human being but I am reliant on the arms which are components of the body.

Is it something like that with the psyche, where if a certain part, like memory, is made unavailable, I will become helpless without it?

Sense of identity control

The connection between the sense of identity (ego) and the intellect is made by a dart of energy which pours out of the sense of identity in the form of ray of light. It is shaped like a dagger.

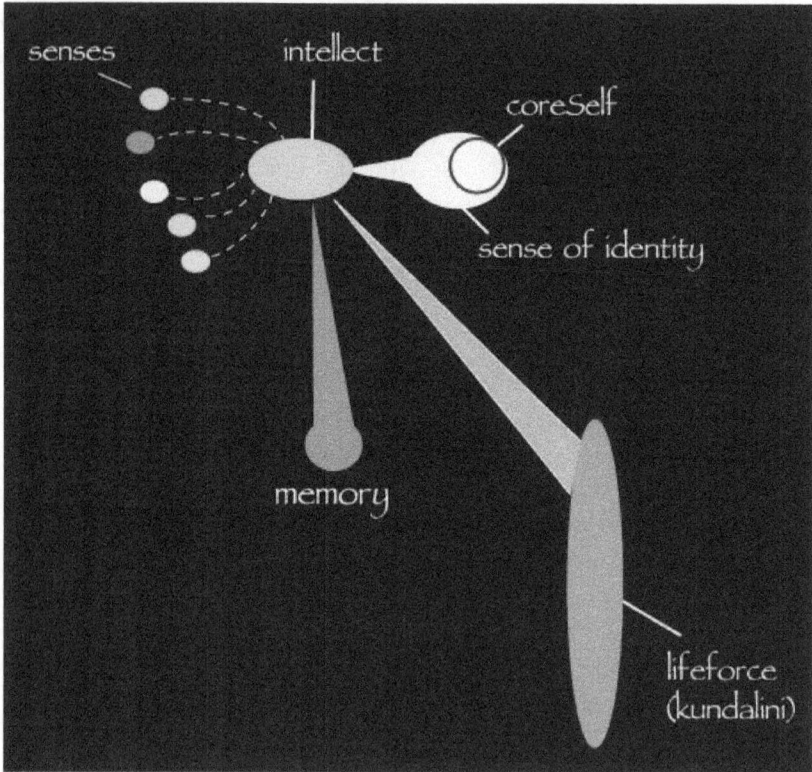

Even though the sense of identity surrounds the coreSelf in all directions, still for there to be communication between the sense of identity and the intellect, the identity fires a dart of interest.

This makes contact with the intellect. From that the vrittis or mental and emotional expressions manifest.

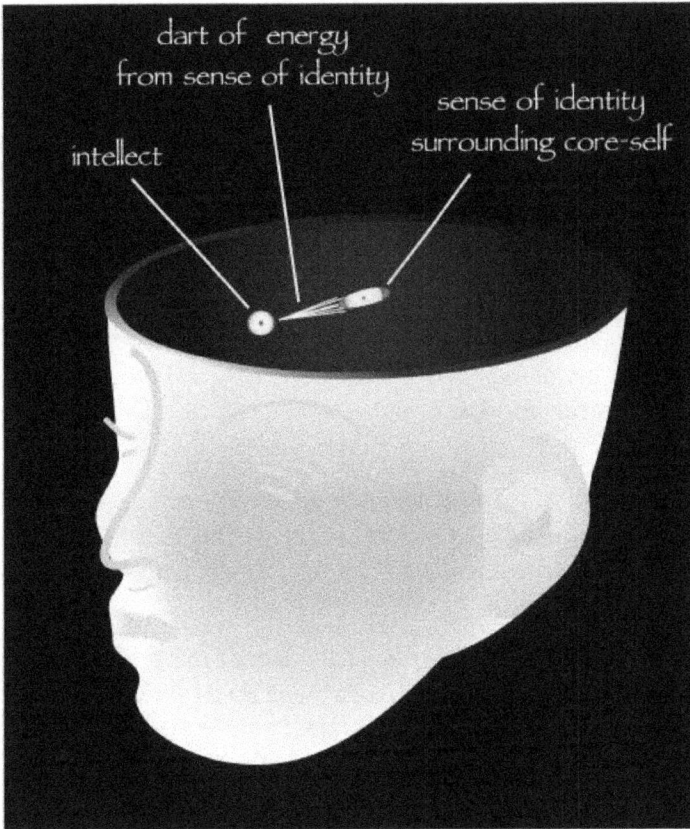

dart of energy
from sense of identity

sense of identity
surrounding core-self

intellect

The importance of this is that if the coreSelf could control the ray which the sense of identity emits, the core could isolate itself from the ravages of the intellect which really means being protected from being influenced by the senses, the kundalini and the memories. That is full compliance with Patanjali.

Many meditators think that if they get rid of the ego, all problems will be solved but that is a losing battle because no individual will eliminate identity. One may suspend it for a time but not eliminate it. By itself the sense of identity is a neutral psychic aspect. The problems begins when it connects haphazardly to the intellect.

Since we are endowed by nature with a lack of control of the very psyche which we are, there must be an effort to change the natural arrangement. A yogi must aspire to control the energy which leaves the sense of identity and touches the intellect.

In meditation when there is a thought, what is the process of the generation of it? How is it perceived in the mind? What determines its rejection or acceptance by the coreSelf?

For this discussion the part which concerns us is the part where the sense of identify reaches out to connect with the intellect. How does the ego get information from the intellect? Can the ego be segregated from the intellect? Can the self keep the ego with it in such a way, that the ego has no freedom to contact the intellect impulsively without first getting permission from the self?

Non-essential yogi

During meditation this morning Rishi Singh Gherwal asked me to mention that a yogi needs to come to the place where he or she can understand that his or her existence in this physical world and also in the lower adjacent astral world, is unnecessary.

He said this.

So long as one thinks that one can be useful in these creations one will not make the full effort for yogic success. This means that one will not feel the necessity to take the yoga disciplines. One may do the practice haphazardly but not sincerely as recommended.

As great as one may be, the plain truth is that this creation does not need one. One is not essential to this. This will go its own way. One will never dent this.

Does one feel that one is necessary? If perhaps one admits that one is not essential, why invest in this endlessly even though whatever one does will have no lasting impact.

Did you not notice that Rama, the son of Dashratha and Kausalya was here? Krishna, the son of Devaki and Vasudeva was here. Jesus the son of Mary was here. Still, this system continues in its own way without the impact of those superpersons.

Wise up! Understand that this will continue in its own way with its own nature. Turn away from this.

Naad Shift (February 2011)

Naad sound is usually heard from the inside of the head as if it comes from the outside through a space near the right or left ear.

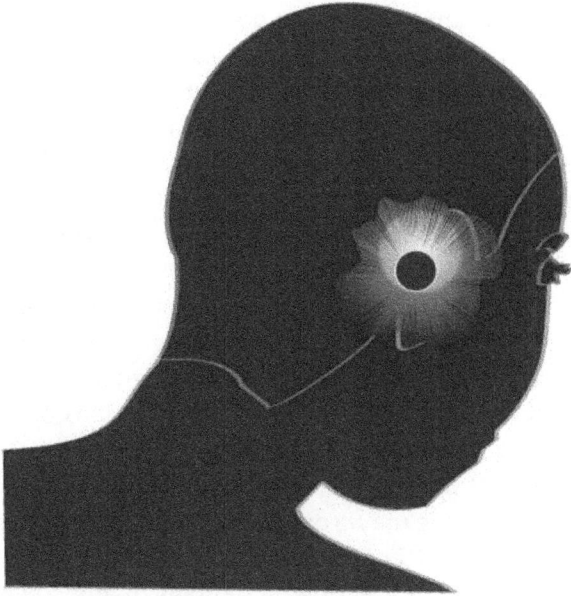

naad sound blaring outside of psyche by right ear

In this morning meditation, naad was heard from a shifted position which was above and a little to the back of the right ear.

After doing breathing infusion and sitting to meditate, and after assuming a position in naad, shifting the coreSelf from its default position, I went forward again after about ten minutes in naad. I checked to determine if the intellect was in a stilled condition. It was. Soon after this there was a flash of light as if a piece of glass was illuminated. That occurred about two feet ahead of me. Then there was pitch darkness in the intellect. (That two feet distance is mystic not physical distance.)

Then there was a series of lighted random lines and a lighted rectangular mirror-like object through the third eye but that lasted for only six seconds and then disappeared.

I resumed focus in naad and moved to where naad was located. Periodically I would find myself out of naad and then I would resume naad focus. The intellect created no images.

I did however see Rishi Singh Gherwal in another part of my subtle head but he gave no directions.

Distance in subtle world (February 2011)

Physical distance is perceived through the physical body, where you can perceive an object and make an estimate of its distance in relation to a standard scale. Others can measure thet distance with a rule to verify it.

Some people feel that everything done is relative to one's perceptions and biases, but physical reality is not dependent on individual preference. This is why one can be given a measure of a certain number of feet or meters, and that can be verified with a standard measure.

Mystic distance uses psychic eyes. One makes the observations, forms conclusions and makes judgment on the basic of other perceptions like intuition, subtle body eye vision, third eye vision, intellect vision and energy perception.

A psychic object could be two feet distant from the intellect but it was as if the third eye was like a glass pane through which one perceives the objects. If you are perceiving something through the intellect and then through the third eye. It is like seeing through two lens of a telescope. The distance can be judged on the basis of measures used in this world but those measurements are not physical. They are psychic distances.

In the astral world one may cross the Atlantic Ocean to travel from Africa to North American in a matter of 2 seconds. Sometimes when the astral body does this, it happens so fast that one only knows that one was in African and then one was in America. One does not perceive the distance because the rapidity of travel is such that it moves faster than one can measure.

There may be another experience where in the astral body, one tries to move it one inch and cannot move or one takes ten minutes of physical time to move that distance.

Self, self, selves and individual psyches.

There is spiritual family relationship with similar limited selves and with the Supreme Self. This is a perpetual kinship. This existence comprises person energy as

- limited selves
- limited psyches
- Supreme Self
- supreme psyche

This existence comprise these four person realities. In addition there are external environments which are outside the limited psyches.

An example is when a person has a third eye experience and sees into a supernatural place which is outside the third eye which is an orifice on the psychic membrane of the psyche.

The relationship between the individual and these environments hinges on the type of body he/she is in synchrony with. These forms either attenuate or amplify the desires and powers of the individual in relation to the facilities in that environment.

If the environments are not taken into account, the idea of unity is flawed because the selves are inevitably involved with environments.

Question is this:

Can there be just an environment of selves with no environment. Or stated otherwise, can there be such a situation where the selves are themselves the environment and there is nothing else?

In the *Bhagavad Gita* Krishna listed two types of selves, namely a limited self (atman) who is in the individual limited psyche (ksetra-Sanskrit for psychological environment), and a Supreme Self (paramatma-adhyatma) who is in all psyches.

Krishna's view was that there is a limited psyche. In that existential environment, there are two selves, namely a limited one and the Supreme One. Krishna never said that the limited one could become the Supreme Self, even though he did place the responsibility for the limited self's spiritual development and liberation upon the limited self itself.

Krishna said that the limited self was (kshara) subject to harassment and the Supreme Self was (akshara) immune to it. To explain the social distinction of each in practical terms, Krishna told Arjuna that Arjuna could not remember past births and therefore was at a disadvantage while Krishna remembered past births and had by virtue of that insight the ultimate intelligence.

Nobody has to agree with Krishna's ideas but at least we need to know what they are. Then we can understand where we agree or disagree with him.

Social life of a yogi (February 2011)

This morning Rishi Singh discussed the social life of a yogi and the acceptance of the outlay of reality scattered by time. He remarked:

"A yogi is better off to cooperate with time. He should allow time to manage everything except the yoga practice. For practice the yogi should squeeze it in here and there when time relaxes the pressure for social obligations. So long as one is pressure by the obligations one should serve with a positive attitude, with no resentment or sulking. One never knows if one may be compelled to take another body or if the present body will be in a helpless condition in the future when one must receive services from others.

"The uselessness of material existence does not in any way eliminate the physical reality. It does not cancel the service obligations which accrue from favors rendered by others to the yogi in the present or past lives. One should repay for these services on the schedule which is presented by time. One will never be the master of that lay out because there is

already such a master in the form of Krishna's Vishvarupa, His universal Form.

"Saying that Krishna is not the master of time and that we all are makes no sense, no more than a prisoner who is sentenced by a judge giving the argument in court that he is a human being and the judge is a human being and therefore the judge cannot have authority to confine others. It is better to accept that there is a Supreme Being controlling this and that whosoever that person is, that Person is the architect of time. One is not in control of this.

"It is not that one has to repay every past obligation. That is not the point. Yogis who are liberated no longer have to deal with the issue of the supervisory Time but so long as one is not liberated one would be sensible to be prompt in reciprocating with time, otherwise even one's attempts at spiritual disciplines will be thwarted because time has this situation under its rigid control.

"Whatever is due for others because of past services rendered by those persons, will have to be given to them either willingly or by force. No matter what one's philosophy is and no matter if one feels that personality is an aberration or illusion, one will still have to return favors voluntarily or as inconvenience by the pressures put on by Time."

Rectangular kundalini (February 2011)

Please look at this verse from Patanjali Yoga Sutras. This happened during meditation this morning:

प्रवृत्त्यालोकन्यासात्सूक्ष्मव्यवहितविप्रकृष्टज्ञानम्॥ २६ ॥

pravṛitti āloka nyāsāt sūkṣma vyavahita viprakṛṣṭajñānam

pravṛttyālokanyāsāt = pravṛtti – destined activity, the force of cultural activity + āloka – supernatural insight + nyāsāt – from placing or applying; sūkṣma – subtle; vyavahita – concealed; viprakṛṣṭa – remote; jñānam – knowledge.

From the application of supernatural insight to the force producing cultural activities, a yogi gets information about what is subtle, concealed and remote from him. (Yoga Sutra 3.26)

Even though this happened it did not occur on the basis of how Patanjali presented this verse. His presentation has to do with the direct application of supernatural insight of a yogi to cultural activities. However a yogi cannot directly apply insight like this unless his insight is well developed and is steady. If the yogi was not isolated and is not fully developed in the supernatural body on the appropriate level, he cannot do what Patanjali described.

This does not mean however that a yogi who is not as developed will never have such experiences. He may but it will happen by the grace of providence, as if it occurred accidently, by chance or good luck. It is very important to report honestly about yoga progress and not to canvas people with a pretense of advancement that one does not have.

After doing some 45 minutes of breath infusion, I sat to meditate. At first I noticed two factors one was naad sound which was a little higher in frequency than it usually is. If naad is higher in frequency or if it changes frequency there is a reason even though a yogi may not know why that occurred. In this case, naad assumed a higher frequency because the kundalini energy was shooting out the top back of the head. It was grazing the naad sound on the right side of the back. This grazing caused naad to have a change in frequency.

To note the experience I positioned the self in the kundalini energy. It was like if a person moved into the path of air flow which blew through a vent under pressure. The kundalini energy was clean and clear like sunlight but it moved with force through the back top of the head. It was in a rectangular shape channel

Most reports about kundalini from yogis is its movement through the spine in a circular shaped central channel called sushumna. In this experience kundalini was rectangular about two inches by four inches passing through the top back of the head. This is a case of having an experience which is different to convention. This is why I asked students not to do meditate with preconceived notions and to be openminded and report what happens rather than to visualize as described in a book. Drop visualization. Be patient. Wait for the experience.

After observing that I moved into naad which is my reference in meditation. Being in naad as usual, something suddenly happened where I saw a flash of a scene in Australia of a lady in an orphanage with aborigine children. The lady used a white body. The children were dark skinned.

When this flash occurred it was as if I was there physically in Australia. In other words the subtle body synchronized into the physical frequency there. This was for no more than three seconds but it was distinct.

I was then resituated in naad sound. I realized that this was an example of what Patanjali said in the sutra quoted above.

प्रवृत्त्यालोकन्यासात्सूक्ष्मव्यवहितविप्रकृष्टज्ञानम् ॥ २६ ॥

**pravṛitti āloka nyāsāt sūkṣma
vyavahita viprakṛṣṭajñānam**

*pravṛttyālokanyāsāt = pravṛtti – destined activity, the force of cultural activity +
āloka – supernatural insight + nyāsāt – from placing or applying; sūkṣma – subtle;
vyavahita – concealed; viprakṛṣṭa – remote; jñānam – knowledge.*

**From the application of supernatural insight to the force producing cultural
activities, a yogi gets information about what is subtle, concealed and
remote from him. (Yoga Sutras 3.26)**

What is the psychic mechanism which operates this mystic transfer
which would be done deliberately by an advanced yogi?

The answer is that this is operated by providence, where certain
consequential energies are released from deep memory when a yogi
accidentally reaches a certain plane of consciousness through breath
infusion.

Why those specific fated circumstances? Because those ideas are the
ones which are next in line in the subconscious memory.

In other words if it could, providence would transport me to that
orphanage to serve there as an assistant to that lady. A yogi does sometimes
utilize such information and goes to do such service in his subtle form,
thereby satisfying a providential account on the astral planes.

Mental chatter for meditation

Initially one can expect that there will be mental chatter during the
meditation. It will be there even during the breath infusion which is done
before the meditation. However once you get a set sequence you will find
that this problem fades away, that is if you are consistent with a daily
practice. If you are not consistent with a daily schedule, this problem will
never go away.

Mental chatter is nature's harassment system. It is not just humans who
are plagued with that, ever other species of life even the most primitive have
that problem. Each species think even though each does not have the
equipment to vocalize thoughts.

Mental chatter will not going go away by Nature's grace. It will leave only
by long endeavor along the lines given by Patanjali. You can imagine how
serious of a problem it is, that Patanjali declared both correct deduction in
thinking and erroneous notions in thinking as impediments to meditation. It
is a serious problem. In fact, the more one makes the effort to meditate, the
more it will seem to plague the person, even though in fact what happens is
that the more one meditates, the more one observes how one is controlled
by thoughts.

Any beginner who gets the idea that overnight he or she will conquer
the thought harassment system will be disappointed. It will happen after

consistent and sincere practice for many years. And as soon as one ceases practice nature will resume the harassment.

I have relatives who know that I have little or no interest in social affairs. Still, even though they are aware of that, they do not hesitate to involve me. That is the way it is for advanced or novice yogis.

Even though during the infusements when one is occupied with vigorous breathing one may not notice thoughts, there will come a time if one persists in the practice where when infusing the system one will notice the involuntary subtle mental activities. Not noticing thoughts does not mean that there are no ideas. The stage of no thought is a rare, just as when people admit not to have dreams, the fact is that they do not recall dreams.

When doing breath infusement, the attention is occupied doing that. Even though thoughts arise one may not be conscious of them. Or one may become aware of a thinking sequence after it began, where initially one was dazed and could not have an objective grasp on the thinking pattern.

During breath infusion or meditation, when one reaches the stage where one becomes aware of thoughts one should send some infusement energy into the mental location where the thoughts appeared.

Disappearing light

During meditation one may suddenly see a glow of light, which when one tries to peer at it, it recedes gradually or vanishes quickly. A yogi should not try to control or compel this light but should observe it with a gentle atttide. He should not pursue the light.

When you sit to meditation if you become aware of light, train yourself to move into the naad sound, and then look forward gently without grasping the light, without trying to possess it or trying to make it stationary for your satisfaction.

Spiritual experience / Providence permitting (February 2011)

This morning Rishi Singh Gherwal sent one of his yogi friends (Rimpoche) to speak to me. At first during my exercises, I saw them. In the distance they were tiny like two ants. Suddenly the other yogi appeared in my subtle head. I recognized him as a Tibetan yoga teacher who was filmed previously in a video about Tibetan tumo yoga.

He checked my practice. During a certain part, he showed an arm-shoulder shake and said that the idea was to be sure that the whole system was energized. Every part of the subtle body which kundalini services should be properly energized. Every bit of the old prana, old subtle energy in all areas should be flushed out.

As if to make a joke, he said,

"You cannot expect that the God will clean this for you. You must do it yourself. Or put it in this way, if it is something that you can do, then for sure know that the God will not do it for you. You must do it yourself."

I replied, "These are aggressive practices. People prefer something passive."

He said,

"This is not for everybody. Those who require other methods may use other systems. We use these because we get the results intended. There is no controversy about methods. It depends on what one desires and how far one is willing to go to accomplish that. One more thing, tell people that what they do not experience will not be desired by them. Once you experience other higher states, you may be willing to work to attain those, otherwise if there is no experience, if providence does not reveal a certain level to you, there will be no reason to do practice for those accomplishments.

"Many people get experiences through taking hallucinogenic drugs, but a human being no matter how great he is cannot force a high experience. The highest levels are off limits even through drug usage. These cannot be experienced or even dreamt of unless providence allows one to go there. As soon as one is allowed, one may desire to reach those places, otherwise there is no reason to do anything to transit from the natural locale one is destined to inhabit."

Soon after this he left. Rishi came but did not say anything. I resumed naad location meditation. Then I came forward in the subtle head to see if the intellect misbehaved. It was silent as if it did not exist. The third eye opening activated.

Tibetan secret technique (February 2011)

During exercises, the Tibetan yogi Rimpoche explained that while in the India system of the chakras, there is much focus on the sushumna nadi spinal passage, in some of the Tibetan traditions, especially the one which came through Marpa, Naropa and Milarepa, the stress is simply on one chakra which is the navel center in the front of the body. This is not the navel chakra because that chakra is on the spine.

Rimpoche said this,

The spinal chakras are more like the prime minister and other officials of a government. These people have some intelligence, charisma and managing power but they cannot do anything by themselves. Can you imagine what the prime minister would be if there were no other persons surrounding him, carrying out his wishes? He would be nothing. In some cases if the prime minister were challenged to a fist fight he could not defend himself effectively. But if his bodyguards are nearby, no one dares to attack him.

We discover that without their accessory expansive influences the spinal chakras are merely hollow authorities. Rishi Singh asked me to explain this because I would write the conversation. Others can use the information in the future even after you leave your body. When will that be? Better write this today. Who knows if for you there will be a tomorrow?

It is good that you have clairvoyant and clairaudient ability. That is rare nowadays with so much trash-chatter in the minds of human beings. From our view point the main issue in the physical body and in the adjacent subtle form, is the frontal navel chakra. Destroy that and you are free. What did Patanjali say about that chakra? I heard he said something to the effect that when that center is shattered, then the yogi gets intimate knowledge about the layout of the psyche.

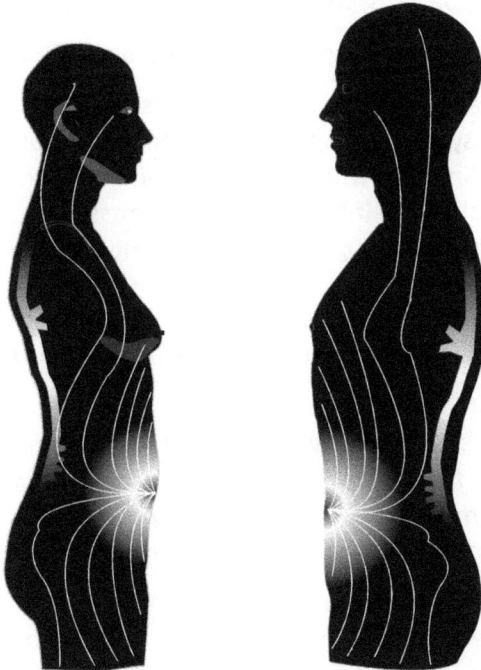

We looked at your translation. Ha! You did a good job of it. There are a few mistakes in your work. You said the word kaaya *means body. Well I do not know what dictionary or intuition you used but it means psyche not body. What does body mean? To some it means the physical system, to others it means the physical and subtle body combined.*

Let us use your words except for that one word. Translate it like this:

नाभिचक्रे कायव्यूहज्ञानम् ॥ ३० ॥

nābhicakre kāyavyūhajñānam

nābhi – navel; cakre – on the energy gyrating center; kāya – body; vyūha – arrangement, lay out; jñānam – knowledge.

By complete restraint of the mento-emotional energy in relation to the focusing on the navel energy-gyrating center, the yogi gets knowledge about the layout of his *psyche*. (Yoga Sutra 3.30)

Our lineage lays down this claim that if you were to change the construction of the navel area, so that the energy ingested does not coalesce there, and instead goes straight to muladhara without having interest in the sex-reproduction apparatus, then your spiritual struggle is over.

Yogi Bhajan: Resistance to responsibility (February 2011)

Yogi Bhajan came during the morning session. At first he defended the Indian yoga chakra system saying that it was only the visualization and passive meditation people in India who were mistaken about the kundalini and the navel chakra. He asked me if I remember his stress about flushing that front expansion of the chakra during the late 1960s and the early 1970s. I did recall what he said.

Yogi went into the topic of why so many of his Western disciples did not remain consistent at the practice. Many resumed their former social ways. He said:

"These guys, the males who came to me, were mostly afraid of responsibility. Thus even though they practiced, when females would approach them for relationship, they considered the approach to be merely a sexual one. They were afraid of a commitment for a family with children.

"That was the stumbling block for them. I encouraged many to take a spouse, raise a family and be a responsible member of society. I even showed them how to start businesses like Health Food stores, Boutiques, small constructions services, auto repair and so on. They could not stick with anything because they did not perceive the value of responsibility.

In India, because without family one cannot get a body and without a body one cannot use a human form for self-realization, the elders stress responsibility for family under the name of dharma.

"In the West family life is seen as a necessarily social utility. But in India, it is also considered the same way in addition to its value for spiritual realization. If someone does breath infusion daily, and meditates, he will see his way through the morass of social life and will at the end of this life achieve some spiritual elevation."

Parallel world with ships (February 2011)

This morning at the very end of the meditation session, I found myself in an adjacent parallel world where my father is presently staying. He is deceased. He was a seaman in immediate past life. Heaven knows how I got to that place but it was due to his power over my subtle body.

At first we were on land. He said that he wanted me to get some money to him while I was out at sea. The presumption was that I would take a job on a ship in that parallel world for the purpose of getting him some badly needed funds.

Because of the power of his thinking over my subtle body, I was immediately transported to a ship which was docked to a pier. One of the officers on the ship approached me. When I tried to introduce myself, he mumbled something and walked away. Then one of the ordinary seamen approached. We spoke but the mental phasing of this seaman's ideas were just like a foreign language. He had difficulty understanding what I said to him.

I asked about my quarters on the ship. Immediately, as if there was a speaker system in my head, I got a reply from my father saying that I should leave all money with my father since on crewmen usually frisk the property of others and remove valuables.

I did not send a reply thought to my father. In the meantime, the officers on the ship moved the vessel out to sea. Using this present material body I get seasick when travelling on ships. It flashed in my mind that for sure I would get sick. However I did not. Nor did any occasion arise for eating anything. There seem to be no need for anyone to eat in that parallel world. My mind had residual ideas from the lifestyle on earth. These served as a reference even though much of it did not apply to that astral place.

As the ship moved out to sea, there was a flash idea in everyone's mind that the captain of the vessel would visit his woman-friend who was on land. Suddenly the ship appeared to be moving through the land, just as if the land was water. In fact when it arrived at the woman's house, the large ship moved up to her house by the mental commands of the captain. It moved through all solid objects just as if everything was seawater. Land was like water. The ship floated through the land the same way it would in water.

At this point in the experience, I was called on this physical side. My astral body left that place and synchronized into the physical form.

I mentioned this experience to give some idea about how one deals with parallel worlds and also with ancestors, departed people who have some rights to use and command one's body, even the subtle one.

When my father first contacted me he thought that I would need money only for family responsibilities for a wife and children and that whatever other money I had should be for him.

This is the situation with relatives. They have no idea about spiritual practice. They take nothing else into account. Note the control the father of my body has, even though he is deceased.

Who owns this body?

Does the father or mother own it?

Does the grandparent own it?

Does the president who starts a war and conscripts it to battle, own it?

Does a disease like cancer take control of it?

Do the children of the body own it?

Does the spouse own it?

Yogi Bhajan: viewing video media (February 2011)

Today when I sat to meditate, Yogi Bhajan was present. He commented on what happens when one views video media. He explained,

"If the mind is strongly attracted to the media, it is engraved on the intellect. The track may be a weak or strong one depending on the strength of the attraction the person feels to the scenes viewed.

"For yogis it is no different. A yogi should not feel that he can view media without a corresponding effect on meditation. If you view media you should expect a setback in meditation. Do not think that you have a yogic process which will easily erase images in the mind if they are strongly etched into the intellect.

"Be an adult about it. The point is that a yogi should not view media unless he is prepared to scrub it out of the memory and intellect when it sabotages meditation."

The methods of removing the images and other impressions which are in the intellect or which penetrate it from memories during meditation, vary from person to person.

It is like the three guys who committed a robbery. They were arrested. One guy was the son of the governor. He called his father and was released. Another guy called his friend who was an attorney. He paid bail and was released. The other guy had no influencial relative or legal counsel. He remained in jail.

This was further illustrated at the trial. The governor's son got a suspended sentence but he paid a fine of ten thousand dollars. The one with the attorney served one week in prison, pay a five thousand dollar fine and did community service for one month. The poor nobody was given a three month sentence with one week of hard labor. Meditation is similar in that one person has it easy and another has difficulty, all depending on the strength of practice, the past life yoga efforts and the present social situation.

Right now I do meditation like the governor's son. If there is an image, I go to the intellect and directly confront it. Or I may not go into the orb but may go to a distance from it, like going into the naad sound and then the orb becomes silenced since its power supply ceases if I am not in connection with it. Another method which I use is to infuse the default location of the orb. I bombard the thought energy with breath energy.

There is also the factor of what type of thought it is. Where did it originate? In what format does it express itself in the mind?

I can however give a general advice which is that in the beginning it is best not to confront a thought or image distraction. Initially because of not having power over the intellect and not knowing how to deal with it, one should get at a distance from it. This means mental or psychological distance, distance in the mystic terrain of the mind.

Go at a distance. Stay at a distance until the intellect ceases production of the thoughts or images. Since the self is attracted to the orb's fascinations this is not as easy as it sounds. It is natural to be attracted to positive or negative ideas which are illustrated in the mind. Each person must fight this attraction power in the psyche by learning how to turn away from what is desired as well as what is morbid but compelling. One must learn how to be happy in not satisfying the curiosity about illustrations produced in the mind.

Just as we are attracted to sweet foods and we helplessly eat these even though we may suffer as a result, so we are attracted to mental ideas which should be abandoned as soon as we realize we are under their sway. It is an uphill battle.

Part 8

Intellect jump (February 2011)

This morning after doing about forty-five minutes of breath infusement in various postures, I sat to meditate. The last fifteen minutes of that session was done to infuse various parts of the subtle head, specifically the back top, middle region and the intellect in the frontal region.

Before infusing the head, I raised kundalini through the spine. It released energy into the chest region with tingling sensations. Through the spinal column in the neck it entered the head.

When I sat to meditate, there was fresh energy rushing here and there in the subtle head. I checked for naad. After identifying that, I moved into its location. I noticed that Yogi Bhajan was in the subtle head. He directed me to move back to the default coreSelf position which is in the center of the subtle head. As soon as I did so, the intellect jumped to a position above the core.

I cannot remember the intellect taking that position within recent history of meditation. I checked to see the cause of its relocation and saw that it did so because of the way the subtle energy struck and entered it.

During the breath infusement session, Yogi Bhajan instructed me to force fresh energy into a band which was around the intellect.

This is what caused the orb to jump to a position above the coreSelf. The intellect had peaceful bliss energy in it.

Intellect bruised (February 2011)

This morning in meditation, I jumped into the intellect at its default location which is in front of the coreSelf, towards the front of the head, toward the brow chakra.

When I entered there was one bruise spot. This is like entering a semitransparent globe or oval shape object. The bruise was on the surface membrane and it did not penetrate into the orb. It was from a thought which reached me from some persons who wanted to contact me yesterday to make social demands.

Because I avoided the contact, those persons felt neglected and sent a resentment which bruised the orb. Such is this social life that one must tolerate unfavorable incidences and not get upset because others make unreasonable demands.

The orb was clear on the inside. It has no thoughts, images or other expression.

Meditation disturbance (February 2011)

In the sense that I had to deal with social relationships having to do with deceased persons whom I knew some years ago, this morning meditation was a disturbance. It was however a good practice session. These people, being now deceased, changed their view about the value of yoga practice and meditation. They realized that Christianity's idea about going to heaven on the basis of church attendance and being saved, turned out for them to be invalid.

They are on the astral planes. When I was in Trinidad around 1973, I tried to explain reincarnation and the value of meditation but these persons were on the course of improving the social status. They neglected such conversations.

The exercise session was good. It was for forty-five minutes. Immediately after I sat to meditate. During the breath infusion, I managed to raise kundalini through the chest area, on the right side, on left side and through the center and then into the brain. This passage through the chest is called middle front kundalini as compared to through the spine which is back kundalini. It is the same kundalini from the base chakra but it may traverse different passages.

This happened while these persons, who are on the astral side only, conversed with me. I kept practicing even though they preferred for me to focus on relating to them.

When in yoga one has an obligation to a teacher or to teachers, one cannot afford not to practice even if others demand attention.

When I saw to meditate, those persons on the astral side backed away for about thirty minutes. Then they pestered me again. During the 30 minutes when they backed away, they examined my subtle body. They noticed the changes in it in terms of how kundalini energy was distributed through it.

One person compared the lights in my subtle body to theirs and saying that perhaps one of these days, he would become a great yogin.

Even though they were present near me, I overheard their conversations from a distance. My subtle body was so infused with energy that dimensionally it was far away from them.

During the first thirty minutes, I heard naad but it moved from its default position by the right ear to the top right side of the head. It sounded distant. When I tried to go into its source-point I could not reach that place. I then decided to stay where I was. I listened to it.

The intellect was completely silent. The frontal part of the head was blank. I saw none of my yoga teachers. After those first thirty minutes, my subtle body lost the breath infusements charge which elevated it above where those astral beings from Trinidad were. It returned to the dimension they were in. They were very happy about that. They began conversing. I pretended to get involved. I socialized with them. Except for one person in the group, the rest of them have no spiritual aptitude.

The idea that we are all the same and there is no difference and that we all have the same spiritual potential is to be contested. Some individuals are earth bound. Not even God can move them from the lowered planes. I do not see how they are all the same. There are definitely different grades of selves just as we see materially we have some persons who are brilliant scientists and other who are just plain dumb.

I do subscribe to the idea that people should be treated fairly and that everyone should be given due concern but that will never cause equalization in full terms because existence itself is against that. After this creation developed for billions of years both in the physical and supernatural levels, no being will change this in any substantial way.

We can be as kind as Jesus Christ and as non-violent as Mahatma Gandhi, and still this existence will continue with manifest disparities. There is absolutely no evidence that everything will be equalize and that everyone will have the same relative value. Perhaps that is the very reason why we have to be so careful not to exploit others.

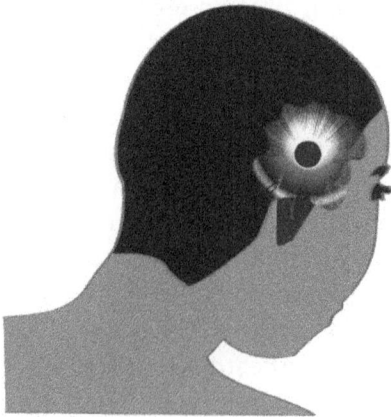

naad sound by right ear

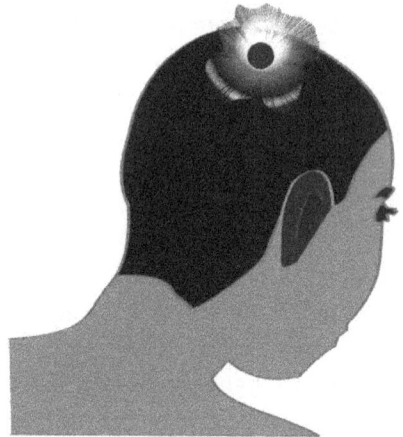

naad sound in shifted position
at right top back of head

Etheric body (February 2011)

The causal place is the level from which the subtle dimensions emerge. That production was magical so that the trace of it is non-obvious and is not perceptible with the psychic tools which we are currently using.

There could be something higher than the causal plane but that reality would be non-perceptible to anyone on this side of the existential divide. Indian (India) books list a spiritual world which is higher than the causal plane. It is sometimes called brahman, parambrahman, akshara dhama, vaikuntha and shivaloka.

The etheric plane is the plane which the subtle body assumes as soon as the physical system dies. In other words, it is the ghost world. This etheric plane is part of the astral dimensions. The astral planes are diverse. The astral body may change in vibration to synchronize to a particular dimension.

Think of the status of the physical body when it is under the influence of alcohol and when it is free of that influence. In both cases it is the same body but the state of mind and the operation of the body varies in each state. Similarly, the same astral body may be experienced differently according to the astral level it is synchronized into.

Etheric projection and astral projection are the same when the word etheric means the astral body in a certain phase or in a certain vibrational level.

When etheric means the body which is experienced just after death of an old physical body, that form cannot be projected until the physical body becomes old and diseased and terribly sick, like in the case when people have tuberculosis, terminal cancer, terminal AIDs and other terrible sicknesses which cause the astral body to be lacking in energy by virtue of its affiliation with a diseased physical one.

When that happens, the person experiences an exhausted or energy depleted astral body which has little wholesome energy. When that body is displaced from the dead physical one, it is experienced as a different astral form, as an etheric body with dark energy and with unwholesome sickly energy which takes that person to lower astral planes where devilish entities exist.

The causal body is not a body in the physical or astral sense. It is a place where there is compresses psychic energy. It is a cove. It is not manifested as a distinct form like the astral body. It is not projected but from that causal energy the astral body forms and from the astral body, the physical bodies are created. The causal body consists of compressed ideation energy. When an idea is first put on paper say like when an architect draws the plan of a building that is like the astral body. When the construction of the building is produced, that is like the physical body. When the building gets old and begins to fall apart and then is demolished, that demolished form when the building disintegrates is like the etheric body which is experiences by aged diseased persons who pass away.

This morning meditation session was intense but there were some people from India who were present. These were five persons who are sannyasin monks. Some are deceased. They argued about their processes of spiritual discipline which did not work to give the results intended after leaving the physical body. I did the exercises as they argued about methods of spiritual advancement.

These exercises lasted for one hour. Then I sat to meditate. In the meditation the intellect was quieted by virtue of the infused breath energy. The core self moved to the top of the head but the crown and brow chakra were absent. This was a silent meditation practice where the energies were quiescent.

No thoughts or images arose but off in the distance the swamis chatted and mentioned incidences which occurred when I was in their association some years ago. It was useless to discuss anything with them about pranayama practice because when a person does not do pranayama, that person has no idea of its advantage and cannot comprehend its value.

Hellish realms hereafter

Generally speaking people who pass away have astral life thereafter which is quite similar to the usual dream existence endured during their life time. If someone regularly had scary dreams, upon passing that person would have similar experiences. The astral body will be drawn to the same astral territories once it disengages fully from the physical system. Those who had mostly positive but just materialistic associations in dreams will go to similar places in the astral world after death. Those who were in divine associations will go to those places in turn.

Sometimes a person on the basis of religious beliefs and expectations, does experience a flash of heavenly life or a flash where they perceive a divine being like Jesus Christ but for most people that does not continue. The subtle body assumes the usual dream form, just as when the person lived physically the attention to Christ or whatever Deity or religion was part-time only. The main interest was to achieve and maintain the status in social life, continues.

Koreans feed their ancestors

Some South Koreans observe Jesa rituals for respecting and feeding ancestors. For the departed soul, the living family performs rituals three times a year (Lunar New Year, Thanksgiving, and the ancestor's birthday).

A table is set in the senior father's home for the grandmother or grandfather or both. It is covered with fresh-cut fruit, dried sweets, meat servings, dried fish, and whatever else the family desires. The picture of departed person is set in front of the table and the family acknowledge them.

Then senior family members give water and bow two or three times while wishing good things. This continues down the family line until the youngest children appear before the shrine of the ancestors and offered water and wished good things.

This is primarily done by Buddhist Korean families. Some feel that the ancestors need food to survive in the afterworld and that they return as human relatives in the future.

At one ceremony, the grandson took a couple cigarettes and put them on the table since the deceased elder was a smoker. One may wondered why they would do that since it would encourage a bad habit if he was reborn. However, the object of the ceremony is not to reform old habits, but to please and appreciate the service rendered to the family by the ancestor.

In addition, the ceremony which is led by the senior male in his house allows him to exercise leadership over the family and reinforces the culture of respect that exists in the Korean society. The older members in society receive a great deal of respect. The Korean language even has four or five different ways to say everything based on the age of the person to whom one addresses.

The offered items have psychic energies which are taken by the departed relative. The departed person would only take what he or she was used to eating while living on this side.

Because the ancestor is focused back into this world, he or she carries a psychology which is suited to this existence and not to the astral places. Their needs from the former life continue. People usually think that they will adapt to a heaven or a divine world, even to all-pervasiveness but it does not work in that way because one is already adapted to this existence and unless one can radically change that while using the physical body, one cannot adjust in the hereafter.

Nobody should waste time thinking of adjusting the psychology after death. The place to do that is here. The time for that is now.

Unless we are sure that the living descendants are more psychically powerful than the ancestor, it would be a miscalculation to think that they can reform the old geezer. The other thing is that even if they are more powerful, his or her pious merits may be greater and in that case, they will be held under the spell not of the ancestor but of the ancestor's contribution to that family line in the past life.

This culture of ancestral respect is neglected by modern descendants who are themselves older relatives reborn but who forgot the past life. One may now wonder about the relevance and value of such cultural nuances. In some old cultures the memory of the past life of a person functions as an instinct which causes that person to respect elders, but with changes in civilization people are freed from tradition and consider it to be irrelevant.

Meditation session

This morning exercises lasted for one hour and so did meditation. In a way, it may be said that one hour of exercises supports one hour of meditation, meaning that the infused energy fizzes out after the equivalent time of meditation and then one finds the self back on the normal social level once again facing the challenges of human life in a world filled with nature's intrigue for the evolutionary ravages forced on the creatures by the disciplinary dictatorial time factor.

A yogi friend from South America sent a text message by phone yesterday, requesting that I call him. I did so last night before resting. This same person was there with me in the astral world before I arose for meditation. He was present during the exercise session and then left soon after. He was not present during the meditation session.

He is wrapped up in various social issues but I told him that even though sometimes I do advise him on more efficient ways to discharge social responsibilities my business with him has to do with his yoga practice and nothing else.

During the exercises, I aroused kundalini into the chest region. It rose into that region like little sharp bliss energy needles. I then did some more infusion of breath energy and rose it into the central head twice. Once it rose and went into the shoulder and into the arms. Due to that I had to hold the arms in special postures to allow the kundalini to pass into the arm nadis more efficiently.

Rishi Singh Gherwal expressed the opinion previously that the entire psyche has to be dealt with and not just the head and spinal column. His view is that if any part of the psyche is not energized, it may cause a yogi to remain on a lower level, even if other parts of the psyche were elevated to higher planes.

Those yogis who deny that they have an individual psyche and that they are individual spiritual units are in for a rude awakening because if they fail to purify that psyche and if they think that they will become nothing at some stage and will be devoid of individuality, they will find out otherwise after leaving the body.

During the last 20 minutes of the exercises, I focused on the head of the subtle body and during the last ten minutes I worked on infusing the intellect. It was not troublesome. It was not producing thoughts but it had a bruise-spot on the front right side of it, which came from the thoughts of my friend in South America.

The other psychic component which was troublesome was a memory bubble which was above the intellect. It had within it an image of a news report I view yesterday. I directed some infused breath energy into the bubble. That demolished it. At first when I sat to meditate, for about 15 seconds or so, I was lost in the mental terrain just like a person who suddenly arrived in a large forest and did not know north from south. After those fifteen seconds my instinct for finding naad sound was felt. I located naad behind me, to the right. Like a lost explorer who resumes the sense of direction I went to it immediately.

After becoming absorbed in naad, I checked the mind chamber in the head of the subtle body. There were no disturbances. I settled deeper in naad. There was a soothing fog light which descended from above. I decided not to try to trace it since these lights usually have a way about them where they disappear as soon as one tries to track them. This light stayed for a time. After that there was another light which spread in a rectangular way. This effortless meditation lasted for one hour. I noted when I began. I noted when it finished.

Kundalini at crown chakra

Not everyone who has a kundalini experience at the crown chakra becomes enlightened in the way Buddha was enlighten or in the way that Paramhamsa Yogananda was enlightened.

Some persons lose objective consciousness when the kundalini rises and hits the crown chakra. Instead of become enlightened these persons go off into nothingness and come back to this world with no memory of the experience and no objective understanding of what occured.

In Yoga, there is something which is called *jada samadhi*. It is Sanskrit for stupid or dumb. There is an experience in which a person enters higher awareness but does not have the objectivity to understand what it is and has no coherent memory of the experience.

The beings in this kind of world are evolving upward. That means that if you were to move something like a rattle snake into the human species that entity would be very vicious and would be in a prison shortly. Stated differently you cannot successfully elevate a person way beyond their normal instinctive evolutionary behavior. One cannot take an alligator, put the self using that body into a human one and expect that person to become a saint.

If a coreSelf in a vicious species is relocated into the human species, that core will carry its mentality so that its kundalini will act in a similar way to that of the vicious species. It will adapt to the human situation but it will also express lower instincts.

To enlighten someone, one must locate a highly evolved self who can absorb the higher qualities and tendencies whereby when the kundalini is aroused, there is recognition of higher reality.

Yogeshwarananda once told a story of being in North India with some yogis. One yogi was a guy who always insisted that everything was the same and there was no diversity and that any such duality was illusion. They were invited into a home and since they were considered to be holy men, yogis of repute, meals were prepared for them.

When they sat to eat, the other yogi who was the advaita type (non-dualist/oneness advocate) was served a different meal. Yogeshwarananda noticed but he did not say anything. He ate his meal but the other yogis was in distress to eat his.

Later Yogesh spoke strictly to the lady of the residence to complain about the meal given to the other yogi. The woman replied that this yogi always said that everything is one and there is oneness and nothing else, that there was no duality and that it did not matter what you ate since it was all the same. She prepared a meal for him using a pound of salt because she felt that for him there would be no difference since he always advocated that it was all the same."

Making sense of subjective states in meditation

In some experiences of kundalini arousal to the crown chakra the yogi does not know what happened within the experience, but there is a method for becoming objective during such experiences.

The yogi should observe what happens in the psyche as he does the breath infusion practice. He should peer down into the body to see what happens. He should keep eyes closed during the exercises so that the mind is forced to look inside and is not distracted by external objects.

He should apply the anus lock, sex lock, neck lock, mind focus lock and other compressions which he will discover as he practices. These locks cause confinement and guidance of the risen kundalini and cause it to be channeled in a disciplined way so that one can observe and accommodate it.

During breath infusion it is important to do a series of breaths, then to observe how that energy is retained and distributed in the psyche. However one should not hold the breath after the accumulated energy was distributed. As soon as the accumulated energy is distributed, one should begin another serious of breaths or resume normal involuntary breathing. If one holds the breath after it was distributed, the system will switch to using polluted energy which should be exhaled from of the body. This use of polluted energy may cause the coreSelf to lose objectivity where it will have no recall or register of the experience and will experience an absorption in a retardative mood as *jada samadhi*.

My selfless acts squashed by fate (February 2011)

This morning meditation was interrupted by two persons. One was a yogi who is in another country and who wanted advice on how to practice. The other was a deceased man whom I was in association with as a neighbor some 25 years ago. This person contacted with me during the night. He got an astral link to me through a person who was in my household at the time.

At first during the night he wanted to speak of old times, about the things he did during the life of his last body and about some things he did in my association but then after some time it came to the punch line which was if any of my descendants could sponsor him a body. I told him that I had no objection to it and that if he needed my approval he had it.

He was happy to hear that. During the exercise session which lasted for about fifty minutes, he was present. He spoke as I practiced. After a while his astral body disappeared. There was absolutely no change in this person's attitude or desire even though his astral body make its last exit from his physical body some twenty years ago.

One thing of interest is that I knew this person in Poplar Bluff, Missouri, where he was a neighbor to the back yard. Now in the astral world he lives in a similar type of building with similar construction and objects. It appears that wherever his astral body goes, his home environment goes with it. When he visited he showed me how his stuff arranged in the exactly the same way as before and his astral form did not travel to Missouri to do this. It did that where he located my astral body.

Another thing of interest is that he has zero spiritual interest. He is as happy as a lark just as he was when he was physically present. Even though he is conscious that he is not in the physical world and that he would like to be part of the physical history of the world, he has no interest in inquiring about the spiritual self or the astral body. His only interest is to be again on the physical side. He does know however that he needs to get near someone who would be his parent. That is the only part of reincarnation that holds his interest.

The most important observation about this person is that when he was a neighbor, he used to offer to help now and again with one or the other things, and I would help him in turn. Now during the conversations with him, his mind remembered those favors he did. It put those things forward as basis for which he should get a body through my descendants. The point is that even if someone does something selflessly, the good intent has no meaning because the person has no control over the future.

Destiny may require that one should facilitate such selfless acts as a bargain at a future time when one becomes needy and must trade a previous selfless act for another favor.

Being selfless with the best intent may be a great quality for a human being but providence may at its convenience, confiscate such selfless acts or the resulting piety generated and use it as a bargaining chip in another circumstance.

This is like when a person saves up money in a bank account during their working years, then in the elderly years, the person falls sick and enters an institution in a crippled state. The hospital administrators then take action to use the money saved up by the person to pay for the medical services rendered. Even though the account was deposited for other reasons such as bestowing money to the patient's children or for a favorite charity the patient can do nothing to stop the hospital for using the funds.

Making a selfless act does not take away fate's overriding authority to disregard a person's plans. Fate could turn such selfless actions into selfish contributions by using the said energy in a selfish way for the person's interest at some future time.

Starfield (February 2011)

In general if one perceives starfield behind closed eyes, these are subtle energies which constantly move here and there in the mental environment. Just as we have clouds moving in the atmosphere, and we have dust particles, solar radiation and many other types of energies in the local atmosphere of the earth and also in outer space, we also have many energies in the mental environment.

There are also various dimensions. One's perception can jump into any of these levels where one may see this or that reality or energy. It does happen where a yogi's perception becomes psychic or supernatural. Then he sees microwave or infrared energy or light frequencies which are not perceptible to physical vision.

One should know the self which perceives the starfield. Is that self in the starfield like a bird which flies in a star-lit night?

Coherent meditation

To make the transition from abstract experiences to having objective coherent meditative states, one should be attentive within the psyche while doing the breath infusion. Look down into the body to perceive energy movements. If possible keep eyes closed during the exercises so that the mind is fully attentive within the psyche and is not distracted by objects outside the body.

Apply the various contractions like the anus lock, sex lock, neck lock, third eye lock and other checks which one discovers as one practices. These cause suppression of the aroused kundalini. It channels kundalini in a disciplined way so that one can observe and accommodate it. Increase the sense of responsibility is social dealings since this will cause a certain amount of kundalini power to be invested in social life and it will not retain excess energy which challenges one negatively when kundalini is risen into the head.

Moving up a notch or two in the evolutionary status is the way to accomplish the removal of abstract transcendence but that is not done through conceptualizing. It is done by action in which one's behavior reflects the increased sense of responsibility.

Lastly, when kundalini first arises in the spine direct it to other parts of the body, so that it penetrates the nadis in the other parts. When it accomplished that, direct it to enter the head.

Little self and itself (February 2011)

During this morning session Rishi Singh Gherwal was present but as a presence only. He did not use a subtle body or a miniature subtle form as most yogis do when they enter the head of a student. As I practiced there was a lady from the Virgin Islands who discussed her background growing up in the islands.

During the night she showed the place where her body grew up and also the cultural nuances of that place. After listening to her, I began practice at 4 am instead of 3 am. This is another effect of association, where when a yogi associates with non-yogis either physically or astral, the practice is affected.

By fate the lady was hurled on my path through life. I could not ignore her but all the same I was aware that the association sabotaged the practice.

In any case, Rishi noticed the lady and heard what she said. He looked into the memory imprint which was in the intellect. He read its contents. Without the lady's knowledge, he said that it was okay for her to be there during the session but he directed me to shift attention to another part of the intellect. When I did that I became less conscious of her speech but she was not aware that my attention shifted. Soon after she disappeared.

A yogi who is serious about spiritual life should understand that social associations which have no strong interest in cultivating spirituality, is a danger. If one is not careful one's spiritual practice will be reduced to nil.

Once that lady left, Rishi discussed the importance of having a yoga guru and of being obligated to that person to make spiritual progression, to rise early to practice, to be attentive during practice, to be consistent and loyal to practice. He said this, "The construction of the human psyche is such that one cannot make full progress unless one has an obligation to a greater person.

No limited person can make full progression by himself or herself without a connection to a greater yogi.

"From the self, one cannot motivate the self enough. One needs a yoga guru to push one and to demand a certain amount of practice. In your case, you have me. You have Yogeshwarananda. You have Atmananda, Shivananda and others. You are lucky. With us breathing down your neck, you will not become lazy with practice. "If we are deducted from the circumstance what will be left, except your little self. Then how much can that little self demand of itself. How much can that self elevate itself?

"Remember Arjuna. Krishna told him to lift himself, to elevate himself spiritually, to act in a manner for the long-ranged spiritual wellbeing, even to use himself to help himself Arjuna needed to be inspired and urged by the Supreme Being."

During the exercise session, kundalini arose in a rare way which is to rise into the nadis which are in the thighs, legs and feet. This feels like if there are cramps which have a bliss energy rather than an annoyance feeling.

In that experience kundalini flares and travels in a downward direction. Beginners doing bhastrika pranayama practice are usually familiar with kundalini rising up the spine. If one continues to practice, one becomes aware of kundalini rising up the front of the body or up the middle of trunk and in other parts, but rarely does kundalini rise and travel in a downward direction.

During the exercise session I did some thigh stretches. Rishi showed how to blow breath energy into the thighs to remove the lusty force and stagnant energy there.

When I sat to meditate, I was alert to naad. After about two seconds I was focused on it. I could not find its root or source point but it was positioned by the right ear. Rishi then said, "Be attentive to naad. Ignore everything else."

After that he disappeared.

Sunlight astral body (February 2011)

Exercises this morning lasted a little longer than usual. Rishi Singh manifested about forty minutes into the exercise when I finished the session. He said that I should do another twenty minutes since he felt that the subtle body was not infused sufficiently.

Just before he arrived, I managed to direct kundalini into the center of the trunk of the body. It spread upwards. This meant that kundalini did not go through the customary sushumna central channel in the spine. Instead it left the base chakra and coursed through the central trunk of the body. One has to contract the muscles around the spine and those in the chest, to cause kundalini to course upwards in that way.

Previously during the night in the astral world, I spoke to several persons. Just before rising for about one hour, I was with a deceased monk and with another person from the religious sect that monk was an official in. They were both arrested in the astral world by some persons who had grievances against them.

The one who still uses a material body, would of course escape as soon as his gross body would require the subtle one to synchronize into it but the other one who has no physical form might remain in the prison where those people held them.

After the exercises, I sat to meditate. Rishi Singh gave details about the social life of a yogi, stressing that a yogi who feels that he will fix the social situation is more or less wasting time. He said this,

"They should understand that the entities who are biased towards material existence and to the games that people play in the social world, will not be convinced of reincarnation. They cannot on their own come up with a solution to the problems of the world. In fact the material existence and the social construction of the world will continue indefinitely because that is the nature of social involvement.

"A yogi should know that his or her main business is to side step this sociology. Once one gets a body, one has an obligation in the social history of mankind. Take care of that efficiently but do not feel that you can change or reform this situation entirely. That is not possible because the way the world was before one took a body is the exactly way the world will remain after one is willingly or unwillingly deprived of the body.

"When we study the Mahabharata about the life of the Pandavas who were personal friends and agents of the Almighty Krishna, we realize that even though they fought for good principles, still in the end, things regressed. They had to leave it all behind. That means that one does the best in the service of righteous lifestyle but deep inside one knows that one wastes time. One will not bring about a permanent change in anything in the material world.

"Therefore work diligently for spiritual life. Do your best in the social field and leave the matter there. There is no point in running up against the people who lack spiritual vision and who are always siding with blind materialistic instinct. Spiritual life is a like a narrow corridor. Social life is like things seen through openings in the corridor. Do not allow those things to distract you in such a way as to cause you to leave the spiritual corridor. Do not go over into any of those windows into the social world

and cause the self to be projected out of the corridor of spiritual discipline. Each yogi must take steps to protect the self."

During the meditation session, I reached naad on the right side near the ear but a little high up in about one second after sitting to meditate. Rishi Singh was nearby and he sent an idea that I should tell the yogis that they should try their best to comply with Patanjali. Rishi said this, "Yogananda and others stressed meditation on the third eye but you do not get that instruction from Patanjali. Why is that? Did Patanjali not know of the brow chakra? The reason is this: The real problem is not the brow chakra. It is the thought generation organ which in the Gita is listed as buddhi."

Patanjali nailed it with his description of its functions, listing five functions. Even if a yogi cannot see that psychic organ, the yogi can located it by finding the location where those five functions take place and become evident to the self in the head of the subtle body.

Focus on that organ and keep it from generating what it normally does. If you do not see it that is okay. Still work on it as instructed by Patanjali. Have faith in Patanjali. Do not doubt Patanjali. Study Patanjali over and over until you become familiar with what he proposes. Practice to achieve what he described as the accomplishments of yogis.

After about one hour of meditation, the astral body separated from the physical one but the astral one keep the lotus posture which the physical one was it. I realized that it had floated to a high table which was in another dimension but I did not recall that it was the astral form. When it began to float about I was a bit worried that it might fall.

However when it resumed fusion into the physical body, I realized that it had entered one of the sunlight dimensions in which the subtle body itself is made of sunlight and the objects in that place, are of light. This means the vegetation, the landscape and everything as contrasted to this world where most of the solid objects are made of physical substance.

I did not see any other person in that other dimension. The location was devoid of other human beings.

Sun beings (February 2011)

In that experience I used a sunlight body but not on the sun planet. It was in a dimension somewhere else, in a world that is near this earthly situation.

There are people living on the sun. They were there for millions of years, using durable bodies that last that long. Those bodies are made of nuclear energy. The problem for a yogi is getting there and staying there once he or she gets there since usually a person using an earthly body is earth-bound because of his or her natural attachments to the earthly culture and process.

Even if the coreSelf is not attached to the earthly life, that does not matter. In the final analysis if kundalini is attached, no matter if one believes in God, no matter if one attains this consciousness or that consciousness, one cannot leave the earthly plane of existence and will again come out crying from a woman's uterus.

Philosophy and even meditation capability does not free one from such a fate if the kundalini is not completely purged of its tendency for earthly forms in some species of life in this type of physical existence.

When one takes a new body, one forgets the past life or lives. One gets crazy again as an innocent little infant, crying and laughing. One does not recall the past. In a new body one shifts into a new mind. One is ignorant of reincarnation.

Back in the 1970s, I astral projected to the sun planet but as time would have it that ability was lost. There are however many persons living in many other dimensions in the space between this planet and the sun. They also use sunlight bodies even though they are not on the sun itself. Jesus Christ for instance is in the earthly atmosphere but he uses a sunlight body.

Some meditators are of the view that we can create a negative or positive mood and by self-effort be miserable or happy. Actually the energy we use for either a positive or negative outlook is sourced from the sun and moon. It is not that we are independent to an absolute degree.

Enter the orb (February 2011)

This morning the exercises session was great with kundalini rising into the chest on the left and on the right side alternately. It also rose and went through the buttocks electrifying those areas.

To make kundalini go to the right side and then to the left side, one has to do certain stretches as soon as one stops infusing the breath and one feels that kundalini will move. By making a stretch to the left, kundalini became pulled to the left side which is termed ida nadi in Sanskrit. This does not only mean the main coursing of energy to the right and left of the spine but to the nadis which branch from the spine and spread throughout the subtle body.

When kundalini moves into those areas it drives out stale subtle energy and causes those areas of the subtle form to be filled with light. Kundalini usually remains at the base chakra and conducts its operations for the maintenance of the body from there. When it rises it usually does so by spreading its power through the sexual organs. This causes sexual arousal. When it spreads through the chest region, one interprets that as affectionate feelings, love.

In yoga, the idea is to cause kundalini to electrify the entire subtle body not the sex area and human social affection concerns. Kundalini has access to every cell in the body. This may be realized by persons who are sexually involved and who can take some time during sexual experience to note what happens when there is sexual climax, when all the cells of the body are forced to contribute energy to the sexual experience.

It is difficult however to make this observation because of the intense feelings which we interpret emotionally and mentally as pleasure. This pleasure bars us from making an objective assessment of how kundalini causes the intense focused feelings of pleasure with the genitals being the main focus.

When I sat to meditate, it took about three minutes before I linked to naad. Why is that? For one thing it was a successful session because kundalini rose several times during the infusion. I directed it in the proper channels. I infused the intellect with energy. I also infused the third eye because I because aware that it was affected when I infused the intellect.

Why did it take a full three minutes to get on to naad sound?

The reason is that somehow or the other there was a persistent thought which entered the orb, a thought from someone else. It penetrated the orb and did not budge even after the orb was infused. I entered the orb and then went to the thought force and confronted it head on. Then it disappeared.

Usually the coreSelf is outside the orb but in this case because of the persistence of the foreign thought, I entered the orb. This is like entering a bubble which is dark inside but which is spacious and which has a subtle object inside which is like a small jelly fish.

After getting rid of that thought force, I got out of the orb and headed to the right back of the head to be in naad sound.

After fifteen minutes with naad, I looked forward and noticed light where the orb was located. It was like when there is a moon in the sky which is on the other side of the planet and hence cannot be seen, but which lights up a cloud with a glow of light in the night sky.

Relocating to the sun planet (February 2011)

Last night I was bombarded by several persons who were socially involved. It is important to understand that no matter how important a social problem is it is really nothing in contrast to the universal situation.

For me it is important to wonder about and ponder on what happens on the sun, how the celestial beings live here and how I could move there when this body is finished. In contrast the social situations of human beings on this planet is not that interesting.

What we do socially which is so important, as a *do or die* type of thing like a mortgage bill, romance, the marital situation, the educational and career accomplishments, are very insignificant when we consider that for the most part, we can only guaranteed these things for ourselves for one hundred years for the most. No one can say for certainty that any of these accomplishment will have a lasting impact in human history what to speak of the entire planet or the sun planet or the Milky Way galaxy in which we are float.

For me a big problem is how to assume a sunlight body and move to the sun planet when this physical system dies. That is of interest to me, not what we are doing here, and the little things that poke us here and the overwhelming sense of self-importance as physical beings.

The next body

One old man whom I spoke to last night in the astral is over seventy-five years of age. He heads for the grave, as people say and yet he is preoccupied not with his impending death but with the life of his descendants.

For this investment in relatives what will he get in the next life? He has the idea of reincarnation but is he miscalculating. Is he sure that the family which he worked hard to socially upgrade, will welcome him as their child in his next life? Is he sure that his daughter or granddaughter will willingly allow him to take birth when he requires it and will not be involved with a career and consider career not childbearing to be the priority? If she allows that even how long will she allow him to suckle her breast? Will she simply insert a bottle of formula in his mouth and leave him at the daycare?

Seeing Krishna (February 2011)

The exercise session this morning was great. I directed kundalini into a little blank space which is above the genital area and in the center of the body. Kundalini rose into the chest and then into the head thrice.

Near the end, Rishi Singh Gherwal became present but he had little to say. During the exercises I had a problem with the intellect. Within it there were three bruised areas. I infused breath to get rid of that. It took some time. Rishi had an attitude of checking to see if I did the exercises with care and attention.

After this session, I sat to meditate. Rishi disappeared at that point. Because I entered the intellect to do battle with some social energies it took fifteen minutes to reach naad sound in the back left side of the subtle head. After fifteen minutes, those energies vanished.

I meditated for about one hour. I had a feeling to recline the body and continue meditating. During this the subtle body separated. I found myself in a dimension where Yogesh floated. The subtle body he used looked like a material form at about the age of 35 years. Above him was Lord Krishna, way in the distance. There was a thread of energy going from Lord Krishna to the yogi.

When I saw Lord Krishna, he had an attitude which said that I should listen to the yogi and not try to communication with Krishna.

Yogesh spoke to me. He was annoyed. Somehow I cried over it. I am not a person who easily goes to tears. Yogesh complained about the lack of practice of yoga by human beings overall and also especially because many persons who do a little yoga, has no serious interest in it and do not practice the elementary part of yoga, the first five stages of practice listed by Patanjali. Yogesh said that without mastering that, they cannot succeed.

The conversation was distressing. For myself, I already failed in my mission, since I convinced only a few people about doing the elementary stages. Most people who do yoga want to do what Patanjali coined as samyama, which is the three highest states combined into one practice, where one stage graduated into another higher stage, moving from dharana, dhyana and then finally samadhi. But Yogesh thinks that is not going to happen in fact because of not being proficient in the lower five stages.

Discrimination (March 2011)

Compulsive behavior and habits on the physical level usually mean more of the same on the astral plane. Last night I dealth with a deceased monk, who was without any change. In fact his compulsive behavior increased as he moved here and there in the astral world trying to exploit situations and use people to fulfill desires.

Someone does not improve in behavior once he is deceased. It usually spirals into an increase in passion and compulsion, with desires getting even more of an upper hand, with reason and analysis almost totally absent. Discrimination is more a human physical body accessory and it hardly feeds over into astral experience.

Discrimination is developed in physical existence because of the challenges one encounters and the opposition put up by gross existence to the fulfillment of a compulsive desires. In the astral world there is less opposition. Subsequently, one goes crazy with the compulsions.

If however one practices restraint, reflection and deep considerations on the physical level, some of that will carry over to the astral planes. One will not be victimized there with a near total lack of discrimination. Discrimination is an alien feature but it proves to be useful once it is developed in physical existence. It curbs sexual compulsions and helps the person to avoid mistakes.

Merging with objectivity (March 2011)

This morning meditation was a bit strange. I did an intense session of rapid breathing, Kundalini rose and spread in different direction many times during the practice. At one time kundalini spread under the armpits and then shot out through the arms. Once it shot down into the pelvic area and spread there like tiny laser beams with a bliss feeling.

For about fifteen minutes at the end of the exercises, I worked on the head of the subtle body. There were foreign thoughts in the subtle head. Usually these thoughts are in the area of the frontal lobe of the brain. Usually they attached themselves to the intellect which is in that location. But the thoughts sensed that the intellect resisted them. To avoid it they stayed high up in the head of the subtle body. Even though they did not contact the intellect directly, they used mental space and mental energy to manifest themselves to me. This happened even during the earlier part of the exercises, even though then I ignored them since I wanted to focus my attention down into the body.

Just when I decided to deal with these thoughts, I sensed the presence of two persons. These persons were the source of the thoughts. I also sensed some energy from Rishi Singh Gherwal, which he left behind in my subtle body. That energy had an instruction content which meant that thoughts which manifest without the assistance of the intellect, should be dealt with in the same way just as if they were manifest by the intellect. I moved close to one thought and infused its space with rapid breathing. That one disappeared. I used the same technique on the other thoughts.

These two energies were hanging in the mind like jelly fish floating in the ocean with long tentacles dangling.

As soon as I sat to meditate, I noticed naad sound in the back top of the head. At first I was distracted by a tiny thought energy which was about to be enlarged. I confronted it and it disappeared. Then I went to the top back of the head. When I got there I became part of the light which came from the naad sound and which was spread through the subtle head. I was part of this light subjectively but with objective awareness of it.

Even though I was part of the light, I could not use it. It was as if you were a tiny part a ray of light which came from light source like a bulb or a sun. There, because you are a composite part of it you are not in a position to use the light or to objectively view it.

The other important thing is that I could not turn around to see the source point of the light because I was emitted from the source, being pushed away from it without the ability to turn to view it. I could see the other rays of light near to the ray of which I was a part. I could see the ray energy ahead of me but not the ray energy behind me. Time wise, I was in that light for five minutes. Then suddenly I was dropped out of it into a dark mental space.

Trash in my mind (March 2011)

I organized files in a computer and eliminated those which were no longer needed or have become useless for one reason of the other. It is amazing at the quantity of trash which accumulates in a computer. I wondered how many memories in the conscious and subconscious compartments are pure trash, pure social trivia but which the mind carries as if those ideas were more valuable than diamonds or gold.

At the age of 50, one should begin taking out old memories which have no continuity value into the next life. When these memories are rediscovered, one should do the very best to neutralize them so that no energy is spent by the mind and emotions for their maintenance.

If one fails to do this, one's mento-emotional energy will be clogged. One may be dotish as the years of the body goes by and the memory support one received in youth from the brain, no longer serves one and one is left as a pure imbecile.

Heaven hereafter (March 2011)

One thing is to realize that each religion promises a heaven which tallies as a natural outcome of the cultural basis of that religion. Take for example the religion of the Viking warriors. That gave an award of entering a heaven in which the warriors would have eternal bodies with facial appearance just like the ones used on earth, but which had no disease or discomfort and which was capable of eating hearty feasts on a daily basis.

Putting aside this general pattern of the religions, we may consider evidence in the form of dream states, particular lucid dreams and conscious astral projections.

What forms do we use in astral projection? What perceptive senses are operating during lucid dreams?

Teacher-student relationship (May 2011)

I was at a taekwondo student testing session today. I recalled some things which I observed years ago in the Philippines with Arthur Beverford. There were two important rules which he stressed:

Before you begin bow to the teacher

Before sparing with a fellow student bow to that person without losing focus

In Western countries, the idea of bowing to the teacher is taboo. No one is supposed to bow to anyone for anything. During the session, the teacher had to repeatedly told students to turn and bow to the master teacher who was there to observe their martial art proficiency.

Even though they had no objections to the bowing procedure, you could see that it was unnatural for them. Why bow to a teacher in the first place? There is this feeling that one should demand an education.

The first rule about bowing to the teacher is completely different to the second rule about bowing to a fellow student before sparing.

In the first situation, one bows to the teacher because he is one's superior. One depends on him to develop the particular discipline. It is assumed that his superiority will hold the entire lifetime. In other words, you will not advance beyond him because his advancement accelerates as yours improves.

In the second situation, one bows to a fellow student because he is a student of one's teacher. He is dependent on the teacher. One also bows to him to signal that one will spar by the rules taught by the teacher. In this case one remains focused on the fellow student. This action of not bowing with the eyes is not to challenge the other person. It is to observe movements since if one does not observe, the other person may attack when one is inattentive.

The whole thing about respecting and bowing to a teacher, has to do with student obligation. In the West everything, nearly everything, is based on its commercial value. One gets an education from a University if one pays for it financially. Since one paid, one had no obligation to the professors.

In the East, before, money was not the means of the education transfer. Service to the teacher and fulfillment of the teacher's wishes were the means. In some cases money played into that but money was not the standard means.

One would take lessons from a teacher, even if one could not pay a penny to him. One would learn but one was obligated. Even in the *Mahabharata,* there is the story of Drona who taught the Pandavas and their rival cousins, and who at their graduation, required that they used the martial skill achieved, to subdue King Drupad. As fees, Drona wanted martial service to seize a kingdom. There is another case with the same crafty Drona, where he required an aborigine to amputate his right thumb as the teacher fees.

The problem with bowing to teachers, with treating them in the Eastern way, is that the student is not free to do what he or she would with the skill achieved. It can only be used in the service of the teacher and in a way that is approved by the teacher. With a commercial school no such stipulation applies. The teacher cannot levy a service nor a moral standard for use of the training.

I learnt kundalini yoga practice from Yogi Bhajan in 1973. This morning he came astrally to tell me to put a restriction on someone whom I introduced to the practice and who thinks of teaching another person.

If I had learnt it with commercial exchange where I paid Yogi Bhajan, he would have no way to instruct me to place a restriction on a person who learnt the practice from me. The Eastern system is restrictive.

While observing those martial arts students, I realized that they were focused on the opponent, on defeating opponents. That reminded me of a conversation I had with Arthur Beverford over 30 years ago.

When I approached him to get a clue from him about anyone teaching yoga in the Philippines, he told me to wait until the martial arts class was over. I sat and waited. When it was finished, he introduced himself as the disciple of Rishi Singh Gherwal. He told me to meet him for half hour sessions of yoga practice on certain days.

This was arranged so that there would be the martial arts session and there would be the yoga teaching. I was the only yoga student. Sometimes someone else would be there. They would practice even though they were not serious about yoga. After the asana postures, we meditated.

Originally when Bodhidharma (the Buddhist Monk) went to China, there was martial arts training but soon after one sat to meditate. There is not much mention about asana postures training in that story.

Anyway after a few sessions, Arthur Beverford asked me to join the martial session. I was disinclined to it but I took two sessions and ceased that.

When Beverford returned to the USA, I got in touch with him. He was near Ojai in Ventura County, California. There he had students and gave lessons at a place in the small town. His sons were advanced black belts. About two weeks after I got to his place, I had an astral projection, where my astral body took past life information from the causal body. Then the astral form did the martial arts forms with precision and rapidity.

I discussed this astral experience with Beverford. He suggested that I learn the art physically. He said, "That is the thing, that the information has to be brought over physically again through practicing again."

It means that if one mastered something in the past, if one wants to demonstrate the proficiency in a new body one has to practice again. For me, and this is something I did not tell Beverford, the proficiency in martial arts was accessed in the causal body and was cancelled out there, because it has absolutely no spiritual value. One does not make spiritual progress by focusing on an opponent because in the spiritual world, there are no opponents. The only place where one can use such skills is in a world where one will find opponents and in such places, it has all value until the opponents find a means of transcending that skill, as happened in Japan when some samurai masters and their students were mowed down by gunfire and the Meiji period came to an abrupt end.

Defense has all importance if one plans to keeping on taking birth in a world which is like this one but otherwise it has no value. Ultimately one should see that when all is said and done, advantage outside of one's psyche is useless. We do need advantage but it is in reference to the psychic organs in the mind which make us into their slaves.

inSelf Yoga™ is the martial arts practice within the psyche, going on between the core-self and the perception equipment. Bodhidharma went to China to teach that because that is what Gautama Buddha mastered but when Bodhidharma got to China, the people were not evolved enough to appreciate Buddha's achievements. Bodhidharma considered their level and taught martial arts.

Those who became proficient reached the realization that it was a waste of time. They took a hard look at the achievements of Gautama Buddha and shifted to internal conquest.

Buddha's father was told by an astrologer that Buddha would be either a world conquering monarch or the most enlightened person. Buddha's father did everything possible to make his son become a monarch but the effort failed because Buddha noticed that the real problem in life was an introspective one. His martial arts practice was between himself and whatever it was in his psyche which chased after impermanent things.

Index

About the Author

Michael Beloved (Yogi *Madhvāchārya)* took his current body in 1951 in Guyana. In 1965, while living in Trinidad, he instinctively began doing yoga postures and tried to make sense of the supernatural side of life.

Later in 1970, in the Philippines, he approached a Martial Arts Master named Arthur Beverford. He explained to the teacher that he was seeking a yoga instructor. Mr. Beverford identified himself as an advanced disciple of *Śrī* Rishi Singh Gherwal, an Ashtanga Yoga master.

Beverford taught the traditional Ashtanga Yoga with stress on postures, attentive breathing and brow chakra centering meditation. In 1972, Michael entered the Denver, Colorado Ashram of *kundalini* yoga Master *Śrī* Harbhajan Singh. There he took instruction in bhastrika pranayama and its application to yoga postures. He was supervised mostly by Yogi Bhajan's disciple named Prem Kaur.

In 1979 Michael formally entered the disciplic succession of the Brahmā - Madhava-Gaudiya Sampradaya through *Swāmī* Kirtanananda, who was a prominent sannyasi disciple of the Great Vaishnava Authority *Śrī Swāmī* Bhaktivedanta Prabhupada, the exponent of devotion to Sri Krishna.

However, yoga has a mystic side to it, thus Michael took training and teaching empowerment from several spiritual masters of different aspects of spiritual development. This is consistent with *Śrī* Krishna's advice to Arjuna in the *Bhagavad Gītā*:

Most of the instructions Michael received were given in the astral world. On that side of existence, his most prominent teachers were *Śrī Swāmī* Shivananda of Rishikesh, Yogiraj *Swāmī* Vishnudevananda, *Śrī Bābāji Mahasaya* - the master of the masters of *Kriyā* Yoga, *Śrīla* Yogeshwarananda of Gangotri - the master of the masters of *Rāj* Yoga (spiritual clarity), and Siddha *Swāmī* Nityananda the Brahmā Yoga authority.

The course for kundalini yoga using pranayama breath-infusion was detailed by Michael in the book *Kundalini Hatha Yoga Pradipika*. This current book was composed from meditation and breath-infusion notes which were originally shared in staple bound booklets as Yoga Journals.

Michael's preliminary books relating to this topic are *Meditation Pictorial*, *Meditation Expertise*, and *Meditation ~ Sense Faculty* (co-author). Every technique (kriya) mentioned was tested by him during pranayama breath-infusion and *samyama* deep meditation practice.

This is a result of over forty years of meditation practice with astute subtle observations intending to share the methods and experiences. The information is published freely with no intention of forming an institution or hogtying anyone as a disciple.

Publications

English Series

Bhagavad Gita English

Anu Gita English

Markandeya Samasya English

Yoga Sutras English

Hatha Yoga Pradipika English

Uddhava Gita English

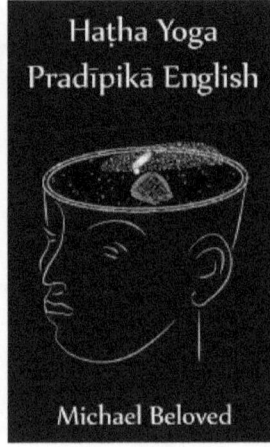

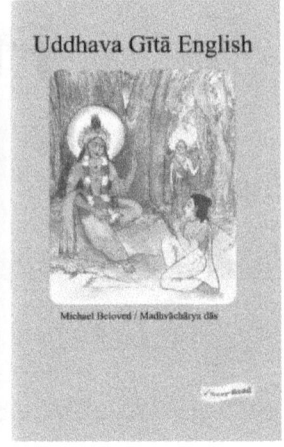

These are in 21st Century English, very precise and exacting. Many Sanskrit words which were considered untranslatable into a Western language are rendered in precise, expressive and modern English.

Three of these books are instructions from Krishna. **In Bhagavad Gita English** and **Anu Gita English**, the instructions were for Arjuna. In the **Uddhava Gita English,** it was for Uddhava. Bhagavad Gita and Anu Gita are extracted from the Mahabharata. Uddhava Gita was extracted from the 11th Canto of the Srimad Bhagavatam (Bhagavata Purana). One of these books, the **Markandeya Samasya English** is about Krishna, as described by Yogi Markandeya, who survived the cosmic collapse and reached a divine child in whose transcendental body, the collapsed world was existing.

Two of this series are the syllabus about yoga practice. The Yoga Sutras of Patañjali is elaboration about ashtanga yoga. Hatha Yoga Pradipika English, is the detailed information about asana postures, pranayama breath-infusion, energy compression, naad sound resonance and advanced meditation. The Sanskrit author is Swatmarama Mahayogin.

My suggestion is that you read **Bhagavad Gita English**, the **Anu Gita English, the Markandeya Samasya English,** the **Yoga Sutras English,** the **Hatha Yoga Pradipika** and lastly the **Uddhava Gita English**, which is complicated and detailed.

For each of these books we have at least one commentary, which is published separately. Thus one's particular interest can be researched further in the commentaries.

The smallest of these commentaries and perhaps the simplest is the one for the Anu Gita. We published its commentary as the Anu Gita Explained. The Bhagavad Gita explanations were published in three distinct targeted commentaries. The first is Bhagavad Gita Explained, which sheds lights on how people in the time of Krishna and Arjuna regarded the information and applied it. Bhagavad Gita is an exposition of the application of yoga practice to cultural activities, which is known in the Sanskrit language as karma yoga.

Interestingly, Bhagavad Gita was spoken on a battlefield just before one of the greatest battles in the ancient world. A warrior, Arjuna, lost his wits and had no idea that he could apply his training in yoga to political dealings. Krishna, his charioteer, lectured on the spur of the moment to give Arjuna the skill of using yoga proficiency in cultural dealings including how to deal with corrupt officials on a battlefield.

The second Gita commentary is the Kriya Yoga Bhagavad Gita. This clears the air about Krishna's information on the science of kriya yoga, showing that its techniques are clearly described for anyone who takes the time to read Bhagavad Gita. Kriya yoga concerns the battlefield which is the psyche of the living being. The internal war and the mental and emotional forces which are hostile to self-realization are dealt with in the kriya yoga practice.

The third commentary is the Brahma Yoga Bhagavad Gita. This shows what Krishna had to say outright and what he hinted about which concerns the brahma yoga practice, a mystic process for those who mastered kriya yoga.

There is one commentary for the **Markandeya Samasya English**. The title of that publication is Krishna Cosmic Body.

There are two commentaries to the Yoga Sutras. One is the Yoga Sutras of Patañjali and the other is the Meditation Expertise. These give detailed explanations of ashtanga Yoga.

The commentary of Hatha Yoga Pradipika is titled Kundalini Hatha Yoga Pradipika.

For the Uddhava Gita, we published the Uddhava Gita Explained. This is a large book and requires concentration and study for integration of the information. Of the books which deal with transcendental topics, my opinion is that the discourse between Krishna and Uddhava has the complete information about the realities in existence. This book is the one which removes massive existential ignorance.

Meditation Series

Meditation Pictorial

Meditation Expertise

CoreSelf Discovery

Meditation Sense Faculty

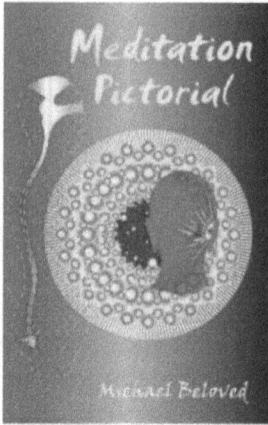

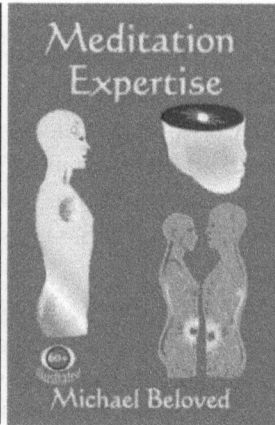

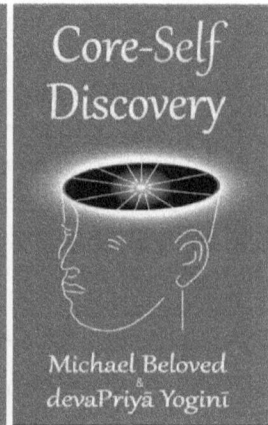

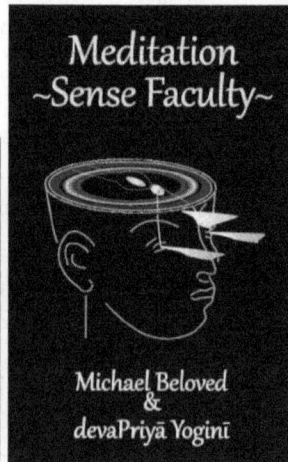

The specialty of these books is the mind diagrams which profusely illustrate what is written. This shows exactly what one has to do mentally to develop and then sustain a meditation practice.

In the **Meditation Pictorial**, one is shown how to develop psychic insight, a feature without which meditation is imagination and visualization, without any mystic experience per se.

In the **Meditation Expertise**, one is shown how to corral one's practice to bring it in line with the classic syllabus of yoga which Patañjali lays out as the ashtanga yoga eight-staged practice.

In **CoreSelf Discovery**, (co-authored with *devaPriya Yogini*) one is taken though the course of pratyahar sensual energy withdrawal which is the 5th stage of yoga in the Patañjali ashtanga eight-process complete system of yoga practice. These events lead to the discovery of a coreSelf which is surrounded by psychic organs in the head of the subtle body. This product has a DVD component.

Meditation ~ Sense Faculty (co-authored with *devaPriya Yogini*) is a detailed tutorial with profuse diagrams showing what actions to take in the subtle body to investigate the senses faculties. The meditator must first establish the location and function of the observing self. That self must be screened from the thoughts and ideas which usually hypnotize it.

These books are profusely illustrated with mind diagrams showing the components of psychic consciousness and the inner design of the subtle body.

Explained Series

Bhagavad Gita Explained

Uddhava Gita Explained

Anu Gita Explained

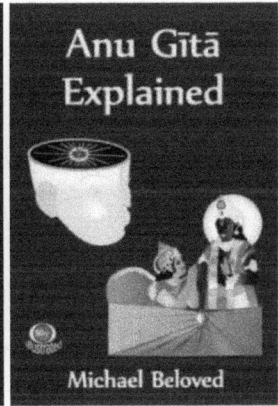

The specialty of these books is that they are free of missionary intentions, cult tactics and philosophical distortion. Instead of using these books to add credence to a philosophy, meditation process, belief or plea for followers, I spread the information out so that a reader can look through this literature and freely take or leave anything as desired.

When Krishna stressed himself as God, I stated that. When Krishna laid no claims for supremacy, I showed that. The reader is left to form an independent opinion about the validity of the information and the credibility of Krishna.

There is a difference in the discourse with Arjuna in the Bhagavad Gita and the one with Uddhava in the Uddhava Gita. In fact these two books may appear to contradict each other. In the Bhagavad Gita, Krishna pressured Arjuna to complete social duties. In the Uddhava Gita, Krishna insisted that Uddhava should abandon the same.

The Anu Gita is not as popular as the Bhagavad Gita but it is the conclusion of that text. Anu means what is to follow, what proceeds. In this discourse, an anxious Arjuna request that Krishna should repeat the Bhagavad Gita and again show His supernatural and divine forms.

However Krishna refuses to do so and chastises Arjuna for being a disappointment in forgetting what was revealed. Krishna then cited a celestial yogi, a near-perfected being, who explained the process of transmigration in vivid detail.

Commentaries

Yoga Sutras of Patañjali

Meditation Expertise

Krishna Cosmic Body

Anu Gita Explained

Bhagavad Gita Explained

Kriya Yoga Bhagavad Gita

Brahma Yoga Bhagavad Gita

Uddhava Gita Explained

Kundalini Hatha Yoga Pradipika

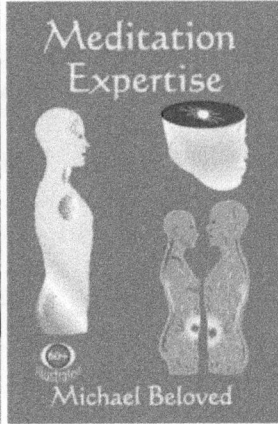

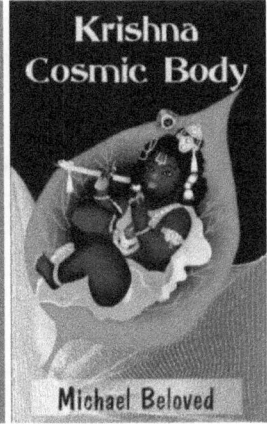

Yoga Sutras of Patañjali is the globally acclaimed text book of yoga. This has detailed expositions of yoga techniques. Many kriya techniques are vividly described in the commentary.

Meditation Expertise is an analysis and application of the Yoga Sutras. This book is loaded with illustrations and has detailed explanations of secretive advanced meditation techniques which are called kriyas in the Sanskrit language.

Krishna Cosmic Body is a narrative commentary on the Markandeya Samasya portion of the Aranyaka Parva of the Mahabharata. This is the detailed description of the dissolution of the world, as experienced by the great yogin Markandeya who transcended the cosmic deity, Brahma, and reached Brahma's source who is the divine infant, Krishna.

Anu Gita Explained is a detailed explanation of how we endure many material bodies in the course of transmigrating through various life-forms. This is a discourse between Krishna and Arjuna. Arjuna requested of Krishna a display of the Universal Form and a repeat narration of the Bhagavad Gita but Krishna declined and explained what a siddha perfected being told the Yadu family about the sequence of existences one endures and the systematic flow of those lives at the convenience of material nature.

Bhagavad Gita Explained shows what was said in the Gita without religious overtones and sectarian biases.

Kriya Yoga Bhagavad Gita shows the instructions for those who are doing kriya yoga.

Brahma Yoga Bhagavad Gita shows the instructions for those who are doing brahma yoga.

Uddhava Gita Explained shows the instructions to Uddhava which are more advanced than the ones given to Arjuna.

Bhagavad Gita is an instruction for applying the expertise of yoga in the cultural field. This is why the process taught to Arjuna is called karma yoga which means karma + yoga or cultural activities done with yogic insight.

Uddhava Gita is an instruction for apply the expertise of yoga to attaining spiritual status. This is why it is explains jnana yoga and bhakti yoga in detail. Jnana yoga is using mystic skill for knowing the spiritual part of existence. Bhakti yoga is for developing affectionate relationships with divine beings.

Karma yoga is for negotiating the social concerns in the material world. It is inferior to bhakti yoga which concerns negotiating the social concerns in the spiritual world.

This world has a social environment. The spiritual world has one too.

Currently, Uddhava Gita is the most advanced and informative spiritual book on the planet. There is nothing anywhere which is superior to it or which goes into so much detail as it. It verified that historically Krishna is the most advanced human being to ever have left literary instructions on this planet.

Even Patañjali Yoga Sutras which I translated and gave an application for in my book, **Meditation Expertise**, does not go as far as the Uddhava Gita.

Some of the information of these two books is identical but while the Yoga Sutras are concerned with the personal spiritual emancipation (kaivalyam) of the individual spirits, the Uddhava Gita explains that and also explains the situations in the spiritual universes.

Bhagavad Gita is from the Mahabharata which is the history of the Pandavas. Arjuna, the student of the Gita, is one of the Pandavas brothers. He was in a social hassle and did not know how to apply yoga expertise to solve it. On the battlefield, Krishna gave him a crash-course on yogic social interactions.

Uddhava Gita is from the *Srimad Bhagavatam (Bhagavata Purana),* which is a history of the incarnations of Krishna. Uddhava was a relative of Krishna. He was concerned about the situation of the deaths of many of his relatives but Krishna diverted Uddhava's attention to the practice of yoga for the purpose of successfully migrating to the spiritual environment.

Kundalini Hatha Yoga Pradipika is the commentary for the Hatha Yoga Pradipika of Swatmarama Mahayogin. This is the detailed process about asana posture, pranayama breath-infusion, complex compressions of energy, naad sound resonance intonement and advanced meditation practice.

This is the singular book with all the techniques of how to reform and redesign the subtle body so that it does not have the tendency for physical life forms and for it to attain the status of a siddha.

These books are based on the author's experiences in meditation, yoga practice and participation in spiritual groups:

Specialty

Spiritual Master

sex you!

Sleep Paralysis

Astral Projection

Masturbation Psychic Details

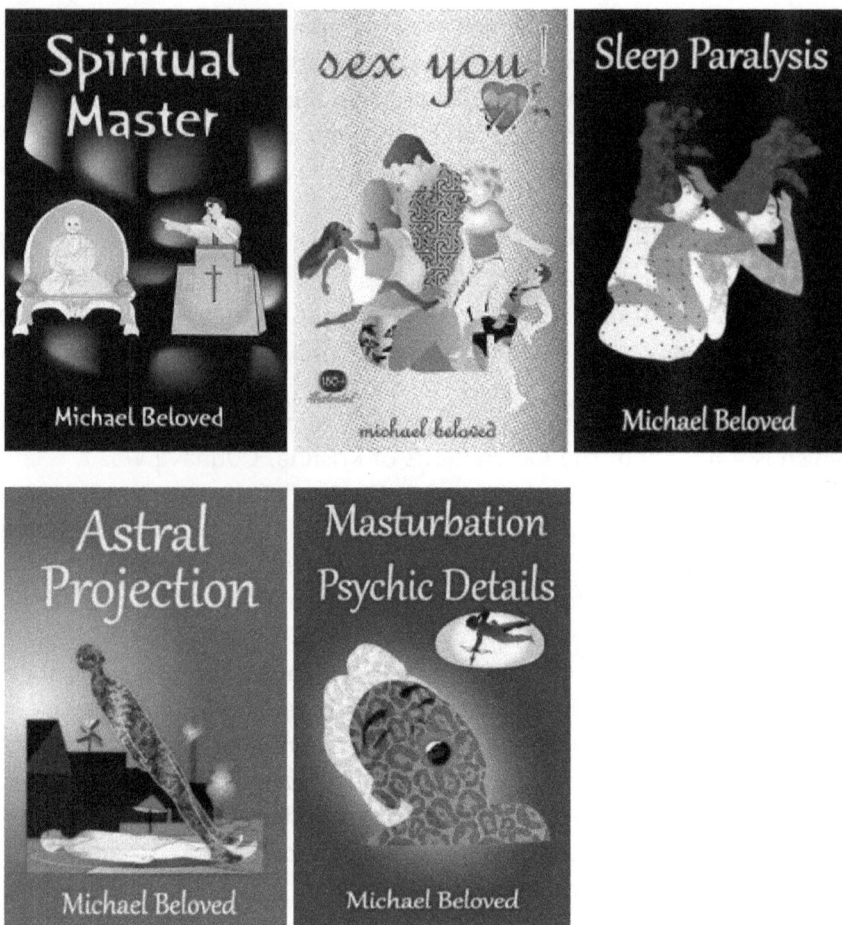

In **Spiritual Master**, Michael draws from experience with gurus or with their senior students. His contact with astral gurus is rated. He walks you through the avenue of gurus showing what you should do and what you should not do, so as to gain proficiency in whatever area of spirituality the guru has proficiency.

sex you! is a masterpiece about the adventures of an individual spirit's passage through the parents' psyches. The conversion of a departed soul into a sexual urge is described. The transit from the afterlife to residency in the emotions of the parents is detailed. This is about sex and you. Learn about how much of you comprises the romantic energy of one's would-be parents!

Sleep Paralysis clears misconceptions so that one can see what sleep paralysis is and what frightening astral experience occurs while the paralysis is being experienced. This disempowerment has great value in giving you confidence that you can and do exist even if one is unable to operate the physical body. The implication is that one can exist apart from and will survive the loss of the material form.

Astral Projection details experiences Michael had even in childhood, where he assumed incorrectly that everyone was astrally conversant. He discusses the lifeForce psychic mechanism which operates the sleep-wake cycle of the physical form, and which budgets energy into the separated astral form which determines if the individual will have dream recall or no objective awareness during the projections. Astral travel happens on every occasion when the physical body sleeps. What is missing in awareness is the observer status while the astral body is separated.

Masturbation Psychic Details is a surprise presentation which relates what happens on the psychic plane during a masturbation event. This does not tackle moral issues or even addictions but shows the involvement of memory and the sure but hidden subconscious mind which operates many features of the psyche irrespective of the desire or approval of the self-conscious personality.

inVision Series

Yoga inVision 1

Yoga inVision 2

Yoga inVision 3

Yoga inVision 4

Yoga inVision 5

Yoga inVision 6

Yoga inVision 1, the first in this series, describes the breath-infusion and meditation practices during the years of 1998 and 1999. There are unique, once in a lifetime as well as recurring insights which are elaborated. inFocus during breath-infusion and the meditation which follows is an adventure for any yogi. This gives what happened to this particular ascetic.

Yoga inVision 2 reports on the author's experiences from 1999 to 2001. Each day the experience is unique, illustrating the vibrancy of practice. Many rare once-in-a-lifetime perceptions are described.

Yoga inVision 3 reports on the author's experiences from 2001 to 2003.

Yoga inVision 4 reports on the author's experiences from 2006 to 2009.

Yoga inVision 5 reports on the author's experiences from 2006 to 2008.

Yoga inVision 6 reports on the author's experiences in 2010.

Online Resources

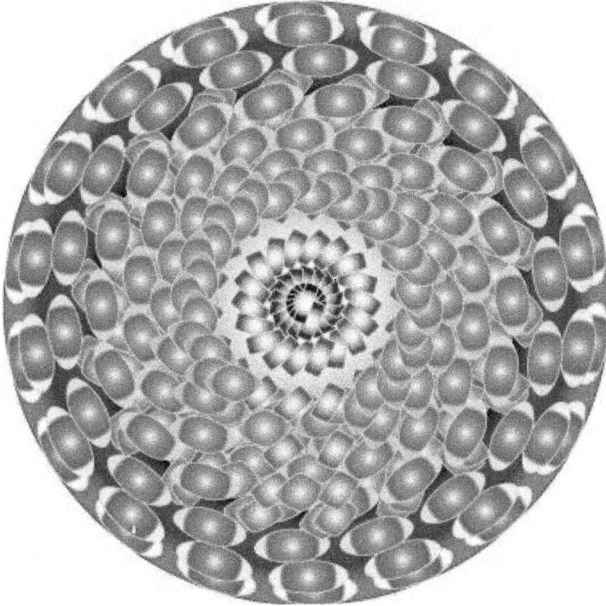

Email: michaelbelovedbooks@gmail.com
              axisnexus@gmail.com

Website: michaelbeloved.com

Forum: inselfyoga.com

Posters: zazzle.com/inself

www.ingramcontent.com/pod-product-compliance
Lightning Source LLC
Chambersburg PA
CBHW022005090426
42741CB00007B/897